T0327669

Option
Trading

Founded in 1807, John Wiley & Sons is the oldest independent publishing company in the United States. With offices in North America, Europe, Australia, and Asia, Wiley is globally committed to developing and marketing print and electronic products and services for our customers' professional and personal knowledge and understanding.

The Wiley Trading series features books by traders who have survived the market's ever-changing temperament and have prospered—some by reinventing systems, others by getting back to basics. Whether a novice trader, professional, or somewhere in-between, these books will provide the advice and strategies needed to prosper today and well into the future.

For a list of available titles, visit our web site at www.WileyFinance.com.

Option Trading

Pricing and Volatility
Strategies and Techniques

EUAN SINCLAIR

WILEY

John Wiley & Sons, Inc.

Published by John Wiley & Sons, Inc., Hoboken, New Jersey.
Published simultaneously in Canada.

For general information on our other products and services or for technical support, please contact our Customer Care Department within the United States at (800) 762-2974, outside the United States at (317) 572-3993, or fax (317) 572-4002.

Wiley also publishes its books in a variety of electronic formats. Some content that appears in print may not be available in electronic books. For more information about Wiley products, visit our web site at www.wiley.com.

Library of Congress Cataloging-in-Publication Data:

Sinclair, Euan, 1969-
   Option trading : pricing and volatility strategies and techniques / Euan Sinclair.
       p. cm. – (Wiley trading series)
   Includes index.
   ISBN 978-0-470-49710-4 (cloth)
   1. Options (Finance)   2. Pricing–Mathematical models.   I. Title.
   HG6024.A3S5622 2010
   332.63'2283–dc22   2010003139

Printed in the United States of America

10 9 8 7 6 5 4 3 2 1

To my parents

Contents

Preface

Traders tend to be a pragmatic group. They are largely interested in results. Actually some become so focused on results that it becomes a hindrance. This tendency can be a handicap, as the way to achieve good results is to focus on good processes and let the results take care of themselves. Good traders learn this.

But good traders are still intellectually parsimonious. They want to know what works, but seldom more than the minimum they need. When I'm feeling uncharitable I regard this as characteristic of the uncurious, dull people I have had the misfortune to work with, and indeed some were like this. More realistically, however, this is less a reflection on the traders themselves, most of who were intelligent people with a wide range of interests, and more a reflection on the nature of trading.

Trading is complex, changeable, and potentially emotionally draining. Once a trader has learned a sensible, statistically valid, profitable method, he is better off concentrating on exploiting it rather than continuing to experiment.

So a perfectly valid question when told something is "Why do I need to know this?" As a general answer, in the case where everything else is equal, the trader with more knowledge will make more money. He will also be more easily able to adapt to new markets and opportunities.

It is possible to trade options successfully without knowing about the Black-Scholes-Merton model, or any other pricing model. But for the traders who do this, everything is a special situation. They have to individually learn every nuance with no organizing principle. It would be like trying to learn chemistry without knowing about the periodic table. Black-Scholes-Merton provides a simplifying framework. Traders who know this can then learn other things more easily, because they use less energy remembering the otherwise unconnected facts.

Throughout this book I will tell you things that are truly useful and not merely "interesting." Trading is interesting only if it is profitable.

However I have no interest in, or intention of, making this an easy read for the "average person." The reason for this is that the "average person" will not succeed as a trader, so I would be making things more difficult for myself by oversimplifying. The text would be longer and more boring. Trading is hard and options are complicated. Much of this book will require work and thought. It is not meant to be a light read; it is meant to be a thorough treatment.

I want this book to be the only book an intelligent, diligent person would need in order to go from knowing nothing about options to being able to trade professionally at a legitimate trading operation (a bank, a hedge fund, or a market making firm).

PROFESSIONAL TRADING

It is commonly believed that 90 percent of those attempting to trade will lose money. This is a difficult number to verify. First, the people in possession of the data needed to prove this are members of brokerages and clearing firms, and they have no interest in publicizing the fact that the vast majority of their customers fail. Second, we cannot learn much by interviewing traders as there is the problem of survivorship bias (the only people who will identify themselves as traders are those who have not gone bankrupt), and all people tend to exaggerate their successes and minimize their losses.

But even if this figure is somewhat exaggerated, its implications are startling. Most people will fail at trading. The normal excuses for this large-scale failure rate given in trading books or seminars (when it is even acknowledged) take one of two forms.

- Traders do not know the correct techniques, where "correct" corresponds to whatever the particular expert is trying to sell.
- Traders do not have the psychological discipline needed to stick with their plan. This is laughable. I know of no other field of endeavor where failure to perform a skill is routinely blamed on psychology. Would you seriously listen to a basketball coach who told you that the *main* reason you were not in the NBA was your lack of discipline and desire? While great players are also psychologically strong, no amount of desire and resolve would turn me into a professional level player. Being undisciplined might be a personal failing, but it is by no means the most important one. This is also true in trading. Psychological coaching can help a winner, but it will not make a winner.

Hundreds of books discuss these subjects, but the survival rate of traders gets no better. Yet the proprietary trading desks of banks continue to be profitable (even in the carnage of 2008) and hedge funds proliferate. Why can professionals consistently do what the amateurs cannot? Why are the same groups successful year after year? In many fields the answer to this question is obvious: it is because they are better. For example, a professional basketball player is doing what I do, but he does it much better. Trading is different. Professionals do not generally have more knowledge, more skill, or more psychological mastery. They make money because they are playing a totally different game.

Many people completely fail to see this. They are encouraged in this view by the proliferation of financial news media. There are several full-time business television channels, daily newspapers, business radio stations, and various Web services that offer to bring people the "inside" view of the markets. They do not. If anything, they give their consumers a false sense of the depth of their knowledge. Particularly misleading are the occasions when a floor trader is interviewed and asked for his views on a particular market. The answer will invariably *sound* useful, containing an analysis of the market's technical and fundamental factors. But successful traders do not care about these things and asking a floor trader for his opinion on them is like asking Tiger Woods for tennis lessons. He is a great sportsman and he hits a ball with an implement, but his tennis views and opinions are no more likely to be valid than those of most other people.

Knowledge is still crucial, but for derivatives traders it is not technical analysis or fundamental analysis that is important. They need a sound knowledge of market structure and arbitrage relationships. The way they consistently make money is through arbitrage and its weaker relatives: quasi-arbitrage, statistical arbitrage, and structural arbitrage.

We will be talking a lot about winning and losing. These can be emotionally loaded terms. No one likes to be called a loser, and, particularly if you are under the age of 40, you have probably become accustomed to having your self-esteem boosted to the point where you think that even if you lose money you still are not a loser. This is the wrong way to think. That is exactly what you are and if you want that unpleasant fact to change, you first need to accept it.

Being a loser does not make you a bad person. On the contrary, many of the things winners do would make them bad people in any normal setting. Winners (while not setting out to be deliberately unpleasant) are fiercely competitive, obsessive and often morose and cranky while trading. We do not trade to make friends; we trade to make money.

There is a common misconception of the successful trader as existing in a state of preternatural calm. Of course this would be nice, but one cannot sustain this state while at the same time maintaining the necessary level of obsession. Edges are so small, that you must be a complete control freak. You need to obsess over every detail.

All of this may sound very negative. It could be construed that way. On the other hand, I'm going to give you a path that has a far greater chance of success. In contrast to the 90 percent failure rate cited earlier, over 50 percent of the people I have ever known in this industry are still in it, meaning that they are competent professionals. Those who succeed are not distinguished by special intelligence. They have learned to put themselves in market niches that give them an edge. This is the most important trading decision they have made. If you also do this and are not stupid, lazy, or dishonest, you can also succeed.

Trading success is measured in money, but people who are purely motivated by money might want to reconsider trading as a career choice. We've already pointed out the colossal failure rate. But even traders who "succeed" may not make great fortunes. Many traders manage to stay in the game without accumulating great wealth. Most of these people could probably have achieved about the same income in another job. Further, a more conventional career choice would follow a standard path of professional development. A lawyer with 20 years of experience might be a partner in a law firm or a judge. A trader does not have these opportunities. If he wants to keep trading he will be in the same job as he was when he started.

So why trade? The reason to become a trader is the same reason someone should choose any career: Because that is what they do and who they are. Eventually this consideration overwhelms all others. As G. H. Hardy said in, "A Mathematician's Apology," "I do what I do because it is the one and only thing that I can do at all well. . . . If a man has any genuine talent he should be ready to make almost any sacrifice in order to cultivate it to the full."

THE ROLE OF MATHEMATICS

A (very annoying) colleague once asked for something to read about option trading that "was not mathematical." This really is not possible. All of the concepts behind the structure, pricing, and trading of options are inherently mathematical. This is true of all trading.

Nonetheless there is a large group of traders who vociferously state their distrust of mathematics. The most charitable thing I can say about these people is that they really are not thinking about what they are saying. Do they really doubt that a trader who makes a million dollars a year is better than one who loses a million dollars? After all, this is a question that can be decided only by using the appropriate mathematics. This case is simple. Is A greater than B? But just because a situation is less clear-cut does not necessarily make the application of mathematics irrelevant. In fact, I hope to show that more complex situations need the most mathematical analysis.

I do not claim that everything is about mathematics. Intangibles matter. Leadership, inspiration, grit, and heart are all important. But they matter only if they lead to something tangible. And results are always tangible. Causes may not be.

A skilled mathematical trader will use math and statistics to simplify the world. A good mathematical model takes a very complex situation and makes it possible to identify a cause and an effect. All traders do this. "If nonfarm payroll comes in under expectations, the market will rally," is an example of a trader using a model in this way. He has not expressed it in an equation, but it is the same process. Someone can choose to simplify the world in a different way to you. This is not a problem. It is a good thing. You can always learn from divergent viewpoints.

A good model has to be based on the appropriate selection of inputs. To predict the score of a baseball game, for example, we might consider the number and type of hits each team averages, how often players take walks and how many runs the pitching staffs give up. Our predictive model will then be some function of these variables. But if we were to also include the population of each team's home city, then our prediction would clearly rest on an unstable foundation. Fundamental knowledge is necessary to avoid this situation.

So I need to assume a certain amount of mathematical literacy, and it is not immediately obvious where to draw this line. I've basically decided to assume that someone who wants to be a serious option trader should have picked up the mathematics of a good high school education. This includes algebra, logarithms, and exponentiation and basic calculus. The Black-Scholes-Merton (BSM) formalism requires more complex mathematics to do properly. We avoid this by doing it improperly. I think we can get the essential points across this way. An option trader need not be able to give a rigorous derivation of this equation (those who first did so were rewarded with Nobel prizes), but should be able to follow an informal discussion of it.

I make an exception for statistics. Here I assume that you know far less, and discuss probability distributions, descriptive statistics, inference, and sampling. There are two reasons for this. First, I've found that many people come into finance with a strong background in mathematics or the physical sciences. To these people calculus is simple, but their grounding in statistics is generally weak. Second, many successful traders have had only a basic understanding of the mathematics behind BSM and certainly have no idea of the differences between calculus and stochastic calculus.

This is not generally a great problem. But misunderstanding statistics and probability can, and does, lead to disastrous decisions.

THE STRUCTURE OF THIS BOOK

This book is roughly divided into three parts. First we will introduce options, both historically and conceptually. Next we use the no-arbitrage principle to introduce option pricing. We examine both static arbitrage relationships and the dynamic hedging approach. The last, and largest, part of the book is about how to actually trade options.

In Chapter 1 we discuss the history of options and other financial derivatives. I think these stories are interesting, but even if they were not interesting, they would be important. Sadly, option traders will often find themselves in situations where they need to defend their profession. This can happen in social situations, which is annoying, but it is also a topic of political debate. Traders cannot reasonably expect much public sympathy, but they need to be able to conduct a coherent defense of the morality, necessity and desirability of the existence of their business. Understanding the history of derivatives and particularly the way that they have been blamed for many past financial catastrophes can only help do this.

Chapter 2 introduces options and option markets. While this is undoubtedly boring material, it is probably the most important chapter in the book. Unless the reader has a solid grasp of basic definitions and nomenclature, he will not be able to go any further.

Chapter 3 is the first chapter in the pricing section of the book. We introduce the concept of no arbitrage and use it to derive relationships between call and puts and options of different strikes and maturities. Again, many of the proofs here are tedious, but the results must become second nature and good traders will become familiar enough with the principle of no arbitrage to be able to apply it to the analysis of unfamiliar structured products.

In Chapter 4 we work through the two most important option pricing models: the binomial tree and the Black-Scholes-Merton (BSM) model. These are not the most important models because they are the most useful. Neither one is actually used in practice much anymore. However, they provide the conceptual basis for most other models, and traders need to become familiar with their assumptions and how we compensate for these in practice.

Chapter 5 examines the solution to the BSM model and introduces the famous greeks, the sensitivities of the option price to various parameters and variables. Although the equations we give are tied to the BSM formalism, the nature of the greeks is not. The behavior of the greeks is more fundamental than this. Options really do have these dependencies irrespective of the particular pricing model we use. This is important: we want to become familiar with *options*, not with option pricing models.

By this point we will know what options are, and how they are priced. Next we can learn how to trade them. Chapter 6 looks at the various strategies that can be constructed from simple calls and puts. Many books do this, but most do so from the perspective of a customer who is trying to construct a directional bet with certain risk characteristics. As professional traders, we generally will not be doing this. We will usually be interested in the volatility aspects of a given position. Nonetheless we still need to know what the standard positions and strategies are.

Option pricing models are not magic. They are incredibly helpful trading tools, but they still need inputs in order to generate option prices. The most important of these is volatility. Chapter 7 shows how to measure and forecast volatility. Chapter 8 is somewhat complementary. Here we consider the nature and behavior of implied volatility: the volatility that the option market is using at any point. The interplay between implied volatility and realized volatility is central to the theory and practice of option trading.

While trading does involve instinctual actions it also has a number of aspects that can be quantified. There are a number of indisputable mathematical truths that need to form the basis of any sensible trading operation. In Chapter 9 we introduce the concept of expected value, the general idea of hedging and the idea of trade sizing: looking at a trade as a part of a continuing business plan rather than a single unrepeated bet.

Chapter 10 discusses the basic ideas and strategies of market making. Not all option traders will be market makers, but all traders can benefit from understanding their behavior. At the very least this will improve a trader's ability to execute trades.

In Chapter 11 we examine volatility trading, in particular, how to hedge and what to expect when we do. Volatility trading is a viable stand-alone strategy, but it also needs to be understood by any trader using options. Option traders inevitably take positions in volatility even if this is not their principal focus.

Expiry trading gets a separate chapter: Chapter 12. Nothing about expiration is really fundamentally different from any other time, but everything that happens is far more extreme. It provides opportunities for good trading, but also risks that are much larger than at other times. Risk management is the most important thing for an option trader to do. Everything a trader does, and everything in this book, is about risk management. All trades must be evaluated by both their return and their risk. But there is another level of risk management to consider as well. At this level, we think far less about the probability of an event, and much more about the consequences of its occurrence. This is just one of the many inconsistencies that a trader must become comfortable with. We spend a lot of time estimating probabilities of events before we do a trade. But we also need to make sure that in no state of the world, no matter how unlikely, can the trade cause us to go broke. This type of analysis is covered in Chapter 13.

Acknowledgments

M any people helped me with this project, but deserving of particular thanks are those who did proofreading. At the risk of forgetting someone, special thanks go to Julien Gosme, Rich Ghazarian, Nicolas Tabardel, Chetan Mehra, Christopher Merrill, DN, Alexander Chiang, David Rasho, Derek G. Nokes, Elizabeth S. Duquette, and Benjamin Portheault.

I'd also like to thank all of the traders I have worked with. Some need to be thanked for the cautionary tales they provide and some for the valuable advice and education they gave me. Notable members of this second group are Art Duquette, Don Perettie, David Little, and, in particular, Raoul Rodriguez, who pointed out to me that "if you shut up and listen you might not be in that clerk's jacket forever."

CHAPTER 1

History

In our view, however, derivatives are financial weapons of mass destruction, carrying dangers that, while now latent, are potentially lethal.
—Warren Buffett, letter to shareholders, 2002

D erivatives have often been characterized as dangerous tools of financial speculation, invented by mathematicians who are out of touch with reality, then sold by unscrupulous salesmen to gullible customers who do not understand the risks they are taking. They have been blamed for most periods of modern financial turmoil, including the 1987 crash, the bankruptcy of Barings Bank, the meltdown of Long Term Capital Management, and the current "subprime crisis." Like many populist misconceptions, there are germs of truth in this straw man, but the full truth is far more nuanced, complex, interesting, and profitable to those who understand.

Derivatives are as old as recorded history. The first reference we have to derivatives is in Genesis 29. Jacob entered an agreement that obligated him to work for seven years in exchange for the hand of Rachel. However, after Jacob had fulfilled his part of the contract, Rachel's father, Laban, defaulted on his obligations and made Jacob instead marry his elder daughter, Leah. So Jacob entered another agreement in which he again worked for seven years in order to marry Rachel.

- This was a *forward agreement* where Jacob paid (in labor) in return for something (Rachel) to be delivered at a certain time in the future (seven years).

1

- Laban *defaulted,* by not carrying out his obligations under the contract, making this not only the first derivative we know of but also the first default.
- Jacob may not have been a great trader. He entered a contract at a high price, was cheated, and then did the same thing again.

The first unambiguously historical reference to options is in "The Politics" by Aristotle. He tells the story of the philosopher Thales of Miletus who lived from 624 to 527 B.C. It seems that Thales eventually grew tired of hearing variants of the question, "If you are so smart why aren't you rich?" and resolved to show that learning could indeed lead to riches. According to Aristotle:

> *He, deducing from his knowledge of stars that there would be a good crop of olives, while it was still winter raised a little capital and used it to pay deposits on all the oil-presses in Miletus and Chios, thus securing an option on their hire. This cost him only a small sum as there were no other bidders. Then the time of the harvest came and as there was a sudden and simultaneous demand for oil-presses, he hired them out at any price he liked to ask.*

Thales actually bought a call option. The deposits bought him the right, but not the obligation, to hire the presses. If the harvest had been poor, Thales would have chosen not to exercise his right to rent the presses and lost only the initial deposit, the option premium. Fortunately, the harvest was good and Thales exercised the option. Aristotle concludes,

> *He made a lot of money and so demonstrated that it is easy for philosophers to be rich, if they want to.*

I do not doubt that the trade was profitable, but at the risk of contradicting a philosophical giant, I need to emphasize that making money is never easy. However, Thales clearly shows that being smart is helpful when trading options.

We can also find other examples of option contracts in the ancient world. Both the Phoenicians and the Romans had terms in their maritime cargo contracts that would today be considered options. It seems likely that options were commonplace in the shipping industry, so we should not be too surprised when their use spread geographically, particularly to another nation with a seafaring history.

The United Kingdom is now one of the world's great financial centers, but the medieval English church was not particularly pro-business. It specifically forbade charging interest for loans. To get around this, a loan would be structured synthetically using the principles behind the put-call parity theorem that we shall encounter later. It could therefore be argued that options are thus more fundamental than mortgages.

The first modern financial scandal involving derivatives took place in another prominent marine trading nation: Holland in 1636. This is an interesting case. Trade in tulips was conducted through a futures market. Dealers and growers would agree on prices before the crop was harvested. As prices rose throughout the 1630s, many German burgomasters began to purchase futures contracts as pure speculation. In February 1637, prices crashed.

Sometimes the reason for this crash is given as the defeat of the Germans by the Swedes in the Battle of Wittstock of October 1636. According to this theory, demand for tulips collapsed as the German nobles had more important things to attend to. However, this is probably a case where we are trying to find a single cause for an event that does not have one. The Battle of Wittstock took part well into the Thirty Years War (1618–1648). In this war, somewhere between 10 and 20 percent of the German population was killed. One could well guess that the German nobles were already concerned about this. Why one battle would cause a crash in the tulip market is not obvious.

Whatever the reason for the crash, the Dutch local politicians were now faced with paying above-market prices for their bulbs and they responded in the typical way for their profession: they changed the rules. After initially trying to renege on their commitments, they turned them into options. Now they would not have to buy the tulips unless the crop prices were higher. As compensation to the short futures holders, they arranged a small premium payment to be made. After this, these options became traded speculative vehicles. One of the most important things for derivative traders to remember is that the contracts exist only as legal contracts. They are hence subject to changes through the legal system. Traders who have forgotten this have apparently been getting hurt since at least 1636, and probably far earlier than that.

The other famous bubble of the period that featured options was the South Sea bubble of 1720. In return for a loan of £7 million to finance a war against France, the House of Lords granted the South Sea Company a monopoly in trade with South America. The company underwrote the English national debt, which stood at £30 million, on a promise of 6 percent interest from the government. Shares rose immediately. Common stock in this company was held by only 499 people, with many members of parliament amongst them. To cash in on the speculative frenzy, the company issued "subscription shares," which were actually compound call options. These fueled the fire, but in September of 1720 the market crashed as the management realized that the share price was wildly inflated. As news of insider selling spread, the price tumbled 85 percent. Many people were ruined. Isaac Newton was rumored to have lost 20,000 pounds (this is equivalent to over one million pounds in today's money). As a result of this crash, trading in options was made illegal in the United Kingdom and remained so until 1825.

Options need not be considered in isolation. Financial engineering is the construction of hybrid derivative products with features of multiple asset classes. This is also not new practice. Early examples were confederate war bonds. The antebellum South had one of the lowest tax burdens of contemporary societies. The hastily assembled Confederacy did not have the infrastructure in place to collect taxes for war financing. In 1863 the Confederacy issued bonds that allowed them to borrow money in pounds. There was also an embedded option that allowed the bondholder to receive payment in cotton. The cotton option gave the bondholder more certainty of payment, as cotton was the south's largest crop. The catch was that the cotton would be delivered in the Confederacy. This bond was probably more important as a political tool rather than a source of financing. These bonds financed only about 1 percent of the military expenditures, but they were seen as a way of conferring legitimacy upon the breakaway states by being listed in London and having William Gladstone, the Chancellor of the Exchequer and future British Prime Minister, among the holders. Of course, the Union won the war and the Confederacy ceased to exist—and defaulted on all of its obligations.

In the United States options began trading in the eighteenth century. By the nineteenth century an active over-the-counter business in equity options had developed. This market had a well-defined structure. Wealthy individuals would sell blocks of puts and calls to brokers who would in turn sell them to smaller speculators. This arrangement helped to mitigate against credit risk, as the smaller traders were only allowed to purchase options and had to pay in full for the options up front. These options were commonly referred to as "privileges," because the purchaser had the privilege of exercising the option and calling (or putting) the stock but was under no obligations.

While the market was active, it was not considered socially acceptable. In 1874 the Illinois state legislature made option trading illegal. Other states followed, often because of the idea that speculation was harmful to "real" businesses and was nothing more than a form of gambling. Option trading was generally considered no more legitimate than trading in bucket shops or even participating in outright financial frauds.

Due to the counterparty risk, this market was mainly one of issuance. The options would trade in a secondary market, but this was far more illiquid. Over the next hundred years, this market developed in size but remained over-the-counter.

During this time, traders gradually developed many of the rules of thumb that we still use today. The equivalence of puts and calls was well understood, as were the ideas behind hedging with the underlying and other options. There were also several option pricing models being used by the more advanced traders. In fact it is likely that traders were using the essential features of the Black-Scholes-Merton model in this period.

The first exchange to list standardized contracts was the Chicago Board Options Exchange (CBOE). These started trading on April 26th, 1973. The publication in the same year of the famous Black-Scholes pricing model (now more correctly referred to as the Black-Scholes-Merton model) also boosted the market as more and more people thought they could now successfully price and hedge options. Initially options were listed on 16 stocks. Today options on thousands of stocks, indices, currencies and futures trade on at least 50 exchanges in over 30 countries.

In addition to this enormous expansion of the universe of underlyings, the total activity has increased exponentially. Figure 1.1 shows the total volume in U.S. stock options annually since 1973.

It is currently popular to advocate a dangerous form of financial Luddism in which derivatives are banned, but we can see that even during the turmoil of 2008, volume continued to rise. The main reason for this large and consistent growth is that derivatives are useful and their users like them. They can indeed be used for foolish speculation, but they can equally be used for prudent risk reduction and profitable trading. Even if the dominant use of options was for speculation, this would seem to be a weak argument against them. Practically anything can be used for speculation. There have been speculative bubbles in baseball cards, stamps, classic

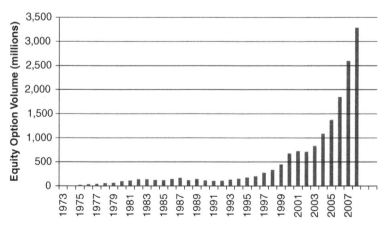

FIGURE 1.1 The Total Annual Volume in U.S. Stock Options

cars, wine, and coins. The subprime crisis was initiated by people buying property they could not afford. Options may well have been a tool in the speculative bubble, but they were not the root cause.

Another thread of this argument against financial options is that no one really understands them. Actually this argument is normally advanced by people who think *they* understand options but no one else does. As with all areas of human knowledge, there are indeed things that we do not understand, but many traders have, through study and experience, developed robust, conservative trading methods. In fact, most professional option traders had a relatively good year in 2008, as the high volatility levels increased the spreads they could charge.

Derivatives are an exceptionally useful tool. They have made financial products such as fixed-rate mortgages with early prepayment options widely available and much cheaper than they would otherwise be. They also allow users to tailor their portfolios toward their ideal level of risk. We could not return to a "simple" financial system without also returning to a "simple" economy with a far higher cost of capital and the lower growth that this would generate.

In any case, as a practical matter, derivatives cannot be *uninvented.* It seems very likely that acquiring a solid understanding of vanilla options will remain useful and profitable.

SUMMARY

- Derivatives are not a modern invention. They have a longer history than either stocks or bonds.
- They have consistently gained in popularity, particularly since they were listed on major exchanges.
- Arguing that they are "too complex" is neither logically or financially sensible.

CHAPTER 2

Introduction to Options

No one said life would be interesting.
—My parents

Boring is good.
—"Squid," with 15 years' worth of option-trading
experience

T he fact that many people try to trade without understanding basic
contract specifications has been illustrated several times in the ETF
space recently.

Consider the case of the ultra-short ETFs. These are funds designed
to return a multiple of the negative daily return of an index. They do this
fairly well. However, due to the ways that returns compound, they will not
deliver the negative return if we look over a longer period. Table 2.1 looks
at the returns of FXI and FXP (which is intended to deliver negative two
times the daily returns of FXI) in October and November of 2008.

We can see from this data that the ETF does a reasonable job of delivering the negative two times return each day. The relationship is not perfect,
as FXP actually averages −1.75 times the daily return of FXI. This is mainly
due to the large bid ask spread slightly distorting the closing prices. But the
important point to notice is that over the full period, the FXI total return
was 9.0 percent and FXP returned −49.2 percent. This is clearly nowhere
close to negative two times the return of FXI. This is not due to any ne-
farious activity on the part of the fund manager. It is purely the effects of
compounding.

TABLE 2.1 FXI and FXP

Date	FXI	FXI % Returns	FXP	FXP % Returns
10/27/2008	19.29		183.01	
10/28/2008	23.15	20.01	118.7	−35.14
10/29/2008	22.34	−3.50	115.48	−2.71
10/30/2008	25.48	14.06	87.03	−24.63
10/31/2008	24.99	−1.92	89.00	2.26
11/3/2008	25.28	1.16	86.00	−3.37
11/4/2008	27.02	6.88	75.20	−12.56
11/5/2008	24.48	−9.40	87.00	15.69
11/6/2008	22.54	−7.92	101.99	17.23
11/7/2008	25.43	12.82	76.32	−25.17
11/10/2008	26.43	3.93	69.50	−8.94
11/11/2008	24.88	−5.86	76.66	10.30
11/12/2008	23.92	−3.86	82.58	7.72
11/13/2008	27.47	14.84	60.40	−26.86
11/14/2008	24.98	−9.06	69.68	15.36
11/17/2008	24.93	−0.20	69.96	0.40
11/18/2008	24.11	−3.29	74.61	6.65
11/19/2008	22.13	−8.21	86.23	15.57
11/20/2008	21.02	−5.02	93.00	7.85

Compounding daily leveraged returns is not the same as delivering a leveraged return over any arbitrary period. This is a mathematical fact. A fabricated example might make the effect clear. Consider two ETFs, X and Y. Y is designed to deliver twice the daily return of X. They initially both trade at $100. On the first trading day, X rallies by 10 percent to $110 and Y accordingly rallies 20 percent to $120. On the second day, X drops back to $100. This is a decrease of 9.09 percent. Y drops by 18.18 percent, as it is designed to do. However this brings the price of Y to $98.18. So after two days, the first ETF is unchanged and the second has lost 1.82 percent. This effect is path dependent and is exacerbated by high volatility.

This should be perfectly obvious to anyone who has read the prospectus. The funds are designed to deliver leveraged, daily returns. They do this. That this relationship does not hold over longer periods is not the fund manager's fault. The fact that customers thought that this should happen is *their* fault. They did not do their homework. However, the trading chat-rooms and message boards indicated that there were plenty of people who were eager to blame others for their ignorance.

This can never happen to a professional. You simply must know all details of your instrument's specifications.

This chapter will test your ability to grind through some fairly dull material. It is, however, vital material. You can forget about exploiting the nuances of trading if you do not know the basic contract specifications.

OPTIONS

Options are a type of derivative. A derivative is a financial instrument whose value is derived from the value of another asset: the underlying. An option gives the option owner the right, but not the obligation, to buy or sell the underlying asset at a specified price any time during a designated period or on a specified date. To gain this right, the owner pays the seller a payment called the option premium.

The fact that an option holder is under no obligation to do anything is worth stressing. The owner of an option can also choose not to exercise the option and to let it expire worthless. This creates an asymmetry that is one of the great appeals of options. The owner can benefit from a favorable move in the price of the underlying, yet does not suffer due to an unfavorable move.

The seller takes the opposite side of this risk in return for the premium. He is obligated to fulfill the terms of the contract if the owner exercises it.

Because options are contracts they can be created without limit (At least this is true in theory. In reality, a market participant's position will be limited by his ability to collateralize it). An option market can never be cornered, and a seller does not have to borrow an option from another person in order to short it.

SPECIFICATIONS FOR AN OPTION CONTRACT

The specifications that define an option contract are: option type, underlying asset, strike price, expiration date, exercise style, and contract unit.

Option Type

There are two basic types of options, calls and puts. A call option gives the holder the right, but not the obligation, to buy the underlying asset at a predetermined price on or by a certain date. A put option gives the holder the right, but not the obligation, to sell the underlying asset at a predetermined price on or by a certain date.

Underlying Asset

Options are available on a number of underlying assets including stocks, indices, and various futures. The underlying asset of a stock option is a certain number of shares of the underlying stock. The underlying asset of an index option is an amount of cash equal to some multiple of the index value (this is sometimes referred to as cash settled). The underlying asset of a futures option is a future.

Strike Price

The strike, or exercise, price is the price at which the option owner can buy or sell the underlying asset.

Expiration Date

The expiration date is the last date on which the option exists.

Exercise Style

The two most common exercise styles are American and European. American options can be exercised at any time before the expiration date (or more practically at a given time on any trading day before the expiration date), while European options can be exercised only on the expiration date. Bermudan options, so named because they fall somewhere between American and European, can be exercised on a given number of days before the expiration date. There are many other options named for geographical areas (for example, Asians, Russians, Israelis, Hawaiians, and Parisians), but these refer to features other than exercise style.

Contract Unit

The contract unit is the amount of the underlying asset that the option owner can buy or sell upon exercise. In the United States, the contract unit for individual stock options is usually 100 shares of stock. For index options, it is an amount of money equal to $100 times the index. For futures options it is one futures contract.

So if a stock option is traded at a price of $3.00, the buyer would need to pay $3 × 100 for each option.

Traders need to be aware of how the contract units and strike price for equity options can be adjusted as a result of corporate actions. If a stock undergoes an integer split, the number of open contracts increases by the split factor, and the stock price and strike price will decrease. For example, if the stock splits two-for-one, the split ratio is two, so the strike and underlying both halve while the number of open contracts doubles. However, if the split is not by an integer ratio, the contract unit increases and the number of open contracts remains unchanged. For example if the stock splits in a 3 to 2 ratio, the contract unit increases to 150 shares, while the stock price and strike price decrease by two thirds. In each case the product of open contracts, contract units, and the strike price remains constant. Other corporate actions such as special dividends, recapitalizations, and rights offerings will be treated in similar fashion.

USES OF OPTIONS

Options have nonlinear payoffs. This allows users to create risk reward profiles that are specifically tailored to their needs (or at least their wants). We look at these strategies in Chapter 6. We also see (in Chapter 4) that the theory of option pricing uses the idea that we can replicate an option position by dynamic trading in the underlying, but this is generally expensive and in practice has many limitations. It also requires continuous monitoring and specialized knowledge. For these reasons, options are not redundant securities. They give traders the ability to do new things.

Option trades can usually be split into hedging trades or speculative trades. Hedges are designed to mitigate current risks, while speculation is designed to create profits. In practice the distinction is one of degree rather than type.

We will spend most of the rest of this book discussing the uses of options. Here we give some simple examples of using options for directional trading, hedging, volatility trading, and as part of a structured product.

Hedging a Long Position with a Put

If we have a long position in the underlying, we can protect ourselves against its price falling by purchasing a put.

For example, we own 1,000 shares of Microsoft (MSFT), which is currently trading at $22. We are worried that it may fall in the short term so we purchase 10 of the one-month $20 puts for a price of $32 each (the quoting convention gives the price as option per share, so these would be offered on the exchange as 0.32). As each option has a contract unit of 100 shares this means we have secured the right to sell all of our shares for $20 for the next month. This is exactly the same as buying insurance.

A fair question at this point is "If the owner thinks the shares are going to fall, why don't they just sell them?" The simplest answer is that maybe they can't. An analogous question is, "If you think your house is going to burn down why not just sell it? Why buy insurance?" The reason is that you need somewhere to live. Further, you hope that even though you have insurance, your house won't burn down. Similarly, sometimes people own large blocks of stock that they cannot sell. During the dot-com boom, a number of companies were acquired in all stock deals where the company owners were given stock in the acquiring company but not allowed to sell it until a certain lock-up period was over. So they would buy puts as a hedge. They hoped that the puts would expire worthless just as we do when we buy house insurance.

This is the simplest way of seeing the fallacy in methods that use the number of outstanding puts or calls to predict the direction of an underlying security. Just because a trader owns some puts does not imply that he expects the underlying to fall. There are too many ways of using options to tell.

It might also be that puts are the cheapest way of protecting the position. The owner could enter a stop order with a broker directing him to sell the shares if the price dropped below $20, but stops have a slightly different payoff to a put. A stop will always be executed if the price reaches a certain level. An option holder may decide not to exercise his option and in fact will usually not do so as soon as the exercise price is reached. Options can act as a stop but they are not the same as a stop order in the underlying.

Although the theory of option pricing is based on the idea that we can replicate an option position by dynamically trading the underlying, this is just an approximation. In practice the subtle distinctions between option behavior and the behavior of the replicating strategy are where professional traders can make money.

Buying a Put (Call) to Speculate on a Fall (Rise)

If we think a stock will fall (rise) we can buy a put (call). This gives us the possibility of making a large profit and only exposes us to the loss of the option premium. Further, by purchasing out of the money puts (calls) (options that would be worthless if exercised against the current underlying price) we give ourselves more leverage than we could obtain by shorting the underlying directly.

Buying a Call as a Hedge

Sometimes our risk is not that an asset will decrease in price. If we are a mortgage provider we will be at risk if interest rates decline. Someone with a fixed rate mortgage will want to refinance if rates fall. The borrower has the option to refinance, so the lender is short this option. He can hedge this by buying bond calls (a bond goes up if interest rates go down). His risk is that bonds increase in value, so the call is a hedge.

Creation of Structured Products

When options are available and liquid, it is possible to use them to create products that are specifically designed for certain classes of investors. An example is the equity-linked note.

Investors are torn between fear and greed. The ideal product is one that allows us to participate in an investment's upside while giving them protection against price falls. It is possible to use vanilla options to construct such a product.

As an example, let's consider the construction of a principal protected, equity-linked note. This product guarantees that at its maturity the holder will receive his principal plus a return that is tied to the performance of an equity index, which we assume initially has a level of 1,000. The noteholders will participate in the return on the index once it increases by more than a certain percentage.

Now the structuring firm (generally a bank or investment fund) will take the interest on the principal and use it to buy calls. Assume that this interest income can buy the one-year calls with an 1,100 strike. At the end of the year, if the index is below this level, the note holder gets his money back. Above this level he will make money as the stock market rises.

Investors love these products because they can be carefully tailored to match their psychological concerns about money. People tend to be scared of losses and resentful if they miss out on large market rallies. On the other hand, the note issuers can make money on these products by taking in a structuring fee that is bigger than their transaction costs. This is a case where both parties benefit.

Volatility Trading

By trading options and dynamically hedging them with the underlying, a trader can take a position that is dependent only on the difference in volatility implied by the option market and the volatility that actually occurs in the underlying during the lifetime of the option.

This can either be used as a stand-alone strategy or to manage the risk in a market maker's position.

Structured Product Arbitrage

Many financial products contain options or option-like features. We have already mentioned the prepayment option that is present in most mortgages. Another example is a convertible bond. This is a bond where the holder receives a slightly lower coupon than a similar but nonconvertible bond, but has the right to convert the bond into the stock of the issuing company at a fixed price. This position could be replicated by buying a bond and a call option. As these positions are the same, they should have the same price. If the price of the components diverges sufficiently from that of the convertible bond, we can profitably sell the real bond and buy the synthetic one, or vice versa.

MARKET STRUCTURE

Exchanges can have slightly different structures both on the trading side (floor trading, electronic or hybrid, market maker or specialist, continuously quoted or response to request, etc.) and in their corporate structure (ownership by members, banks or the public, etc.). There is no way we can cover all of these extensively. This would be boring and fairly pointless. A trader should understand how the general process works and then check on the details of his own markets. Here we will examine the structure of the United States equity option market because it is deep, broad, likely to be useful to most readers, and it is the market with which I am most familiar.

An Option Account

In order to make an option trade, a trader must open an account with a broker. To do this, he must complete the following documents.

- A securities account agreement
- An options account agreement
- The OCC (The Options Clearing Corporation, whose role we will look at later) risk-disclosure agreement, "Characteristics and Risks of Standardized Options"

After this, the trader can place an order.

An Option Order

When placing an order, the trader must specify several things. The order could either be given to a broker over the phone (in which case give the order and have him repeat it to confirm that there are no mistakes) or through the trading software. The trader must specify the following.

- Whether the trade is a buy or a sell
- Whether we are trading a call or a put

- The number of option contracts
- The underlying stock
- The strike
- The expiration month
- The account number
- Whether the option is a market order or a limit order. A market order is one that will be executed as soon as the order reaches the exchange. A limit order will only be filled at the specified price (or better). A limit order may also have further limitations placed upon it such as how long it is to be effective.

Market Execution

Once the brokerage firm receives the order, it either sends it to a floor broker (for an open outcry exchange) or routes it to the exchange computer (for an electronic exchange). The actual mechanics of the trade depend on the type of exchange.

In an open outcry exchange, the order will be yelled into the pit that trades options on the appropriate stock. For example, "I need a market for March 20 calls on Microsoft!" Market makers (traders who aim to make money by collecting the bid-ask spread) respond with a bid price and an ask price: "One bid at one point one." Then the broker shows his size and direction of the customer's trade, "I'll pay one point one for 100."

In an electronic exchange there will be a continuously posted bid and offer for each price. Here the customer will see the current price on his trading software and can enter his order directly, just as he would if he was trading a stock with an online brokerage.

Currently there are six U.S. equity option exchanges.

1. Boston Options Exchange, Inc. (BOX)
2. The Chicago Board Options Exchange (CBOE)
3. The International Securities Exchange (ISE)
4. NASDAQ Options Market (NSDQ)
5. NYSE Alternext U.S.
6. The Philadelphia Stock Exchange (PHLX)

These markets are linked together on a real-time basis through a network capable of transporting orders between each market. This obligates a market maker (or specialist) either to match another exchange's price for an order or else route the order to the exchange offering the best price.

The prices at which the options are quoted and traded must be multiples of some minimum amount that is set by the exchange. This minimum price fluctuation is known as a "tick." Depending on the stock this is either $0.05 or $0.01.

At exchanges with a specialist system, things are slightly different. The specialist is a market maker who also operates as the order book official. As market makers, they fulfill the dealer function by maintaining inventory and trading for their own accounts. As order book officials, they fulfill the broker function by accepting and executing the customer limit orders. However, unlike an order book official at the CBOE, the specialist is not required to show the limit orders to other members. Other traders will also be present, but being the specialist is enormously advantageous. The advantage is so great that most futures exchanges specifically prohibit brokers from also trading for their own accounts. In fact, I have not seen any recent research from a disinterested party that shows or even suggests the superiority of the specialist system. Its only defenders are the specialists themselves.

There is also another market that operates in parallel with the exchanges. This is the "call-around market" where interdealer brokers call a number of market makers and try to obtain a price before trading with the winning market maker on the exchange. This is standard practice for large orders. It is also of slightly murky legality as most exchanges forbid prearranged trades. It seems that they are happy to ignore the prearranging when it happens on private phone lines.

Clearing and the Option Clearing Corporation (the OCC)

The clearing-house is an organization that fills the role of a centralized common counter-party. Instead of traders trading directly with each other, one sells to the clearing-house and the other buys from it. This has two great advantages:

- Traders no longer worry about other traders' credit worthiness. The clearing-house is the counter-party to all trades, and a clearing-house is far more credit worthy than any individual trader or trading firm.
- To close out a trade, a trader does not need to trade with any particular trader. This greatly increases liquidity.

The United States equity options market is served by a single clearing-house, the Options Clearing Corporation (the OCC), which the exchanges collectively own. When a trade is executed on an exchange, it is reported to the OCC. First the buyer and seller confirm the trade details with the brokerage firms involved. If the brokerage is a clearing member, it directly reports to the OCC. If the brokerage is a nonclearing member then it must report through a clearing member. To become a clearing member, the brokerage must be an exchange member and also fulfill higher capital requirements than a nonclearing member. After receiving trade notification, the OCC makes sure that both sides agree. At this point the OCC becomes the buyer from the original seller and the seller to the original buyer. The appropriate cash transfer happens on the next business day.

The Over-the-Counter Market (OTC)

Over-the-counter trading refers to trades that are conducted directly between the counterparties without an exchange as an intermediary. There is one main benefit to trading this way:

- The terms and conditions of the contracts can be negotiated so that they more closely hedge the exposures of the customer. This may be as simple as choosing a strike or expiration that does not match that listed on the exchange, or it could involve several underlyings, a nonstandard payoff, and options whose existence is triggered by some other event (these are known as "knock-in" options).

There are also some disadvantages:

- The counterparties are exposed to credit risk.
- The trade needs to be closed out with the same counterparty, and it is unlikely that the side that needs to close will get a good price due to lack of dealer competition.

There are also some things that are of dubious benefit to the public:

- The market is not transparent. This leads to worse prices. In fact, the banks that were active in the OTC market deliberately kept many products (e.g., variance swaps and credit default swaps) off the exchanges to keep prices free of unnecessary competition.
- There are no universally enforced levels of collateral that need to be posted. This can lead to banks taking more risk than they can handle. Much of the subprime crises could have been avoided if the instruments involved were cleared through an exchange and therefore had to be properly collateralized.

Exercise and Assignment

When an option holder exercises an option, the seller must fulfill his contractual obligations. If the option is a call, he needs to deliver shares. If it is a put, he must purchase shares at the strike price. The exerciser is required to pay the strike price if he exercises a call or to deliver the shares if he has exercised a put.

In order to exercise, a trader must submit an exercise request though a clearing member firm to the OCC. This must be received between 10 A.M. Eastern Time and 8 P.M. Eastern Time before the last trading day. On expiration day notice must be received by 5:30 P.M. Eastern Time. However, on the expiration day, the OCC will automatically exercise all options that expire in the money, unless the clearing member gives instructions to the contrary.

When an option is exercised the OCC randomly assigns the obligation to a clearing member with the corresponding short position. This clearing member then assigns the obligation to one of its customers. The underlying shares must be delivered by 1 P.M. ET on the third business day after the OCC has accepted the exercise notice.

Trading Costs

Costs are incurred at several points in the trading and clearing process. Whenever an option is bought or sold, a commission is charged by the broker. Similarly, commissions are charged on the amount of stock that is required to be bought or sold, when an option is exercised. Fees are also charged by the exchanges and clearing firms each time they handle a customer's order.

Margin

In the options markets the term *margin* has a different meaning from its use in the stock market. To buy stocks "on margin," a trader provides at least 50 percent of the necessary cash and borrows the rest from his broker. In the option markets, margin refers to the cash or securities that a trader posts as collateral to guarantee that he can fulfill his obligations under the options contract. Minimum margin requirements are set by the OCC, but individual brokerage firms often charge more than this.

There are two types of margining to consider: strategy-based margin and portfolio margin. Strategy-based margin is more conservative (from the point of view of the brokerage firm) and is usually applied to customer accounts. Portfolio margin is the standard for market-maker accounts, but since April 2007, some classes of stocks have been approved for this type of margining for all customer accounts.

Strategy-Based Margin   This consists of a number of rules designed to insure the broker against the worst-case scenario for each type of position. Instead of giving every possible case, we will consider some of the more common positions.

Long Calls or Puts   An option must be paid for in full. It is illegal to borrow money to finance the purchase.

Short Calls or Puts   The margin is the greater of:

- The proceeds of the sale plus 20 percent of the value of the underlying minus the amount the option is out of the money; or
- The proceeds of the sale plus 10 percent of the value of the underlying.

The proceeds of the sale can be applied to the initial margin requirement.

Example: We sell the 105 call for 3.00 when the underlying is at 100. First we calculate the greater of

$$\$100 \times 3.00 + 0.2 \times \$100 \times 100 - \$5 \times 100 = \$1,800$$

$$\$100 \times 3.00 + 0.1 \times \$100 \times 100 = \$1,300$$

So the total margin is $1,800 - $300 = $1,500.

Short Calls and Long Stock (a Covered Call)   The margin is 50 percent of the value of the equity. The proceeds of the call sale may also be applied to reduce the necessary margin. No extra margin is required for the call because any losses due to the option will be offset by an increase in the equity.

Portfolio Margin   This margining method uses a pricing model to calculate the loss of a position at different underlying prices above and below current stock price. The largest loss identified is the margin of the position.

Stock positions are tested with price changes of up and down 15 percent. Small cap broad-based indices are tested with 10 percent price changes, and large cap broad-based indices are tested with a move of down 6 percent and up 8 percent. The range is divided into eight equal units, and the loss on the position is calculated at each of the eight points and the two high and low points.

This is the basic method but there are several adjustments applied.

- There is a minimum margin of $37.50.
- "Similar" classes such as SPX and OEX options are assumed to have offsetting risks.
- In addition to the underlying price shift, a volatility shift can also be applied.

SUMMARY

- You should never make a trade until you fully understand the contract specifications.
- When making a trade, err on the side of overchecking the contract details.

CHAPTER 3

Arbitrage Bounds for Option Prices

B efore we even consider any models for pricing options, we can make some statements about option values. These are based on the principle of no arbitrage.

This is probably the closest thing finance has to a fundamental law. Sometimes known as the "law of one price," this states that if two securities are the same, then they will have the same price. If they do not, then traders called arbitrageurs will trade the securities and make a risk-free profit. Making money with no risk is very difficult, so these opportunities tend to arise infrequently. Moreover, once these divergences from value do occur, the trading action of arbitrageurs tends to eliminate the discrepancy. Thus the law of no arbitrage is somewhat self-fulfilling. This concept is crucially important so we will look at some simple examples.

First, imagine we can buy a share of Microsoft on one exchange for $32.00 and sell it immediately on another for $32.02. These shares are exactly the same, so by doing this we would make 2 cents with no risk. Note that to do this our trading costs would need to be less than one cent per share (as we have traded two shares in total). Sometimes what appears to be an arbitrage opportunity is merely a situation with larger than anticipated transaction costs. Second, there will be an instant when we own a share and have not yet sold one (or vice versa). If the price changes in this time we can lose money. This is an example of execution risk.

A far more common form of arbitrage is where two securities are not identical, but they have a well-defined financial relationship that allows us to construct a risk-free portfolio from combinations of the securities. The simplest example of this type is a forward contract.

Imagine that we have an asset, say a stock with a current price of S, which we want to sell at a certain time in the future, T. What is the price, F, at which we would be indifferent about agreeing to sell it? By this we mean that neither we nor our counterparty have any obvious advantage in the trade. In the case where the stock pays no dividends

$$F = S \exp(rT) \qquad (3.1)$$

where r is the risk-free interest rate.

As an example, let's assume we have a stock trading at \$100, interest rates are 5 percent, and we want to calculate the fair value for a one year forward. Equation 3.1 gives this value as

$$F = \$100 \ \exp(0.05) = \$105.13$$

We will prove that equation 3.1 holds, by assuming it does not and showing that this leads to possible arbitrage profits. First assume that

$$F < S \exp(rT)$$

To make a profit we

- Buy the futures contract and sells the underlying. We invest the proceeds from the sale.
- On the expiration date, we take the money out of the bank. It will have grown at the risk-free rate, r.
- We then receive the underlying and pay the agreed forward price using the matured investment to do so.
- The difference between the two amounts is the arbitrage profit.

If

$$F > S \exp(rT)$$

we

- Sell the futures contract and buy the underlying with borrowed money.
- On the expiration date, we deliver the underlying, and receive the agreed forward price, F.
- We then repay the lender the borrowed amount plus interest.
- The difference between the two amounts is the arbitrage profit.

We see that if equation 3.1 does not hold we can make a risk-free profit. So by the law of no arbitrage, equation 3.1 must be true. There are a few things to note:

- The underlying must be an asset we can actually trade. We need to be able to buy it and also to sell it short. If only one of these conditions held we would have an inequality rather than an equality.
- We have assumed that the interest rate we can borrow at and lend at is the same. This is clearly not the case and if we took this into account we would arrive at no arbitrage bands, instead of at a single value.
- We have assumed that holding the underlying gives the owner no benefits. This would be untrue if it was a stock that paid a dividend. In this case we would need to adjust equation 3.1 so that we considered the value of the stock minus the present value of the dividend.

$$F = (S - PVD) \exp(rT) \tag{3.2}$$

- Similarly, we have assumed that holding the underlying does not incur storage costs. For most commodities this is not the case. These costs would behave like a *negative* dividend.
- We have assumed that the interest rate is paid by an entity that will not default. This is the definition of the risk-free rate. Such a situation does not exist. United States government securities are normally used as a proxy for risk-free bonds, but these are neither riskless nor always available in the correct duration. In practice, traders borrow from or lend funds to their clearing firm. As different firms will have slightly different rates this means that each trader may have a slightly different idea of fair value for the futures contract.
- We have assumed that the interest rate is constant. This is important when we are considering the difference between forward contracts and futures. Technically, what we have done here is price a forward, not a future. Forwards are agreed upon between counterparties, whereas futures have an exchange as a central counterparty. Futures are marked to market each day and the amount of collateral a trader needs to post is hence adjusted daily. If interest rates and the underlying are positively correlated, futures contracts will be worth slightly more than forward contracts. This is because when the underlying increases, the holder of the future makes an immediate gain in his account because of the daily settlement. The positive correlation makes it likely that rates have also increased, so the gain can be invested at a higher rate. So gains will be invested at higher rates and losses at lower rates. A forward will not be affected in this way, so a future will be worth more than a forward in this case. Negative correlation will

imply that futures are worth less than forwards. However, in general this difference is too small to bother with and in practically every case we can assume futures are priced as forwards.

- Something that is very important to note is that nowhere have we appealed to a forecast of the future price of the asset. The future contract's price is *not* the expected price in the future. It is merely the price that allows no arbitrage. If the price is expected to be higher in the future it will have to be higher *now* to prevent arbitrage.

This is an example of arbitrage through *static replication*. We did a trade, and then held it until the derivative contact expired. We will see in Chapter 4 that option pricing is based on the idea of *dynamic replication*, where a position needs to be rebalanced in order to maintain the riskless nature of the arbitrage. Obviously, any position that needs to be adjusted will have more risk than one that needs only to be traded once, so at this point we are not dealing with true arbitrage any more.

PSEUDOARBITRAGE

Incidentally, you will often encounter this situation in trading, where a risky trading strategy is referred to as an arbitrage. Other examples include *statistical arbitrage*, where a relationship should hold on average. At least this fairly accurately describes the situation. A less honest example is *risk arbitrage*; the practice of buying shares in a company that has been taken over before the transaction has closed. In such situations, the share price generally does not immediately rise to the announced takeover price but stays a little lower. This is because not all announced transactions are completed. Risk arbitrage traders hope that enough mergers are completed to make up for the times where the deal falls apart completely. This is a valid example of statistical arbitrage, but it is not a true arbitrage at all.

We will now look at the bounds that this principle implies for option prices. If an option price violates these bounds, we would be able to make a risk-free profit. These arbitrage bounds give relationships between calls and puts and the underlying, also between options with different strikes, maturities, and expiration types.

The results in this section need to become second nature, but it is also important to be familiar with the arguments we use for establishing them. This type of thought process will need to be used when a trader has to trade a previously unfamiliar security. As options are now often embedded in other financial products, this process is probably as important to understand as merely remembering the results. Another way to put this is that this chapter is repetitive and dull, but it is also very important. One could argue that traders do not really need to understand pricing models (the argument would be incorrect but at least some defense could be mounted), but all traders need to understand these arbitrage relationships.

AMERICAN OPTIONS COMPARED TO EUROPEAN OPTIONS

An American option is always worth at least as much as a European option. We always have the right to exercise the American option before expiration, but we do not have to. If we hold it until expiry it will be a European option. If we ever find an American option trading for less than an equivalent European option we can create a risk-free profit by buying the American option, selling the European option, then holding the position until expiration. So, using the notation where capital letters denote American options and lowercase letters denote European options, we have

$$c \leq C \tag{3.3}$$

for calls and

$$p \leq P \tag{3.4}$$

for puts.

ABSOLUTE MAXIMUM AND MINIMUM VALUES

The Maximum Value of a Call

A call cannot cost more than the underlying. That is

$$c \leq S \tag{3.5}$$

The first way to prove this is to use the argument from obviousness: the right to purchase an item cannot be worth more than the item itself. However this is both a generally invalid form of proof, and also deprives us of an opportunity to see a simple example of the more general method. We will show that this statement is true by assuming it is not, then constructing a portfolio that can only profit. As we know that arbitrage profits do not just sit around, we can consider the statement proved. This is proof by contradiction and the principle of no arbitrage.

Imagine a European call is trading for more than the underlying. We then choose to sell the call and buy the underlying at a price of S_0. At expiration (time T) our profit will be

$$c - (S_0 - S_T) \tag{3.6}$$

But the second term has to be less than S_0, and our assumption was that $c > S_0$, so this profit must be greater than zero. We have to make money. So for there to be no arbitrage we need to have

$$c \leq S$$

This argument can be modified to apply to American options. Here we cannot assume that our short option position exists until expiry. The holder may decide to exercise before this. But all we need to do is replace the terminal price S_T by the price at exercise, S_{ex}. The rest of the argument is the same.

The Maximum Value of a Put

An American put can never be worth more than the strike price.

$$P \leq X \tag{3.7}$$

This is because the most value a put can ever have is when the underlying goes to zero. In this case the payoff is equal to the strike.

Further, for a European option we know that it will take this maximum value only at expiry. So we need to discount this amount. This gives the lesser bound

$$p \leq X \exp(-rt) \tag{3.8}$$

Minimum Value for a Call Option

The lower bound for a European call option is given by

$$c \geq S - X \exp(-rt) \tag{3.9}$$

To see why this needs to be the case we consider two portfolios. The first consists of one share. The second consists of a call and an amount of cash equal to $X \exp(-rt)$. By expiration the cash will have grown to X, because we will have invested it at the risk-free rater. If the option is in the money it will be worth $S - X$, and the entire portfolio will be worth S. If the option is out of the money the portfolio will be worth X. So this portfolio has value of

$$Max(S, X) \tag{3.10}$$

at expiry.

Clearly the first portfolio will be worth S, so the second portfolio is always worth at least as much as the first. As we are dealing with European options this must also be true today. So

$$c + X \exp(-rt) \geq S \tag{3.11}$$

or

$$c \geq S - X \exp(-rt) \tag{3.12}$$

Example Consider a one-year European call option with a strike price of 95 when the stock is trading at 100 and interest rates are 10 percent. Then the lower bound for the option price is

$$100 - 95 \ \exp(-0.1) = \$14.04$$

Minimum Value for a Put Option

The lower bound for a European put option is

$$p \geq X \exp(-rt) - S \tag{3.13}$$

We can prove this in an analogous way to the argument above. We consider two portfolios. The first consists of a put and a share. The second consists of an amount of cash equal to $X \exp(-rt)$. Again, at expiry this second portfolio is worth X. At expiry if the underlying is below the strike we exercise the put and the first portfolio is worth X. If the option expires worthless because the underlying is above the strike the portfolio will be worth S. So the portfolio has the value

$$Max(S, X)$$

at expiry.

So again we have the situation where the first portfolio is always worth at least as much as the second at expiry. And for European options this relationship holds for all times. So

$$p + S \geq X \exp(-rt) \tag{3.14}$$

or

$$p \geq X \exp(-rt) - S \qquad (3.15)$$

Example Consider a six-month European put option with a strike price of 105 when the stock is trading at 100 and interest rates are 8 percent. Then the lower bound for the option price is

$$105 \ \exp(-0.08 \times 0.5) - 100 = \$0.88$$

These arguments do not apply to American options, but we can state another lower bound for these options. Both American calls and puts have lower bounds given by their intrinsic values.

$$C \geq Max(0, S - X) \qquad (3.16)$$

$$P \geq Max(0, X - S) \qquad (3.17)$$

Imagine this was not the case and we could buy an American option for less than intrinsic value. We could immediately exercise the option and receive the intrinsic value giving us an arbitrage.

Note that this means that European options can trade below intrinsic value due to the effects of discounting. This is never the case for American options.

Unless we are at expiry or interest rates are zero

$$S - X \exp(-rt) > S - X \qquad (3.18)$$

So, together with the fact that American options are always at least as valuable as European options, we can see that the lower bound for the European call must also apply to the American option.

$$C = Max(0, S - X \exp(-rt)) \qquad (3.19)$$

We will discuss the subject of early exercise in more detail (see Chapter 15), but already we have enough to see that we should never exercise a call on a non–dividend paying stock. This is because an in-the-money option has a minimum value, if unexercised, of

$$S - X \exp(-rt) \qquad (3.20)$$

and this is greater than the intrinsic value of $S - X$.

This may seem counter-intuitive, but if a trader wants to realize the profits from a deep in the money call position he will be better off selling the option than exercising it. All we do by exercising early is to pay for

TABLE 3.1 Comparing Calls with Different Strikes

Portfolio 1

Instrument	Initial Value	Value at Expiration		
		$S < X_1$	$X_1 < S < X_2$	$S > X_2$
Long $c(X_1)$	$c(X_1)$	0	$S - X_1$	$S - X_1$
Short $c(X_2)$	$-c(X_2)$	0	0	$-(S - X_2)$
Total	$c(X_1) - c(X_2)$	0	$S - X_1$	$X_2 - X_1$

Portfolio 2

Instrument	Initial Value	Value at Expiration		
		$S < X_1$	$X_1 < S < X_2$	$S > X_2$
Cash	$(X_2 - X_1)\exp(-rt)$	$X_2 - X_1$	$X_2 - X_1$	$X_2 - X_1$

the asset before it is actually necessary and, further, to give up the right to change our mind later.

So long as we never exercise such a call early, the American and European calls will have the same value.

Calls with Different Strikes

What can we say about call options that are identical except for their strikes? Consider two strikes, X_2 and X_1, where $X_2 > X_1$.

Now construct two portfolios: the first consisting of a long position in $c_1 = c(X_1)$ and a short position in $c_2 = c(X_2)$, and the second a cash position worth $(X_2 - X_1)\exp(-rt)$. There are now a number of scenarios to keep track of. To make this easier we drew up Table 3.1.

The first thing to note is that the payoff for Portfolio 1 is always positive. This means that the initial value must also be positive. So

$$c(X_1) > c(X_2) \tag{3.21}$$

Does this result also hold for American options? Clearly it does if the underlying pays no dividends. If also holds in general if we can show that there is no situation where the call spread can have negative value to us. Our long call cannot be a problem because we would only ever choose to exercise it if we made money. Now imagine that the holder exercises our short call, $c(X_2)$. For this to happen, S must be above X_2, and hence X_1. So in this case, we could also exercise our call and obtain a payoff of $X_2 - X_1$.

This means that early exercise considerations do not change the result. So

$$C(X_1) > C(X_2) \tag{3.22}$$

The second thing is that the second portfolio is always worth at least as much as the first. This means that

$$c(X_1) - c(X_2) \leq (X_2 - X_1) \exp(-rt) \tag{3.23}$$

This argument needs to be modified a little for American options. If both calls were exercised early (so $S > X_2$) we would obtain $X_2 - X_1$ in cash and could then invest this. This would make the call spread portfolio worth more than the cash portfolio. To avoid this we need to structure the cash portfolio so that it has a current value of $X_2 - X_1$. This means that if we are in a situation where exercise is optimal we receive this value and can then invest it, so the cash portfolio is never dominated due to earned interest. With this modification we see that

$$C(X_1) - C(X_2) \leq X_2 - X_1 \tag{3.24}$$

As a practical matter, if a trader can ever buy a call spread and receive a credit for doing so (for example, receiving money for buying a 100, 105 call spread) he should do as many as possible. In fact if he can do this trade without an outlay of cash he should do as many as possible. In many cases, both options will expire out of the money and the trade will make nothing, but in some cases it will be profitable at expiry. This is a situation where traders need to take a statistical view. Arbitrage violations will not be profitable in every case, but on average they are. It is like being given free lottery tickets.

Puts with Different Strikes

Now we work through a similar analysis for put options of different strikes. Again we consider two strikes, X_2 and X_1 where $X_2 > X_1$.

Again we construct two portfolios. The first is short a European put struck at X_1 and a long position in a European put struck at X_2. The second portfolio consists of the amount of cash, $(X_2 - X_1) \exp(-rt)$. Table 3.2 shows all the possible values of these portfolios.

The first thing to notice is that the final payoff on the put portfolio is always non-negative. This means that the current value must also be non-negative. So

$$p(X_2) \geq p(X_1) \tag{3.25}$$

TABLE 3.2 Comparing Puts with Different Strikes

Portfolio 1

		Value at Expiration		
Instrument	Initial Value	$S < X_1$	$X_1 < S < X_2$	$S > X_2$
Short $p(X_1)$	$-p(X_1)$	$-(X_1 - S)$	0	0
Long $p(X_2)$	$P(X_2)$	$X_2 - S$	$X_2 - S$	0
Total	$P(X_2) - p(X_1)$	$X_2 - X_1$	$X_2 - S$	0

Portfolio 2

		Value at Expiration		
Instrument	Initial Value	$S < X_1$	$X_1 < S < X_2$	$S > X_2$
Cash	$(X_2 - X_1)\exp(-rt)$	$X_2 - X_1$	$X_2 - X_1$	$X_2 - X_1$

That is, European puts with a higher strike price are always worth at least as much as those with a lower strike price.

We can show that this result also holds for American options if we can show that the payoff of the put portfolio is *never* negative, not only at expiry. If our short put is exercised early, it must be because $S < X_1$. But this implies $S < X_2$ so we could also exercise this put and capture a gain of $X_2 - X_1$. So the possibility of early exercise does not change the result.

$$P(X_2) \geq P(X_1) \tag{3.26}$$

Next we see that the second portfolio is always worth at least as much as the first. This gives an upper bound on the value of the put spread.

$$p(X_2) - p(X_1) \leq (X_2 - X_1) \exp(-rt) \tag{3.27}$$

In the case of American puts we again need to make a small modification, just as we did for call spreads earlier. We need to hold a current value of $X_2 - X_1$ in cash. Now if our short put is exercised early, we can in turn exercise our long put and get a payout of $X_2 - X_1$. This can then be invested and grow at the risk-free rate. But this will also be happening to our cash portfolio, so it will grow to a value at least as great as that of the put portfolio (they will be equal if the puts are exercised as soon as the portfolios are set up). So for American puts we have the upper bound for a put spread given by

$$P(X_2) - P(X_1) \leq (X_2 - X_1) \tag{3.28}$$

The "Butterfly" Relationship

There is an important relationship between three options that differ by strike price. Consider European call options with strikes X_1, X_2, and X_3, where $X_3 > X_2 > X_1$. Now we set up two portfolios. The first consists of α units of $c(X_1)$ and $(1 - \alpha)$ units of $c(X_3)$, where α is defined as

$$\alpha = \frac{(X_3 - X_2)}{(X_3 - X_1)} \qquad (3.29)$$

From this definition we can see that $\alpha > 0$.

The second portfolio consists of one of the middle strike calls, $c(X_2)$. The payoff scenarios for these portfolios are shown in Table 3.3.

If $S < X_1$, the portfolios produce the same result. If $X_1 < S < X_2$, the first portfolio is obviously better. If $X_2 < S < X_3$, portfolio one is again dominant because $X_2 > X_1$. In the final case where $S < X_1$ the portfolios are equal. This is not particularly self-evident but we can check it by substituting the expression for α and doing a little algebra. So Portfolio 1 is at least as valuable in all possible states of the world.

$$\alpha c(X_1) + (1 - \alpha) c(X_3) \geq c(X_2) \qquad (3.30)$$

This also applies to American options, because all the payoffs that we assumed would occur at expiration would just arrive early. So

$$\alpha C(X_1) + (1 - \alpha) C(X_3) \geq C(X_2) \qquad (3.31)$$

The same type of argument also applies to puts.

$$\alpha p(X_1) + (1 - \alpha) p(X_3) \geq p(X_2) \qquad (3.32)$$

$$\alpha P(X_1) + (1 - \alpha) P(X_3) \geq P(X_2) \qquad (3.33)$$

In the special case where the strikes are equally spaced $X_3 - X_2 = X_2 - X_1$ we can see that $\alpha = 0.5$. This portfolio is known as a butterfly. For example, a European call butterfly would satisfy the relationship

$$c(X_1) + c(X_3) \geq 2c(X_2) \qquad (3.34)$$

or

$$c(X_1) - 2c(X_2) + c(X_3) \geq 0 \qquad (3.35)$$

That is, butterflies can never be negative. We will return to this later.

TABLE 3.3 Comparing Three Calls with Different Strikes

Portfolio 1

Instrument	Initial Value	Value at Expiration			
		$S < X_1$	$X_1 < S < X_2$	$X_2 < S < X_3$	$S > X_3$
Long $\alpha c(X_1)$	$\alpha c(X_1)$	0	$\alpha(S - X_1)$	$\alpha(S - X_1)$	$\alpha(S - X_1)$
Long $(1-\alpha)c(X_3)$	$(1-\alpha)c(X_3)$	0	0	0	$(1-\alpha)(S - X_3)$
Total	$\alpha c(X_1) + (1-\alpha)c(X_3)$	0	$\alpha(S - X_1)$	$\alpha(S - X_1)$	$S - \alpha X_1 - (1-\alpha)X_3$

Portfolio 2

Instrument	Initial Value	Value at Expiration			
		$S < X_1$	$X_1 < S < X_2$	$X_2 < S < X_3$	$S > X_3$
Long $c(X_2)$	$c(X_2)$	0	0	$S - X_2$	$S - X_2$

Relationships between Calls with Different Expirations

Consider two European calls that are identical except for their expiration dates. One has time until expiry of T_1 and the other has time until expiry of T_2. We will also assume that $T_2 > T_1$.

Initially we ignore dividends. At the expiry of the shorter dated option it will be worth

$$Max(0, S(T_1) - X) \qquad (3.36)$$

However the longer dated option still has more time remaining. From equation 3.12 its minimum value is given by

$$Max(0, S(T_1) - X \exp(-r (T_2 - T_1))) \qquad (3.37)$$

This is greater than the value of the shorter-term option. So

$$c(T_2) \geq c(T_1) \qquad (3.38)$$

If the underlying pays dividends we need to modify this argument. In this case the longer dated option has the minimum value

$$Max(0, S(T_1) - D - X \exp(-r (T_2 - T_1))) \qquad (3.39)$$

This means that the longer dated option could take a value less than that of the shorter dated option (The way to rationalize this is that if the underlying pays a dividend and this occurs during the lifetime of one option and not another, then in some ways these options are on a different underlying). For American options this could not be true, as the longer dated call could not be worth less than intrinsic value. So

$$C(T_2) \geq C(T_1) \qquad (3.40)$$

Relationships between Puts with Different Expirations

Now let's think about European puts. When the underlying pays no dividends the shorter dated option is worth

$$Max(0, X - S) \qquad (3.41)$$

at expiry.

At this time the longer dated option is worth at least

$$Max(0, X \exp(-r (T_1 - T_2)) - S) \qquad (3.42)$$

TABLE 3.4 The Put Call Parity Relationship

Instrument	Initial Value	Value at Expiration $S < X_1$	Value at Expiration $S > X_1$
Long $p(X_1)$	$p(X_1)$	$(X_1 - S)$	0
Short $c(X_1)$	$-c(X_1)$	0	$-(S - X_1)$
Long Stock	S	S	S
Total	$S + p(X_1) - c(X_1)$	X_1	X_1

So in this case the short-term option could be worth more. This result can be confusing to some traders. It is related to the reason that we will sometimes decide to exercise an American put early. If we exercise we get the cash early and can invest it. So in this case holding the option hurts us. We would rather convert it into the cash position, but this is not allowed with European options. Here we have to wait to get our money. We will return to this point when we discuss the effects of interest rates on options.

This argument also applies when dividends are being paid. However for American options it does not hold. Here

$$P(T_2) \geq P(T_1) \tag{3.43}$$

Put Call Parity

Put call parity is an arbitrage relationship between European calls and puts of the same strike. It states that

$$c - p = S - X \exp(-rT) \tag{3.44}$$

To see why this relationship must hold, we construct a portfolio that is formed by buying a put, selling a call with the same strike, and buying one share of stock. At expiration this takes the values given in Table 3.4.

So at expiry, this position must be worth the strike price. This means that it currently must be worth the discounted value of the strike price. So

$$p - c + S = X \exp(-rT) \tag{3.45}$$

Rearranging this gives the more common, and easier to remember, version above (equation 3.44). This relationship has a number of important implications.

- We can simply rearrange equation 3.45 to obtain

$$c = S - X \exp(-rT) + p \tag{3.46}$$

This says that owning a call is like borrowing money to buy stock and also owning a put. Or it is a leveraged position in the underlying with limited downside.

- For nonzero interest rates, if the options are struck at the spot price ($S = X$) calls are worth more than puts. For the call and put to have equal value we need

$$S = X \exp(-rT) \tag{3.47}$$

or

$$X = S \exp(rT) \tag{3.48}$$

That is, the options must be struck at the forward price.
- We can replicate the payoff from any position with the other three instruments. For example, a call can be replicated with a put, stock, and cash.

This relationship can easily be modified if the underlying pays dividends. We just have to consider the underlying minus the present value of any dividends. The put call parity relationship can be stated as

$$c - p = S - PVD - X \exp(-rT) \tag{3.49}$$

Put call parity does not hold for American options. In the portfolio above where we demonstrated the relationship, we had to sell a call (We could also construct the opposite portfolio which would have required selling a put). In order for us to create a risk-free position we must be assured that this short option will not be exercised. If the underlying pays no dividends the short call in our portfolio will not be exercised. However it is possible that we would want to exercise our put early so we could not be sure that we would receive X in cash at the expiry date of the option. Again we set up two portfolios:

Portfolio 1

| Instrument | Initial Value | Value at Expiration | |
		$S < X_1$	$S > X_1$
Long $c(X_1)$	$c(X_1)$	0	$(S - X_1)$
Cash	X_1	$X_1 \exp(rt)$	$X_1 \exp(rt)$
Total	$c(X_1) + X_1$	$X_1 \exp(rt)$	$S + X_1 \exp(rt-1)$

The second portfolio consists of a share and a put. It may be optimal to exercise the put before expiration. We have two situations to keep track of: one where the put is not exercised and one where it is exercised at time t^*. At this time we sell a share short. We buy this back at the expiration date.

Portfolio 2: No Exercise

Instrument	Initial Value	Value at Expiration $S < X_1$	$S > X_1$
Long $p(X_1)$	$p(X_1)$	$(X_1 - S)$	0
Long Stock	S	S	S
Total	$p(X_1) + S$	X_1	S

Portfolio 2: Exercise

Instrument	Initial Value	Value at Expiration $S < X_1$	$S > X_1$
Long $p(X_1)$	$p(X_1)$	$X_1\exp(r(t-t^*))-S$	$X_1\exp(r(t-t^*))-S$
Long Stock	S	S	S
Total	$p(X_1)+ S$	$X_1\exp(r(t-t^*))$	$X_1\exp(r(t-t^*))$

Clearly at expiration the first portfolio is worth at least as much as the second. So

$$C + X \geq P + S \tag{3.50}$$

or

$$C - P \geq S - X \tag{3.51}$$

This gives a lower bound.

To get an upper bound we start with the European put call parity relationship of equation 3.43, and rearrange slightly to get.

$$p = c - S + X \exp(-rT) \tag{3.52}$$

Also $P \geq p$, so

$$P \geq c - S + X \exp(-rT) \tag{3.53}$$

When no dividends are paid $c = C$, so we get

$$C - P \leq S - X \exp(-rT) \tag{3.54}$$

This gives an upper bound. So for American options on nondividend paying stocks, the put call parity relationship is

$$S - X \leq C - P \leq S - X \exp(-rT) \tag{3.55}$$

If the put is closer to an exercise (i.e., the put is deeper in the money) we will be closer to the lower bound.

Example   If $S = X = 100$, $r = 10$ percent and $T =$ one year the difference between the American call and put values is bounded by

$$0 \leq C - P \leq 100 - 100 \exp(-0.1) = 9.516$$

A similar argument establishes a lower bound when the underlying pays dividends of

$$C - P \geq S - PVD - X \tag{3.56}$$

where PVD is the present value of the dividends. So, the put call parity relationship in this case is

$$S - PVD - X \leq C - P \leq S - X \exp(-rT) \tag{3.57}$$

Boxes

Suppose we have the position where we own $c(X_1)$, are short $c(X_2)$, own $p(X_2)$ and are short $p(X_1)$. That is, we are long the call spread and also long the put spread (Quite why we would be interested in this position will become clear in a moment). This is a box or a box spread. The payoffs for this strategy are shown below in Table 3.5.

No matter what happens, this strategy is always worth $X_2 - X_1$ at expiry. So at any time it will be worth the present value of $X_2 - X_1$. That is

$$c(X_1) - c(X_2) + p(X_2) - p(X_1) = (X_2 - X_2) \exp(-rT) \tag{3.58}$$

A box spread is useful because its risk is entirely dependent on the interest rate. So a trader can manage his interest rate exposure by trading boxes. Often other traders will be equally eager to trade, so the effective

TABLE 3.5 A Box

Instrument	Initial Value	Value at Expiration		
		$S < X_1$	$X_1 < S < X_2$	$S > X_2$
Long $c(X_1)$	$c(X_1)$	0	$S - X_1$	$S - X_1$
Short $c(X_2)$	$-c(X_2)$	0	0	$-(S - X_2)$
Short $p(X_1)$	$-p(X_1)$	$-(X_1 - S)$	0	0
Long $p(X_2)$	$p(X_2)$	$X_2 - S$	$X_2 - S$	0
Total	$c(X_1) - c(X_2) - p(X_1) + p(X_2)$	$X_2 - X_1$	$X_2 - X_1$	$X_2 - X_1$

interest rate bid ask spread will be far smaller than that charged by the clearing house. This analysis is unchanged if the underlying pays a dividend as we are net flat both calls and puts.

Unfortunately, things are not as neat when the options are American. This can be seen by combining equations 3.24 and 3.28 to get

$$C(X_1) - C(X_2) + P(X_2) - P(X_1) \leq 2(X_2 - X_2) \qquad (3.59)$$

This is clearly not as restrictive. American boxes are quoted and traded. Some American options are almost European. If the dividend yield and interest rates are low the early exercise risk is lessened, and they become more like a European option. However, traders should be very careful when selling an American box. It may be the counterparty's way of putting on a trade that will profit if a special dividend is paid when an American call will become far more valuable than it would be without the dividend.

SUMMARY

We now know a considerable amount about options. In fact, many traders rely more heavily on these arbitrage-based relationships than on the predictions of any specific pricing model. We discuss this in detail in Chapter 10, in which we look at market making tactics and strategies.

Generally these statements are true. In making this summary, I will ignore the differences between American and European options and cases where dividends are paid, unless explicitly stated otherwise. These are relationships traders rely on and the subtleties that we covered in the text of this chapter are less important than these generalities.

- American options are worth more than European options
- Longer dated options are worth more than shorter dated options

- Calls cannot be worth more than the underlying.
- Puts cannot be worth more than the (appropriately discounted) strike price.
- Call spreads are positive.
- Put spreads are positive.
- Butterflies are positive.
- Put call parity allows us to transform puts into calls, and vice versa.
- Boxes are the discounted value of the difference between the strike.

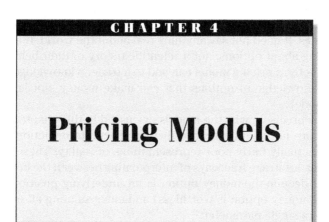

CHAPTER 4

Pricing Models

Essentially, all models are wrong, but some are useful.
—George Box, in "Robustness in the Strategy of
Scientific Model Building." In R. L. Launer
and G. N. Wilkinson, eds., *Robustness in
Statistics.* New York: Academic Press, 1979.

Option pricing involves reasonably complex mathematics. How deeply does a trader need to delve into this? To answer this we need to understand what a model does. What is a model?

A model is a map. It simplifies the world, keeping the detail we need and excluding the rest. It is not meant to be a perfect representation of reality. The only way a map can be perfect is if it is the same size as the world. Then we have gained nothing.

Options are complex. Their prices are dependent on a number of variables and the prices change very quickly. Add to this the fact that one underlying may have hundreds of options associated with it and that these all have relationships to each other, and having a model to make things simpler seems clearly advantageous. That is not to say a model is essential. Many retail option traders, and even some professionals, trade without one, either using options as leveraged directional instruments or to implement the static strategies we look at in Chapter 6.

But a model, used intelligently, greatly simplifies things. It expresses the fast moving option prices as functions of more slowly evolving parameters. It also enables us to compare options of different strikes, maturities and underlyings in a simple framework.

This cannot be overemphasized. A model is a framework for thinking about trades. It need not say anything real about the world. It is a language for thinking about options, not a scientific theory of their behavior. When used correctly, a pricing model can add to a trader's knowledge of options, but it is knowledge of options that can make money, not knowledge of pricing models.

This is precisely why the models discussed in this chapter are so useful. They are not useful because they are accurate depictions of reality. They are actually fairly poor representations of reality. These models are convenient, arbitrage free ways of interpolating between the boundary conditions (a deep-in-the-money option is an underlying position and a far-out-of-the-money option is worthless) and encapsulating all of our uncertainty into a single parameter.

So what does a trader need to understand about his model?

Clearly a trader needs to be aware of the assumptions behind the model, but this knowledge is only useful if he is also aware of how the imperfection of these assumptions affects the model's prices. In many cases this seems to be the missing step. It is easy to recall that the Black Scholes Merton model assumes that the underlying can be shorted and the proceeds invested at a given rate. It is another thing to know what happens to the price of a put when this is not the case.

This will be our focus. We will look at two option-pricing models: the Black-Scholes-Merton (BSM) model and the Binomial Tree model. These are complementary approaches and provide the basis for more complex methods. If a trader really understands these he will be in a good position to understand other models (and will be well ahead of his competitors).

Neither of these models is presented so the trader can use them as practical pricing tools. The BSM partial differential equation has only a closed form solution for European options, and these form only a small subset of tradable options. The binomial model can form the basis of a practical pricing algorithm but it needs to be slightly reformulated in order to converge quickly and smoothly. These models are presented to aid understanding. Few traders need to program their own models anymore, but all should understand modeling assumptions.

But before we can look at particular models we need to discuss modeling in general, and in particular what variables a sensible option-pricing model needs to use.

GENERAL MODELING PRINCIPLES

Traders are not quants, and they should not be expected to have the same depth of modeling ability or expertise. It would be unreasonable to expect an option trader to come up with an option-pricing model. However, a good trader needs to be able to understand models and modeling to a level where he can point out failings and suggest improvements (the process is analogous to that of a race-car driver giving feedback to the engineers). Here we will give a general overview of what to look for in a model. It will consist of a number of parts.

- Have we used the correct mathematical or statistical methods?
- Do the variables we have chosen on which to base our model make sense?
- How should we interpret the results?

Choosing the Tools

Too often we see models where it is obvious the modeler has applied a technique because he is an expert in that method, rather than because it is suitable for the problem. A couple of recent examples I have seen include using quantum field theory to rederive the Black-Scholes-Merton equation, and using the path integral approach to quantum mechanics to predict basketball games. So how should we decide which tool to use?

The answer to this lies in having a fundamental understanding of the problem. For example, the value of an option is clearly (at least after having read the previous chapters) related to the value of the underlying. So a natural way to price options would be to simulate the underlying or to look at its price distribution. The first way of thinking will lead you to Monte Carlo– or tree-based methods, and the second to the Black-Scholes-Merton world. I do not see how anyone could start from a statement of the problem and conclude that quantum field theory was the natural framework for a solution.

Using Suitable Variables

Starting with the wrong variables will inevitably lead to a poor model. Experience is essential here.

A trivial example can illustrate the problem. Imagine we are trying to forecast the number of games a particular NBA team will win next season (which consists of 82 games). We decide that the relevant variables to consider are winning percentage, field goal percentage, and free-throw percentage (ignore for a moment why we would think that these variables are any more predictable in themselves). If we run a regression using historical data we will obtain the regression results

$$wins = 82 \times win\% + 0 \times FG\% + 0 \times FT\%$$

According to this model, shooting ability has absolutely no effect on teams' results. You do not need to know a lot about basketball to be suspicious of this conclusion. What has gone wrong?

The problem is that winning percentage is also a function of the two shooting percentages (the technical term for this is multicolinearity). It is important that the variables we choose are, as much as possible, independent of one another. In finance this can be very difficult, as it often is not obvious what anything is a function of. In other cases, the same variable will enter a problem in two distinct ways. For example, interest rates are necessary variables in all derivative pricing problems as they are needed for discounting future cash flows to their present values. However they also are believed to be determinants of the underlying price, so these two variables are not independent. As we clearly need to incorporate both rates and the underlying, we cannot avoid this problem. However this is not an ideal situation and if the effect of rates on the underlying were stronger, it could cause real problems.

Identifying relevant variables is something of an art form. But a general guide is to:

- Think about possible codependence between the variables.
- Consider if the data that is available is a sensible measure of the effect you are trying to include. For example, a lot of trading strategies include as a factor a variable that measures whether a particular underlying is trending. However, there are many ways to actually measure "trendiness." Does your choice make sense? Is there a better one?
- Decide if you have left anything important out. There will always be something, but are the omissions so important that the results are useless? For example, we know that underlying price is an important variable for an option-pricing model. We also know that stock prices display a day of the week effect, where returns on certain weekdays are stronger than others. Is this a strong enough effect to include?

Interpretation of Results

To do this a trader needs to have the ability to translate the results from the particular mathematical form of the solution into something intuitive. In the case of the BSM pricing model this is usually done by graphically displaying the results. A trader need not be able to solve the differential equation, but he has to be able to understand the results.

The next step is to use the results of the modeling to gain insight. If the model does not help us do this, we have gained nothing. We will just have been playing mathematical games. We go through this process in Chapter 5, where we interpret the solutions of the BSM model.

CHOICE OF DEPENDENT VARIABLES

What variables do we need to consider when pricing options? And how must our model's output depend on these inputs? In Chapter 3 we look at arbitrage relationships between options and the underlying. Here we look at how individual options depend on other variables. Obviously there is some overlap. For example, the relationships between options with differing times to expiry could also have gone here to show how option prices vary with time. However, the interesting thing about that relationship is that it could potentially form the basis for an arbitrage, whereas knowing how an option price varies with the underlying could not, as there is only one underlying for each class of options.

Dependency on the Underlying

Calls are increasing functions of the underlying.

$$\frac{\partial C}{\partial S} > 0$$

$$\frac{\partial c}{\partial S} > 0$$

The reason for this is that the call payoff is

$$\text{Max}(0, \ S - X)$$

That is, the option pays off linearly above the strike. If the stock rises, the option has a greater probability of paying off so it will be worth more. Conversely, puts are decreasing functions of the underlying.

$$\frac{\partial P}{\partial S} < 0$$

$$\frac{\partial p}{\partial S} < 0$$

Dependency on the Strike

For vanilla options, strike is a fixed parameter rather than a variable. However, the payoff of an option is defined relative to the strike—that is, the relevant argument in the payoff function is $S - X$, rather than S. So the dependency of option prices on strikes is opposite that of the dependency on the underlying.

$$\frac{\partial C}{\partial X} < 0$$

$$\frac{\partial c}{\partial X} < 0$$

$$\frac{\partial P}{\partial X} > 0$$

$$\frac{\partial p}{\partial X} > 0$$

Dependency on Interest-Rate Changes

The effect of interest rates is generally far smaller than other parameters. This is both because rates tend to be more stable and also because changes in rates tend to correlate with changes in the underlying and it will be this second effect that dominates. This correlation can be nearly perfect in the case of bonds and interest rate futures: strong as in the case of equities or complex to varying degrees as in the case of many commodities. However, if we consider the effect of rates while holding all other variables constant, we can say a few things.

Calls on equities are affected positively by rising rates. The owner of a call will receive either zero or $S - X$ when it is exercised. If rates increase, the present value of the amount of cash we need to allocate to buying the asset decreases, so the call is worth more.

$$\frac{\partial C}{\partial r} > 0$$

$$\frac{\partial c}{\partial r} > 0$$

This is not true for futures options, as here no cash outlay is required to "purchase" the underlying. Here the interest rate effect is entirely due to the cost of carry of the option premium. This is always negative.

Puts are affected negatively by rising rates. The owner of a put will receive either zero or $X - S$ when it is exercised. If rates increase, the present value of the amount of cash we will receive decreases, so the put is worth more.

$$\frac{\partial P}{\partial r} < 0$$

$$\frac{\partial p}{\partial r} < 0$$

So the difference in rate sensitivity is that in one case we pay cash and in the other we will receive cash.

Dependency on Volatility Changes

While it is probably obvious that option prices should depend on the level of the underlying, the effect of volatility probably is not as evident. Even before we precisely define what we mean by volatility, we can state that options need to depend on *risk*.

If the underlying had no risk, that is if it was perfectly predictable, there would be no need to pay for a product that only had value in certain states of the world. It is only because we are uncertain about the future of the underlying that options have any value at all. And it follows that the more uncertain we are, the more valuable options must be.

$$\frac{\partial C}{\partial \sigma} > 0$$

$$\frac{\partial c}{\partial \sigma} > 0$$

$$\frac{\partial P}{\partial \sigma} > 0$$

$$\frac{\partial p}{\partial \sigma} > 0$$

Dependency on Time Changes

The effect of time on option prices is complicated because it enters in two places. On the one hand, time and volatility have similar effects. Volatility only creates risk if it has time to act; so longer time to expiration leads to more risk and higher option prices. However time also appears with interest rates to act as a discounting factor. Thus longer time to expiration tends to lower option prices. These two opposite effects must both be considered.

Dependency on Dividend Changes

Whether a dividend is paid discretely as in the case of stocks or whether they occur so frequently that we approximate them by a continuous yield (this is often done with indices), the effect of a dividend is to lower the effective underlying price. The holder of an option does not receive the dividend, so he is interested in the price minus the dividend (or discounted by the dividend yield). Thus a larger dividend decreases the value of calls and raises the value of puts.

$$\frac{\partial C}{\partial div} < 0$$

$$\frac{\partial c}{\partial div} < 0$$

$$\frac{\partial P}{\partial div} > 0$$

$$\frac{\partial p}{\partial div} > 0$$

Other Pricing Variables

We have seen that option prices are functions of underlying price, strike, rate, dividends, time, and volatility. Can we make a plausible argument for including any other parameters? Let's go over where we got these inputs.

- Strike and underlying appear in the payoff function.
- Rates, dividends, and time are needed for discounting and because holding the underlying has different costs and benefits from holding the option. From our work on pricing forwards in Chapter 3, we know that this could also include generalized carry costs that can include storage, dividends, and convenience yields.
- The underlying price is a function of volatility and time. Actually the underlying price is a random function that has a certain distribution. So anything else that may plausibly influence option prices through the underlying and its risk will enter the analysis here. For example, stock prices are influenced by earnings, seasonality effects, prices of raw materials, and currency prices, but these can all be viewed as contributors to the shape of the stock's return distribution and do not need to be modeled separately.

With this preamble behind us, we can look at two specific option-pricing models.

THE BINOMIAL MODEL

Examining the binomial model (or binomial tree) is the easiest way to get intuition about option pricing. It is also a very good way to price general options with more complex expiration conditions or payoff structures than the standard exchange traded vanilla options. First we will look at a very

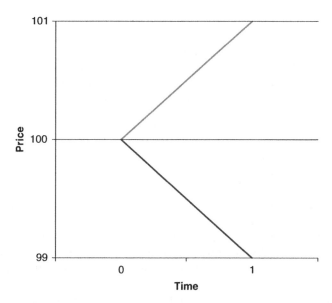

FIGURE 4.1 The Evolution of the Stock Price in the One-Step Binomial Tree

simple "toy" version of the model. Then we will show how it can be extended into a more realistic form.

Imagine that we have a stock that is trading $100. It can either move up $1 with probability, p, or move down $1 with probability, $1 - p$. This situation is illustrated in Figure 4.1.

Now let's imagine that we own the at-the-money call option. This has a strike of 100. If the stock rises we will make a profit of $1. If it drops we make nothing. We will try to hedge this position by selling a quantity, h, of the underlying.

When we have done this, if the stock rises we will make money on our call but lose money on our hedge. Our portfolio will be worth

$$Max(101 - 100,0) - h \times 101 \tag{4.1}$$

If the stock drops we lose money on our option, but our hedge will be profitable. In this case our portfolio will be worth

$$Max(99 - 100,0) - h \times 99 \tag{4.2}$$

For this to actually be a hedge we chose the hedge ratio, h, so that these two expressions are equal. This requires that $h = 0.5$.

Now we are indifferent to the stock's movement. The position has been transformed into one with no risk (this means that we can legitimately discount the portfolio value at the risk-free interest rate, but we will ignore this for now).

So what is the option worth right now? Setting h in expression 4.1 (or 4.2) equal to 0.5, we see that the final portfolio value is 48.5. As this is a risk-free portfolio, this must also be its current value when the stock is at $100. So the value of the call, C, can be obtained by solving the equation

$$C - 0.5 \times 100 = 49.5 \tag{4.3}$$

So $C = 0.5$ is the call value.

Two very important things have happened here:

- We have introduced the idea of hedging. Valuing a risk-free portfolio is much easier than trying to value one with sources of risk.
- The actual probability, p, of the stock moving up did not enter the argument at all. By hedging the movement of the underlying, we made this irrelevant. This is the major breakthrough in option pricing.

To generalize this idea we need to consider the case where the underlying can move up by a factor u, or down by a factor d. So

$$S_{up} = S_0 \times u \tag{4.4}$$

$$S_{down} = S_0 \times d \tag{4.5}$$

We are going to assume that our call has a value C_u if the underlying goes to S_u, and C_d if the underlying goes to S_d. Now we again want to calculate our hedge, h, that makes our long call/short stock portfolio riskless. In the upper state this is worth

$$C_u - h \times S_u \tag{4.6}$$

and in the lower state it is worth

$$C_d - h \times S_d \tag{4.7}$$

Equating these expressions and solving for the hedge ratio we obtain

$$h = \frac{C_u - C_d}{S_u - S_d} \tag{4.8}$$

Using this hedge ratio gives us a risk-free portfolio, so it grows at the risk-free rate, r. Equivalently, the present value of the portfolio will be given by

$$(C_u - hS_u) \exp(-rT) \tag{4.9}$$

where T is the length of the time step in the tree (we could also use the value at the down state in this argument). But we also know that the current value of the portfolio is

$$C - hS \qquad (4.10)$$

Equating these, we can solve for C.

$$C = hS - \exp\left(-rT\right)\left(C_u - hS_u\right) \qquad (4.11)$$

This can be rewritten in a more appealing form if we introduce

$$p = \frac{\exp\left(rt\right) - d}{u - d} \qquad (4.12)$$

Then

$$C = \exp\left(-rT\right)\left(pC_u - (1 - p)\,C_d\right) \qquad (4.13)$$

The variable, p, looks like a probability (in particular, $p + (1 - p) = 1$) and we have written equation 4.13 so that it looks as if the current value of the option is the discounted probability weighted average of its value in the up-and-down states of the underlying. But looking at equation 4.12 we see that the true probability of an up move never enters into our reasoning. That is, p depends only on the size of the up-and-down moves, not their actual probabilities. In other words, the true return of the underlying is irrelevant. This is because we are assuming we can hedge this away. The underlying may well drift, but this drift will affect our option and our stock positions equally, so we will be indifferent.

So how do we interpret p? Let's assume that p really is the probability of an up move in the underlying. Then the expected value of the stock after a time step is given by

$$pS_u - (1 - p)\,S_d = pSu - (1 - p)\,Sd = S\exp\left(rT\right) \qquad (4.14)$$

That is, interpreting p as the probability of the stock moving up is equivalent to assuming the stock grows at the risk-free rate. This is an example of *risk-neutral valuation*: if we set up a hedged portfolio we can always assume that the underlying grows at the risk-free rate. This is a very useful trick because stock returns are very hard to measure and probably close to impossible to predict, but we need to remember that it means all of the answers we get will be true in this risk-neutral world and may not apply in the real world. This is particularly important when we are tempted to attach probabilistic interpretations to things.

Next we generalize to more than one time step. In particular we want to connect our values for u and d, to the distribution of the underlying returns that we are considering. Actually we will only try to match the second moment, the variance. We know that under risk-neutrality the mean can assumed to be the risk-free rate, r, and we will for the time being ignore higher order moments. The variance of the return can be written as

$$\text{var}(r) = E\left(r^2\right) - (E(r))^2 \tag{4.15}$$

So from equation 4.14

$$\text{var}(r) = pu^2 + (1 - p)d^2 - (pu + (1 - p)d)^2 \tag{4.16}$$

Now we set this equal to $\sigma^2 T$ and substitute the definition of p from equation 4.12 to obtain

$$\sigma^2 T = \exp(rT)(u + d) - ud - \exp(2rT) \tag{4.17}$$

To first order in T, this equation has a solution

$$u = \exp\left(\sigma\sqrt{t}\right) \tag{4.18}$$

$$d = \exp\left(-\sigma\sqrt{t}\right) \tag{4.19}$$

These choices mean that we have matched the mean and standard deviation of the underlying price process. However, we have three parameters to choose $(u, d, \text{and } p)$ and only two moments to match. This means we could have made an infinite number of such choices. This choice is "nice" because it is symmetric with respect to u and d, but it is in no way fundamental or even the best choice when actually solving problems numerically.

Now that we have specified the dynamics of the underlying we can price the options. To do this we first construct a tree of underlying prices using the parameters specified by equations 4.12, 4.18, and 4.19. Then we work backward through the tree, pricing the option at each node. An example should make this process transparent.

Example   We will construct a three-step tree to price a one-year option on a stock that is initially priced at $100. This means that our time step is four months or one third of a year. We also want to use a volatility of 0.3 and an interest rate of 0.05.

So we have $u = \exp\left(0.3 \times \sqrt{\frac{1}{3}}\right) = 1.19$ and $d = \exp\left(-0.3 \times \sqrt{\frac{1}{3}}\right) = 0.84$, which leads to $p = 0.505$ from equation 4.12. This gives us enough to construct our tree of underlying prices. This is shown in Figure 4.2.

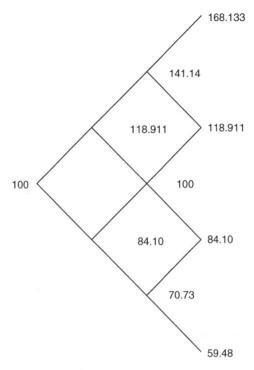

FIGURE 4.2 The Evolution of the Stock Price in the Three-Step Binomial Tree

Note again that the probability of reaching each node does not appear here. This tree shows only the possible levels of the underlying, not the chances of these being reached.

To value the options we start at the terminal nodes, those on the far right side. Here the option will be worth its intrinsic value. So in the case of the vanilla call we are valuing here

$$C = Max(S - X, 0) \tag{4.20}$$

To get the value at the other nodes we probability weight these values and then discount by the interest rate.

$$C = \exp(-rt)\left[pC_{up} + (1 - p)C_{down}\right] \tag{4.21}$$

This is exactly the same calculation that we did above in the toy example of the one-period tree. Figure 4.3 shows this calculation for the top of the tree.

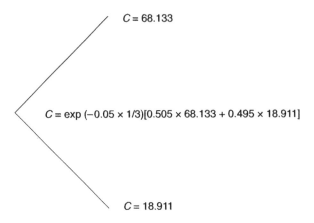

$C = 68.133$

$C = \exp\,(-0.05 \times 1/3)[0.505 \times 68.133 + 0.495 \times 18.911]$

$C = 18.911$

FIGURE 4.3 The Pricing of a Call Option at a Single Node in the Binomial Tree

This process continues back through the tree until we reach the initial node. This gives the current value of the option. This is shown in Figure 4.4.

Note that pricing the options is easy and is also easy to generalize. We can clearly price puts by changing the intrinsic value calculation at the final node to

$$P = Max\,(X - S, 0) \tag{4.22}$$

Other payoffs can similarly be easily accommodated.

It is also straightforward to add the American exercise feature. This is in sharp contrast to the differential equation–based methods where path dependency can be very hard to deal with. All we need to do in the tree is to check at each node whether the option is worth at least its intrinsic value. So the node value for an American call is

$$C = Max(\exp\,(-rt)\left[pC_{up} + (1 - p)\,C_{down}\right], (S - X)) \tag{4.23}$$

Changing the payoff is easy. Most of the difficulty in the tree approach lies in constructing the tree of underlying prices. But this part of the process can also be extended to allow for alternative asset prices (refer to the references given at the end of this chapter for details).

It is important for a trader to understand how the value of an option calculated in a tree converges to the "true" value as the tree becomes larger ("true" is in quotes because in many cases the exact value is unknown and had to be estimated by some type of numerical method. Generally, convergence is examined by using European options as a test case, because in

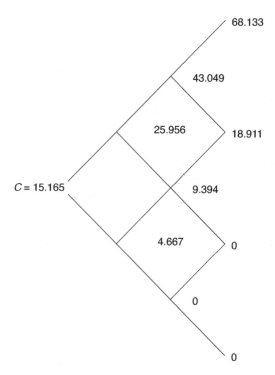

FIGURE 4.4 The Pricing of a European Call Option in the Binomial Tree

this case the true value can be calculated from the closed-form solution to the BSM equation.).

As we would hope, in the limit of an infinite number of nodes (or time steps) the binomial tree converges to the BSM result. The proof of this result is based on the fact that as the number of draws becomes large, a binomial distribution tends to resemble a normal distribution. However, the result should not be particularly surprising, and the proof is not particularly edifying, so we omit it here.

THE BLACK-SCHOLES-MERTON (BSM) MODEL

If we already have gone through a perfectly acceptable method for pricing options, why repeat the process? The tree model gives a simple, reasonably intuitive method for pricing an option. It can also form the basis for a practical numerical algorithm. The BSM approach does not do this as well.

Deriving the BSM differential equation is only half the problem; we then need to solve it. However the BSM approach shows the meanings and interrelationships between the Greeks (the dependencies of the option value on the various model parameters) far more clearly. Return to our analogy of pricing models as languages. It may be *possible* to say anything in any language, but it is far *easier* to say some things in certain languages. There are just some situations where the tree approach is more useful than the differential equation approach, and vice versa.

There are many derivations of the Black-Scholes-Merton equation, most of which focus heavily on the mathematics. They are typically not aimed at traders who tend to have more practical applications in mind. We must always remember that our goal is to identify and profit from mispriced options. How does the BSM formalism help us do this?

We saw in the previous section how to create a delta-hedged portfolio and how useful this concept is. Here we will start from the assumption that a trader holds a delta-hedged portfolio consisting of a call option and Δ units of short stock. Next we will apply our knowledge of option dynamics to derive the BSM equation.

We hold the delta-hedged option position,

$$C - \Delta S_t \tag{4.24}$$

Where C is the value of the option, S_t is the underlying price at time, t, and Δ is the number of shares we are short. Over the next time step the underlying changes to S_{t+1}. The change in the value of the portfolio is given by the change in the option and stock positions together with any financing charges we incur by borrowing money to pay for the position. Over a single time step the change in the option position is

$$C(S_{t+1}) - C(S_t) \tag{4.25}$$

The change in the hedge value is

$$-\Delta(S_{t+1} - S_t) \tag{4.26}$$

And the amount it costs us to finance the position is

$$-r(C - \Delta S_t) \tag{4.27}$$

(To see why this is true we need to consider our cash flows. We bought the option, so we need to finance that cost but we shorted stock so we receive money for this so over a single time step we gain $r\Delta S_t$ from this.)

So the total change in the position value is

$$C(S_{t+1}) - C(S_t) - \Delta(S_{t+1} - S_t) - r(C - \Delta S_t) \tag{4.28}$$

The change in the option value due to the underlying price change can be approximated by a second order Taylor expansion. Also we know that when "other things are held constant," the option will decrease due to the passing of time by an amount denoted by θ.

By saying this we have assumed that we need to consider second derivatives with respect to price, but only first derivatives with respect to time. Why is this valid? The reason is that underlying price moves are a source of *risk*. They are random (at least this is assumed here). The effect of time is a *cost*. Time change is predictable.

Confusion abounds about this point. One of the worst trading decisions an option trader can make is to conclude that selling options purely to buy them back later when they "will be cheaper" is a good idea. Do these people really think that they are the only people to realize that time passes? We will later revisit the relationship between underlying price changes and theta that resolves this confusion. But in general, when making a trading decision you need to be correct and you also need to be *different*. Here the rest of the market is well aware of the passing of time. Where is your edge?

So we get

$$\Delta(S_{t+1} - S_t) + \frac{1}{2}(S_{t+1} - S_t)^2 \frac{\partial^2 C}{\partial S^2} + \theta - \Delta(S_{t+1} - S_t) - r(C - \Delta S_t)$$

$$(4.29)$$

Or, if we define the second derivative of the option price with respect to the underlying as Γ, we obtain

$$\frac{1}{2}(S_{t+1} - S_t)^2 \Gamma + \theta - r(C - \Delta S_t) \tag{4.30}$$

Where Γ is the second derivative of the option price with respect to the underlying. Expression 4.30 gives the change in value of the portfolio, or the profit the trader makes when the stock price changes by a small amount. It has three separate components.

1. The first term gives the effect of gamma. The return is proportional to half the square of the underlying price change.
2. The second term gives the effect of theta. The option holder loses money due to the passing of time.
3. The third term gives the effect of financing. We have already seen that a hedged long option portfolio is equivalent to lending money.

We also see in Chapter 7 that, on average,

$$(S_{t+1} - S_t)^2 \cong \sigma^2 S^2 \tag{4.31}$$

Where σ is the standard deviation of the underlyings returns, or volatility. So we can rewrite expression 4.30 as

$$\frac{1}{2}\sigma^2 S^2 \Gamma + \theta - r(C - \Delta S_t) \tag{4.32}$$

If we accept that this position should not earn any abnormal profits because it is riskless and financed with borrowed money, the expression can be set equal to zero. Therefore the equation for the fair value of the option is

$$\frac{1}{2}\sigma^2 S^2 \Gamma + \theta - r(C - \Delta S_t) = 0 \tag{4.33}$$

This is the famous Black-Scholes-Merton differential equation.

Before continuing, we need to make explicit some of the assumptions that this informal derivation has hidden.

- In order to write down expression 4.24, we needed to assume the existence of a tradable underlying asset. In fact we assume that it can be shorted and the underlying can be traded in any size necessary without incurring transaction costs.
- Expression 4.27 has assumed that the proceeds from the short sale can be reinvested at the same interest rate at which we have borrowed to finance the purchase of the call. We have also taken this rate to be constant.
- Expression 4.29 has assumed that the underlying changes are continuous and smooth.

But something that we have not made any assumptions about at all is whether the underlying has any drift, any return. This is remarkable. We may naively assume that an instrument whose value increases as the underlying asset rises would be highly dependent on its drift. However, the effect of drift can be negated by combining the option with shares in the correct proportion. As the drift can be hedged away, the holder of the option is not compensated for it.

However, note that while the price change does not appear in equation 4.33, the square of the price change does. So the magnitude of the price changes is central to whether or not the trader makes a profit with a delta-hedged position. This result holds as long as the variance of returns is finite.

With appropriate final conditions, equation 4.33 holds for a variety of instruments: European and American options, calls and puts, and many exotics. It can be solved with any of the usual methods for solving partial differential equations.

In this exercise we have derived a form of the BSM equation by working backward from our trader's knowledge of how options react to changes in underlying and time. In doing so, it has given us what we need to know to trade options from the point of volatility.

It is perfectly acceptable to make simplifying assumptions when developing a model. It is totally unacceptable to make assumptions that are so egregiously incorrect that the model is useless, even as a basic guide. So before we go any further, we look at how limiting our assumptions really are.

Existence of a Tradable Underlying   We assumed that the underlying was a tradable asset. While the BSM formalism has been extended to cases where this is not true, notably in the pricing of real options, we will be primarily concerned with options on equities and futures, so this assumption is not restrictive. However on many optionable underlyings liquidity is an issue, so "tradable" is not always a clearly defined quality. For an option to be priced in this framework we must be able to dynamically hedge so liquidity must always be present in the size necessary.

The Existence of a Single, Constant Interest Rate   There is really no such thing as *an* interest rate. Interest rates have a bid/ask spread. We cannot invest the proceeds of a sale at the same rate that we borrow at. It is possible to modify the BSM formalism to allow for this but it makes the equations intractable. Further, interest rates are not constant. This should be obvious as options on interest rate futures and bonds are very active and these would be worthless if interest rates had no volatility.

We generally do not need to take these effects into account because for short dated options, the risk due to interest charges (rho) is insubstantial in comparison to other risks. Further, rho can often be hedged either by trading interest rate futures or option boxes.

Absence of Dividends   We assumed that the underlying pays no dividends or any other income, or has any costs associated with it. To see this, note that in equation 4.27 we associated the risk-free rate, r, with both the call premium and the hedge value ΔS. We could instead associate another rate with this second term.

- If the stock pays a dividend yield, q, this last term would need to be associated with $r - q$ instead.
- The short seller of a stock rarely receives the full proceeds of the sale for investment, as fees must be paid to borrow the stock. This can be accounted for synthetically by assuming an extra dividend yield, q, on the underlying.

- If the underlying was a physical commodity that required storage at a rate of q^*, the rate associated with the hedge would need to be increased to $r + q^*$.

If the underlying pays a discrete dividend (a more sensible assumption than a dividend yield for an individual stock), we can modify the approach by replacing the underlying by the underlying minus the discounted value of the dividend.

$$S \rightarrow S - D \exp(-rt_d)$$

Where t_d is the time until the dividend, D, is paid. This complicates the form of the equations, but does not really change the spirit of the argument.

Ability to Short the Underlying　We also assumed that the underlying asset could be shorted. This is not a problem where the underlying is a future but when it is a stock, shorting is often more difficult. During the 2008 financial crisis large numbers of stocks were illegal to short. This completely breaks the replication argument.

Volatility Is Constant　We have assumed that volatility is a constant, neither a function of time nor the underlying price. Not only is this untrue, but we will be actively trying to trade these changes. There are models that explicitly take into account volatility changes. However, we choose to recognize this limitation and learn to use the BSM model anyway. This is consistent with our philosophy of the model as a framework for organizing our thoughts rather than as an accurate depiction of reality.

Assumptions about the Distribution of Returns　We have assumed that the underlyings changes are continuous so we can continually adjust our hedge. This is not true. Sometimes the underlying has vast jumps. For example, it is not uncommon for the shares of a biotech company to jump by 70 to 80 percent in one day. Modifications have been made to the BSM formalism to price options in these circumstances (and indeed while our derivation of the BSM equation will fail in the presence of jumps, other derivations are still possible), but this is not really the point. These jumps cannot be hedged and the replication strategy fails utterly. We have to learn to hedge this risk with other options. This is the concept of semistatic hedging that traders need to use in practice.

We assumed that volatility is the only parameter needed to specify the distribution of the underlying returns. The mean can be hedged away and we have ignored higher-order moments. This is the same as assuming a normal return distribution or a log-normal price distribution. This is incorrect and is often cited as the biggest failing of the BSM paradigm.

In some ways we can compensate for this failing through the use of a different implied volatility for each option. We revisit this point in some detail in Chapter 8. But we still need the square of the returns to be finite before any of the BSM derivation is mathematically well-defined. We need the return variance to be well-defined. As we discuss in Appendix A, some perfectly sensible looking distributions do not have this property. In fact, the Cauchy distribution has no well-defined moments at all.

However, in practice we will never deal with *populations*, we will deal with *samples*, and all samples have well-defined variances. This is one of the limits of the BSM model. It may not be philosophically or mathematically consistent, but it should be good enough for us to estimate the value of an option from the data we have available. And it is certainly good enough to estimate the relative value of two options. For example, it is very likely that we have made errors that make our estimate of the one-month Microsoft 35 call value incorrect. But it is also highly probable that those same errors impact the price of the 30 call in much the same way, so that our estimate of the spread value is much more robust.

Estimating the volatility of the underlying and hence the value of options from data sampled from an unknown (and probably unknowable) distribution is sensible trading practice. People make these types of estimates all the time. Most of the estimates and valuations we make in life are far worse than this. However, using this type of estimation for risk management is a disastrous idea. Never think you know enough about the distributions to make statements of the probabilities of extreme moves. This is of course inconsistent, but you will just need to get over that.

Much of the remainder of this book looks at what happens to option prices in the "real world," where these assumptions hold to varying degrees but certainly never perfectly.

SUMMARY

- A model is a framework for simplifying the world. It is meant to leave some things out.
- The assumptions behind the model need to be remembered at all times.
- Option pricing models depend on the idea that the directional risk of the underlying can be hedged.
- The magnitude of the underlying price moves cannot be hedged and are of utmost importance to an option trader.
- Option pricing models are most effective for identifying relative price discrepancies.
- Option pricing models are least effective as risk-management tools.

CHAPTER 5

The Solution of the Black-Scholes-Merton (BSM) Equation

I t is very important that traders understand how option prices and the various greeks (derivatives of the option prices) behave. It is understandable if a trader cannot derive a pricing model, but all traders need a thorough knowledge of how option values change in response to changes in the inputs to the model. Here we give equations that describe various aspects of option behavior. We illustrate these results graphically and discuss them. Then we can use our knowledge to look further at the theory of option trading that we introduce in Chapter 4 during our derivation of the Black-Scholes-Merton (BSM) model.

Some of the discussion in this chapter might seem like overkill, and indeed many successful traders only know the characteristics of the major greeks: delta, gamma, theta, and vega. Normally this is all that is required and focusing on the higher-order greeks is distracting. An analogy that I heard recently might be useful. A good pilot normally flies a plane by looking out the window, and by watching and feeling the aircraft's movement and orientation. He rarely glances at the instruments. However, if he needs to fly through a cloud the visual method is useless and his spatial perception will fail. Now he needs to rely on the instruments and he needs to understand what they do. This is not a good time to learn what an altimeter does. Similarly, there will come a time in a trader's career (possibly in a job interview) when he needs to understand the more esoteric greeks and he will not have the time to look them up.

Most options are American. Unfortunately there are no closed-form solutions for American options, so in order to develop intuition we will examine the solution for European options. Obviously there are differences between the two expiration types but these are generally minor. Being able to look at closed-form solutions more than makes up for the slight inconvenience of having to make note of the occasional American wrinkle not captured by the BSM model.

We can solve the generalized BSM model to get closed-form solutions for European calls and puts.

$$c = S \exp((b - r)\, t)\, N(d_1) - X \exp(-rt)\, N(d_2) \qquad (5.1a)$$

$$p = -S \exp((b - r)\, t)\, N(-d_1) + X \exp(-rt)\, N(-d_2) \qquad (5.1b)$$

where

$$d_1 = \frac{\ln\left(\dfrac{S}{X}\right) + \left(b + \dfrac{\sigma^2}{2}\right) t}{\sigma \sqrt{t}} \qquad (5.2a)$$

$$d_2 = \frac{\ln\left(\dfrac{S}{X}\right) + \left(b - \dfrac{\sigma^2}{2}\right) t}{\sigma \sqrt{t}} = d_1 - \sigma \sqrt{t}, \qquad (5.2b)$$

b is a generalized cost of carry parameter.

$b = r$ gives the Black-Scholes stock option model

$b = 0$ gives the Black futures option model

$b = r - q$, where q is a dividend yield, allows us to price options on stock indices where we can approximate the dividend stream by a continuous yield. It also allows us to adjust the effective interest rate for stocks that are hard to borrow.

And $N(x)$ is the cumulative normal distribution function,

$$N(x) = \frac{1}{\sqrt{2\pi}} \int_{z=-\infty}^{x} \exp\left(-\frac{z^2}{2}\right) dz \qquad (5.3)$$

The relationship between the call value and the underlying is shown in Figure 5.1. We also plot the intrinsic value.

The relationship between the put value and the underlying is shown in Figure 5.2. We also plot the intrinsic value.

These figures show that another way to think of the BSM equation is that it is a way to smoothly interpolate between the values the option takes when deep in-the-money, the intrinsic value, and when far out-of-the-money, zero.

Equation 5.1 can also be read in a way that gives more intuition. A call is made up of $N(d_1)$ units of the (appropriately discounted) underlying and $N(d_2)$ units of cash. Similarly a put is made up of $N(-d_1)$ short units of the

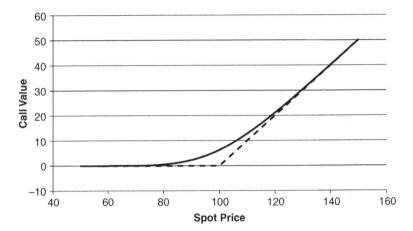

FIGURE 5.1 Call Value as a Function of the Underlying Price

This is for a 100-day option. The strike is 100, interest rates and dividend yield are zero, and volatility is 30 percent.

(appropriately discounted) underlying and a short position of $N(-d_2)$ units of cash.

The relationship between an at-the-money call option and time to expiration is shown in Figure 5.3.

The relationship between an at-the-money put option and time to expiration is shown in Figure 5.4.

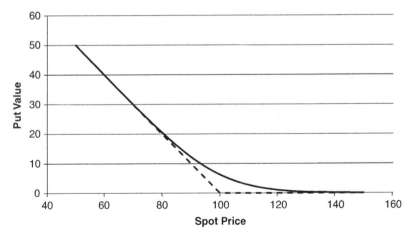

FIGURE 5.2 Put Value as a Function of the Underlying Price

This is for a 100-day option. The strike is 100, interest rates and dividend yield are zero, and volatility is 30 percent.

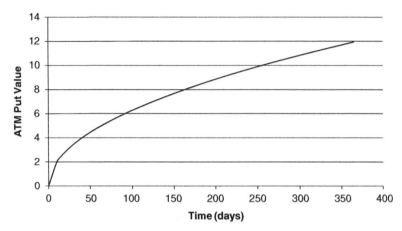

FIGURE 5.3 At-the-Money (ATM) Call as a Function of Time until Expiry

The strike is 100, interest rates and dividend yield are zero, and volatility is 30 percent.

As we can see, Figures 5.3 and 5.4 are identical: when the effects of rates are ignored, the time evolution of at-the-money puts and calls is the same.

A rough approximation for the value of at-the-money options is given by

$$c \approx 0.4S \exp((b - r)\,t)\,\sigma\sqrt{t} \tag{5.4a}$$

$$p \approx 0.4S \exp((b - r)\,t)\,\sigma\sqrt{t} \tag{5.4b}$$

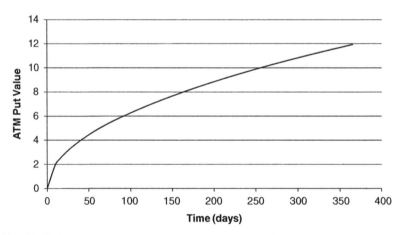

FIGURE 5.4 At-the-Money (ATM) Put as a Function of Time until Expiry

The strike is 100, interest rates and dividend yield are zero, and volatility is 30 percent.

This approximation is easy enough for a trader to estimate in his head. For example, if carry and the interest rate are both zero, this approximation says that the value of a one-year option with volatility at 30 percent is about 12 percent of the value of the underlying. The true value is 11.92 percent.

DELTA

Delta is the partial derivative of the option price with respect to the underlying. It is also our hedge ratio. If the options are priced using the BSM model, the call delta is given by the expression

$$\Delta_c = \frac{\partial c}{\partial S} = \exp((b - r) t) N (d_1) \tag{5.5a}$$

This is always positive.
And the put delta is

$$\Delta_p = \frac{\partial p}{\partial S} = -\exp((b - r) t) N (-d_1) \tag{5.5b}$$

This is always negative.

We can approximate the derivative in the definition of delta by a difference to get the approximation,

$$\Delta = \frac{\partial c}{\partial S} \approx \frac{c (S_2) - c (S_1)}{S_2 - S_1} \tag{5.6}$$

This is the slope of the tangent in the graph that shows the option price as a function of the underlying (Figure 5.1). This is illustrated in Figure 5.5.

The relationship between a call delta and the underlying is shown in Figure 5.6.

The relationship between a put delta and the underlying is shown in Figure 5.7.

These figures show that the magnitude of the put delta is large when the call delta is small and vice versa. This follows naturally from put-call parity. If we start with the standard form of the put-call parity equation,

$$c - p = S \exp((b - r) t) - X \exp(-rt) \tag{5.7}$$

and take the partial derivative with respect to the underlying, we get

$$\Delta_c - \Delta_p = \exp((b - r) t) \tag{5.8}$$

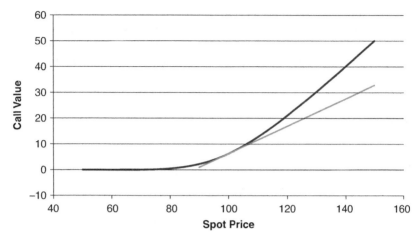

FIGURE 5.5 Call Value as a Function of the Underlying Price

Also plotted is the tangent representing the delta of the at-the-money option.

So for the special case of nondividend paying stocks we have the relationship (where $b = r$),

$$\Delta_c - \Delta_p = 1 \tag{5.9}$$

This is a very useful approximation in the general case (even for American options).

The relationship between an at-the-money call delta and time to expiration is shown in Figure 5.8.

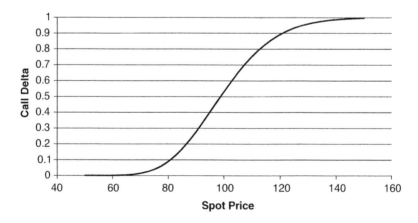

FIGURE 5.6 Call Delta as a Function of the Underlying Price

This is for a 100-day option. The strike is 100, interest rates and dividend yield are zero, and volatility is 30 percent.

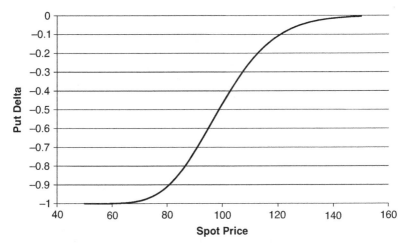

FIGURE 5.7 Put Delta as a Function of the Underlying Price
Parameters are the same as those for Figure 5.6.

Time has a different effect on put deltas. This should be apparent from the delta form of the put-call parity relationship (equation 5.8). The relationship between an at-the-money call put delta and time to expiration is shown in Figure 5.9.

So at the limit of infinite time (or volatility), the call delta will tend toward one and the put delta will tend toward zero. This asymmetry is due to the fact that at high volatility, the stock price is expected to move much higher, but it is bounded on the downside by zero.

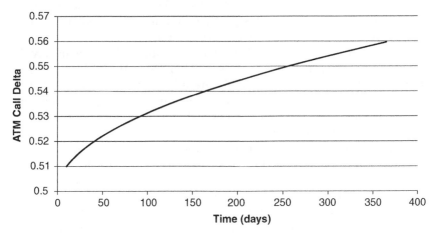

FIGURE 5.8 At-the-Money (ATM) Call Delta as a Function of Time until Expiry
Parameters are the same as those for Figure 5.6.

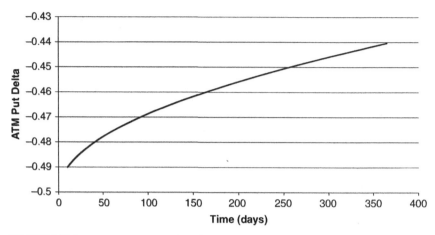

FIGURE 5.9 At-the-Money (ATM) Put Delta as a Function of Time until Expiry
Parameters are the same as those for Figure 5.6.

If we ignore the effects of interest rates, volatility and the square root of time always appear in the same places in the BSM world. Volatility needs time in which to act, so extending (the square root of) time is the same as raising volatility. So the effect of volatility changes is also to raise the delta of a call.

Because the underlying typically moves around much faster than implied volatility or rates, delta is generally the greek that we need to stay most concerned about. We saw in the BSM derivation, that the delta is the amount of the underlying that makes us hedged. A trader needs to constantly monitor the delta of his position and make adjustments to avoid becoming unhedged. This is the basis of volatility trading.

Sometimes traders think of the delta as a probability, specifically that a call delta is the probability that the call expires in the money (in this interpretation the delta of a put is the negative of the probability that the option expires in the money). This interpretation is incorrect. Mathematically speaking, delta behaves like a probability, but it does not have such a clean financial interpretation.

In fact, $N(d_2)$ is the probability that the option expires in the money *in the risk-neutral world*. The probability that a call option will be exercised is the probability that S (at expiry) $> X$, and this is the same probability that $\ln S$ (at expiry) $> \ln X$. This is $N(d_2)$.

What does this say about probabilities in the real world? Not much. A higher delta call will have a greater chance of expiring in the money than one with a lower delta, but the actual numbers do not tell us anything. Clearly in the real world the probability of exercise involves the drift of the underlying, which does not appear at all in the BSM equation (we could replace the risk-neutral drift with the actual drift and use this to calculate a "real" $N(d_2)$, but this is highly unlikely to be correct. If we were this good at calculating expected drifts, we would find easier ways to make money than trading options).

Given that $N(d_2)$ is the probability of finishing in the money in a risk-neutral world, can we say anything interesting or useful about delta?

As we have seen, the BSM equation for a call is

$$c = S \exp((b - r)t) N(d_1) - X \exp(-rt) N(d_2) \qquad (5.10)$$

Let's ignore the discounting factors to make the following imprecise argument a little easier to follow. If delta was the same as $N(d_2)$ we could write this as

$$c = \text{probability of exercise} \times (S - X) \qquad (5.11)$$

But this could clearly lead to negative option values, which, as we see in Chapter 3, cannot happen. The only way around this is to insist that $N(d_1) > N(d_2)$. In this last equation we have assumed that all the uncertainty is in the probability of exercise, and that we know exactly what we will get at that time. This is true for binary options but not in general. Generally we are uncertain about both whether we get anything and what we will get. $N(d_2)$ reflects the first uncertainty and $N(d_1)$ reflects the second.

The upper limit for the value of delta can also be a source of confusion. For a call option, as volatility or time becomes larger, the delta approaches one as the call option takes on the characteristics of the underlying (in the limit of infinite volatility all calls will be in the money). However for a put option the delta will approach zero as the put takes on the characteristics of the strike, which is fixed.

The at-the-money approximation for option values given by equations 6.4, imply an approximation for at-the-money deltas as well. We differentiate these equations to get

$$\Delta_c \approx \exp((b - r)t) \left(0.5 + 0.2\sigma\sqrt{t} \right) \qquad (5.12a)$$

$$\Delta_p \approx \exp((b - r)t) \left(0.2\sigma\sqrt{t} - 0.5 \right) \qquad (5.12b)$$

Revisiting the example of a one-year option with volatility of 30 percent, equation 5.12a gives a call delta of 0.56 and 5.12b gives a put delta of -0.44. The true values are 0.5596 and 0.44032 respectively.

An even rougher approximation for the delta of at-the-money options, is that the call has a delta of 0.5 and the put has a delta of -0.5.

GAMMA

Gamma is the partial derivative of the delta with respect to the underlying. If the options are priced using the BSM model, the call gamma is given by the expression

$$\Gamma_c = \frac{\partial \Delta_c}{\partial S} = \frac{\exp((b-r)\,t)\,n(d_1)}{S\sigma\sqrt{t}} \tag{5.13a}$$

This is always positive.
And the put gamma is

$$\Gamma_p = \frac{\partial \Delta_p}{\partial S} = \frac{\exp((b-r)\,t)\,n(d_1)}{S\sigma\sqrt{t}} = \Gamma_c \tag{5.13b}$$

The relationship between gamma and the underlying is shown in Figure 5.10.

Gamma is high for at-the-money options and is roughly normally distributed. The reason it is not symmetric with respect to the at-the-money price is that it is scaled by the underlying price, S. Gamma is the change in delta for a given absolute move in the underlying. This definition can cause a few counterintuitive results.

First, traders often think that gamma is highest for at-the-money options. This is a workable approximation for short times (or low volatilities) but the maximum is actually at

$$S_{\Gamma\,\text{max}} = X \exp\left(-\left(b + \frac{3\sigma^2}{2}\right)t\right) \tag{5.14}$$

In the example shown in Figure 5.10, this tells us that gamma is maximized when the underlying is 96.37. This effect can become very problematic when either time until expiry or volatility is large and we are looking at the gamma of a far out-of-the-money option. In this case, the peak of the gamma distribution gets pulled closer to zero. This is shown in Figure 5.11.

For these parameters the gamma is maximized at an underlying price of 2.48.

But note that if the underlying were at 2.48, the gamma number would overstate our risk. This is because gamma measures the change in delta due

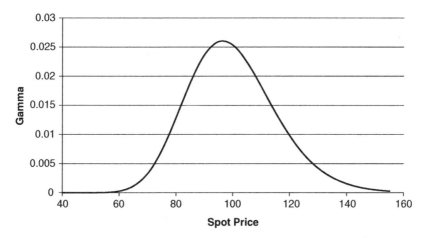

FIGURE 5.10 Gamma as a Function of the Underlying Price
Parameters are the same as those for Figure 5.6.

to an absolute (i.e., dollar) move in the underlying. If the underlying were at 2.48, a one-dollar move would correspond to a 40 percent change. This is clearly a very different magnitude event than a one-dollar change if the underlying was 100. To avoid this issue we can define a relative gamma by

$$\Gamma_r = S\Gamma = \frac{\exp((b-r)t)\,n(d_1)}{\sigma\sqrt{t}} \tag{5.15}$$

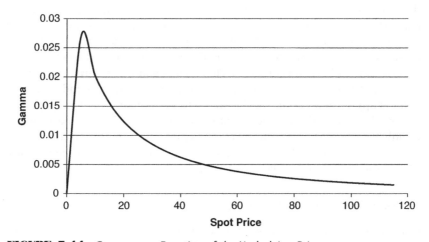

FIGURE 5.11 Gamma as a Function of the Underlying Price
This is for a 10,000-day option. Strike is 100, interest rates and dividend yields are zero and volatility is 30 percent.

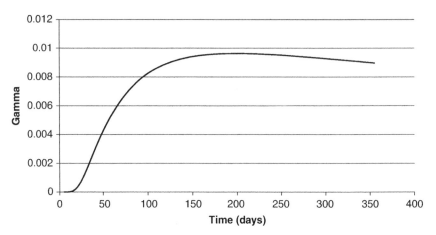

FIGURE 5.12 Gamma as a Function of Time until Expiry for an Out-of-the-Money Option

This is for an 80 strike put when the underlying is 100. Interest rates and dividend yield are zero and volatility is 30 percent.

This could also be more useful for comparing gamma numbers across different stocks. Otherwise the stock with the higher underlying will always appear to have less gamma than an otherwise identical stock with a smaller underlying.

Options are nonlinear instruments: their payoff function is not a straight line. As gamma is the rate of change of delta, it is also a measure of this nonlinearity. It can be thought of as a measure of an option's optionality. This interpretation can guide us when we think about what happens to gamma as we approach expiration. If an option is far out of the money, close to expiry it is worthless and is likely to remain worthless. Its delta is zero and is likely to remain so. This means gamma is zero. If an option is deep in the money close to expiry it will behave like the underlying. Its delta is approximately one and is likely to remain so. This means gamma is zero. However, if an option is at-the-money, its delta will be changing rapidly between zero and one as we cross the strike. This means the gamma of an at-the-money option will become very large as we approach expiry. This is shown below in Figures 5.12 and 5.13.

Gamma Scalping or Gamma Trading

Gamma is important because it tells us how our delta changes in response to moves in the underlying. The fact that the delta changes means that we have to periodically adjust our hedge. This leads to the idea of gamma scalping.

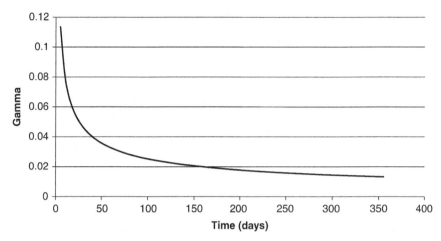

FIGURE 5.13 Gamma as a Function of Time until Expiry for an At-the-Money Option

This is for a 100 strike put when the underlying is 100. Interest rates and dividend yield are zero and volatility is 30 percent.

Example Let's assume we have bought 1,000 of the at-the-money call options that we have been discussing here. These are the 100 strike, 100-day calls when interest and carry rates are zero and the volatility is 30 percent. These cost $6.53. Let's assume that these are standard U.S. equity options, so each option contract is on 100 shares. The delta of these options is 0.531. So our hedge is to sell short $0.531 \times 1,000 \times 100 = 53,100$ shares.

Now the underlying rallies to $105. At this level our delta is 0.651, so to achieve delta neutrality we need to sell an additional 12,000 shares (so our total short share position is equal to 65,100). With an underlying price of $105 our calls are now worth $9.22. So our total profit is given by

$$\text{Option P/L} + \text{Stock P/L} = 1,000 \times 100 \times (\$9.22 - \$6.53)$$
$$+ 53,100 \times (\$100 - \$105) = \$3,500$$

The fact that we made a profit has nothing to do with the fact that we were long calls and the market went up. A similar result would have occurred had the market declined. To see this, let's assume that the market declined by 5 percent instead. Against an underlying price of $95, our calls would only be worth $3.92, so our profit would be

$$\text{Option P/L} + \text{Stock P/L} = 1,000 \times 100 \times (\$3.92 - \$6.53)$$
$$+ 53,100 \times (\$100 - \$95) = \$4,500$$

So we make money in either case. The two obvious questions are

- Why do we make money on a hedged position?
- Why do we make a different amount, for equal sized up and down moves?

The reason we make money is that while our position started off hedged, the effect of gamma caused it to become unhedged and, no matter which way the underlying market moved, we were not carrying a sufficient amount of stock. If we recall the interpretation of delta as the tangent of the call value (Figure 5.5), then it is obvious that this value changes as the underlying moves.

The reason we make more money on a down move, is because gamma is greater below the strike. The delta of the options thus changes by more. As this delta change works in our favor, a bigger change is even better.

- If we are long gamma, underlying moves make us money.

So why isn't everyone long gamma (by owning options) all the time? We actually addressed this in our derivation of the BSM equation but it may not have been apparent at that time. The reason is that gamma has a cost associated with it, theta.

THETA

Theta is the negative of the partial derivative of the option value with respect to time. If the options are priced using the BSM model, the call theta is given by the expression

$$\theta_c = -\frac{\partial c}{\partial t} = -\frac{S\sigma \exp((b-r)\,t)\,n(d_1)}{2\sqrt{t}} - S(b-r)\exp((b-r)\,t)\,N(d_1)$$

$$-rX\exp(-rt)\,N(d_2) \qquad\qquad (5.16a)$$

And the put theta is

$$\theta_p = -\frac{\partial p}{\partial t} = -\frac{S\sigma \exp((b-r)\,t)\,n(d_1)}{2\sqrt{t}} + S(b-r)\exp((b-r)\,t)\,N(-d_1)$$

$$+rX\exp(-rt)\,N(-d_2) \qquad\qquad (5.16b)$$

Theta is usually normalized so that it represents the amount of change in the option value over a day. To do this we would divide the raw theta by 365.

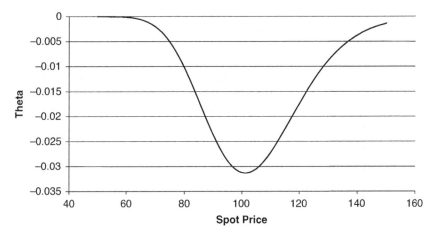

FIGURE 5.14 Call Theta as a Function of the Underlying Price
Parameters are the same as those for Figure 5.6.

The relationship between call theta and the underlying is shown in Figure 5.14.

This function has its shape because at-the-money options have greater volatility value than any others, but by expiry no options will have any volatility value. For these two statements to be consistent the at-the-money options need to decay faster than those in the wings.

Theta obtains a minimum value just above the at-the-money strike. For stock options, where the cost of carry is equal to the interest rate

$$S_{theta \max} = X \exp\left(\left(r + \frac{3\sigma^2}{2}\right)t\right) \tag{5.17}$$

The situation is more complex in general and will be further complicated in the presence of an implied volatility curve.

The expressions for theta each consist of three terms. The meaning of the second and third terms becomes clearer if we again consider put-call parity. Either by directly differentiating equation 5.7 with respect to time or by subtracting equation 5.16b from equation 5.16a we find

$$\theta_c - \theta_p = (b - r)S\exp((b - r)t) + rX\exp(-rt) \tag{5.18}$$

We know that a long call, short put position has no volatility exposure, but this shows it does have time dependency. The time dependency is purely carry. The first term is the carry on the underlying. The second term is the carry on the strike value.

Now we can see that the second and third terms of equations 5.16 just allocate this carry to the call and put proportionally according to their delta (the second term) and the probability of finishing in the money (the third term).

Generally traders think of their theta as representing the amount of money that their position bleeds each day. This is not what theta is. It means no more and no less than "the partial derivative of the option price with respect to time." However, we can remove the two carry related terms and the discounting factor from theta to create a new Greek more in line with what traders are looking for. This has various names, including modified theta, decay, volatility theta, and driftless theta.

$$\bar{\theta}_c = \bar{\theta}_p = -\frac{S\sigma n(d_1)}{2\sqrt{t}} \tag{5.19}$$

This has a minimum value at

$$S_{theta\,\max} = X \exp\left(\left(\frac{\sigma^2}{2} - b\right)t\right) \tag{5.20}$$

If we also ignore the carry terms in gamma we can write down a useful relationship between this volatility gamma and volatility theta

$$\bar{\Gamma} = -\frac{2\bar{\theta}}{S^2\sigma^2} \tag{5.21}$$

This specifically shows us that if we want the benefits of owning options (being long gamma) we pay for it (in the form of the decay from theta).

The Concept of the Breakeven

The "breakeven" is the amount that the underlying needs to move for us to have a P/L of zero. For static option positions, this is a trivial calculation. We will examine a number of examples in Chapter 6.

The concept is also useful when examining the sort of delta-hedged volatility positions that will typically concern a professional option trader. These traders must always know how much the underlying needs to move in any given time interval for their positions to breakeven.

If our position is delta-hedged and volatility is unchanged there are two Greeks that dominate our P/L (at least for smallish moves). This can be directly seen from the BSM equation.

$$\frac{1}{2}\sigma^2 S^2 \Gamma + \theta + r(C - \Delta S_t) = 0 \qquad (5.22)$$

So for a hedged position

$$\frac{1}{2}\sigma^2 S^2 \Gamma + \theta = 0 \qquad (5.23)$$

Or in the version from earlier in our derivation of the BSM

$$\frac{1}{2}(\Delta S)^2 \Gamma + \theta = 0 \qquad (5.24)$$

The effects of theta and gamma cancel each other. If we are calculating the price of an option the BSM equation needs to hold on average. We do not expect this relationship to hold perfectly on any particular day. Nonetheless this equation describes the underlying movement required to make exactly zero profit.

Our daily P/L can be expressed as

$$P/L = Gamma\ P/L + Theta\ P/L + other\ effects$$

Recall from our derivation of the BSM equation that

$$Gamma\ P/L = \frac{1}{2}\Gamma(\Delta S)^2 \qquad (5.25)$$

So, ignoring the other effects, we have

$$P/L = \frac{1}{2}\Gamma(\Delta S)^2 + \theta(\Delta t) \qquad (5.26)$$

where Δt is the time step that we are concerned about, generally a day. Using the relationship between gamma and theta (equation 5.24) we can write

$$P/L = \frac{1}{2}\Gamma\left[(\Delta S)^2 - \sigma_{implied}^2 S^2 (\Delta t)\right] \qquad (5.27)$$

$$= \frac{1}{2}\Gamma S^2 \left[\left(\frac{\Delta S}{S}\right)^2 - \sigma_{implied}^2 (\Delta t)\right] \qquad (5.28)$$

So to breakeven, we need the squared daily return to equal the daily implied variance. Or

$$\left|\frac{\Delta S}{S}\right| = \sigma_{implied}\sqrt{\Delta t} \tag{5.29}$$

VEGA

Vega is the partial derivative of the option value with respect to implied volatility. If the options are priced using the BSM model, the call vega is given by the expression

$$Vega_c = \frac{\partial c}{\partial \sigma} = S \exp((b - r)t)\, n(d_1)\sqrt{t} \tag{5.30}$$

This is the same as the put vega.

This is slightly different in character from the greeks discussed so far. They were derivatives with respect to variables. Vega involves taking the derivative with respect to a parameter. If the BSM formalism was actually correct, the implied volatility would be constant and this Greek could not even be defined. However in practice, vega is a very important risk number for a trader.

Vega is typically scaled so that it represents the dollar change in option value for a one-point change in implied volatility. This involves dividing the raw vega by 100. The relationship between vega and the underlying is shown in Figure 5.15.

Vega reaches a maximum at

$$S_{Vega\,max} = X \exp\left(\left(-b + \frac{\sigma^2}{2}\right)t\right) \tag{5.31}$$

Vega is closely related to gamma. This relationship forms the basis of volatility trading and will be revisited in detail in Chapter 11. The relationship is

$$Vega = \Gamma \sigma S^2 t \tag{5.32}$$

As vega measures sensitivity to volatility, and volatility requires time to manifest itself, vega increases as a function of time. This is shown below in Figure 5.16.

Contrast this with the time evolution of gamma for an at-the-money option shown in Figure 5.13. We see that long-dated options are more sensitive to vega, and short-dated options are more sensitive to gamma. Because

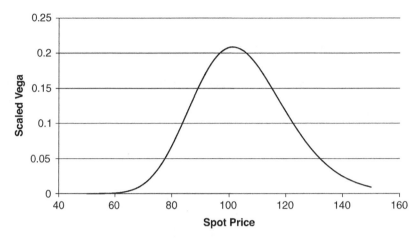

FIGURE 5.15 Vega as a Function of the Underlying Price
Parameters are the same as those for Figure 5.6.

of this, traders will often say they are "buying gamma" if they buy short-dated options and "buying vega" if they are buying long-dated options.

A problem with vega is that all implied volatilities do not move by the same amount. In particular, longer-dated options will have significantly less volatile implied volatilities than shorter-dated options. So it does not really make sense to simply add the vegas. A given dollar amount of vega is far

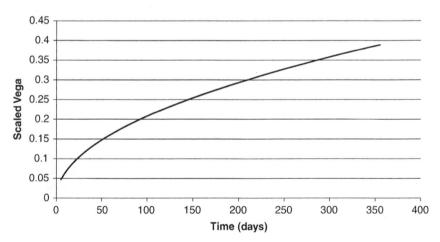

FIGURE 5.16 Vega as a Function of Time until Expiry for an At-the-Money Option
This is for a 100 strike option when the underlying is 100. Interest rates and dividend yield are zero and volatility is 30 percent.

more risky if the volatility is expected to be very changeable than if it is expected to be very stable. To address this, vega is often weighted. There are two common methods of doing this.

- Use a theoretical weighting based on the time until expiration. We choose a base expiration, often the second or third expiration, then multiply the other vegas by the factor

$$w_i = \sqrt{\frac{T_{base}}{T_i}}$$

  So exposure in a six-month option will be weighted by a factor of 0.71 relative to a three month option.
- Use an empirical weighting, based on the observed volatility of implied volatilities. This could be a better solution but it requires more gathering of data and updating of estimates. It also assumes that the measured weights have sufficiently low sampling error and are relatively persistent.

I would probably choose the first approach in most circumstances.

Rho

Rho is the partial derivative of the option value with respect to the interest rate. If the options are priced using the BSM model, the call rho is given by the expression

$$\rho_c = \frac{\partial c}{\partial r} = tX \exp(-rt) N(d_2) \tag{5.33a}$$

And the put rho is given by

$$\rho_p = \frac{\partial p}{\partial r} = -tX \exp(-rt) N(-d_2) \tag{5.33b}$$

Rho is typically scaled so that it represents the dollar change in option value for a one-point change in the interest rate. This involves dividing the raw rho by 100.

The relationship between call rho and the underlying is shown in Figure 5.17.

As we can see, the magnitude of rho is greater for in-the-money options. This is because these options have more premium, so the change in discounting factor is affecting a larger amount.

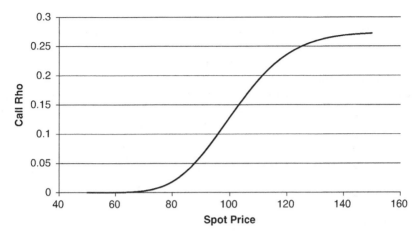

FIGURE 5.17 Call Rho as a Function of the Underlying Price
Parameters are the same as those for Figure 5.6.

In the case of futures options, where the cost of carry on the underlying is zero, rho is given by

$$\rho_c = -tc \tag{5.34a}$$

$$\rho_p = -tp \tag{5.34b}$$

Carry Rho

Carry rho is the partial derivative of the option value with respect to the carry cost. If the options are priced using the BSM model, the call carry rho is given by the expression

$$\rho_c = \frac{\partial c}{\partial b} = tS \exp((b-r)t) N(d_1) \tag{5.35a}$$

And the put carry rho is given by

$$\rho_p = \frac{\partial p}{\partial b} = -tS \exp((b-r)t) N(-d_1) \tag{5.35b}$$

Interest rates are relatively easy to estimate, as there is a liquid market in rates and we can price the options using the appropriate part of the yield curve. Ideally, this is the yield of the zero-coupon government bond with the same maturity as the option.

Carry rates are not as easy to estimate. Generally the most important element is the dividend yield. This generally is not a traded quantity (dividend swaps sometimes exist, but not in most products, and even when they do exist are relatively illiquid). Normally, we estimate future dividends by simply assuming that they will be the same as they have been in the past. Sometimes stock analysts can give further guidance.

Another situation in which traders have to be aware of carry rates is when they need to short stock to hedge their position. A central assumption of the BSM model is that shorting is possible. It generally is, but there is usually a cost associated with it. That is, we cannot short the stock and collect interest on the proceeds of the sale without paying the holder from whom we have borrowed. This process is the basis of the "repo" market. "Repo" is an abbreviation of "repurchase agreement." The stock holder agrees to sell the stock with the agreement to buy it back in the future at a specified price. This price will be larger than the original selling price and defines the repo rate by

$$r = \frac{S_f}{S_i} - 1$$

where S_f and S_i are the final and initial stock prices respectively.

Normally the cost to borrow a stock would be around 10 basis points (0.1 percent), but in certain situations where a stock is heavily shorted the cost can be much greater. In these circumstances the stock is said to be "hard to borrow." During the Internet bubble, many stocks had a very low free float and it was difficult to find stock to borrow. The repo rate was often over 20 percent in these cases.

Repo rates have the same effect on forward prices as dividend yields. A high repo rate lowers the forward. A repo rate is identical to a dividend yield for a stockholder. It is a payment he receives for owning the stock, that the forward holder does not receive. So option traders need to adjust the carry cost in their models to reflect this.

Second-Order Greeks

We have emphasized in our discussion of each greek that they are not constant. Some of these changes are important. It should become second nature to a trader to know how gamma changes with respect to the strike and underlying for instance. However, it will not be necessary to discuss all of the higher order derivatives. For example, I have never had the need to think about my positions' derivative of vega with respect to interest rate. So here I am only going to discuss in detail the few higher order greeks that are essential, noting that we have already discussed how delta, gamma, vega, and theta depend on spot price and time.

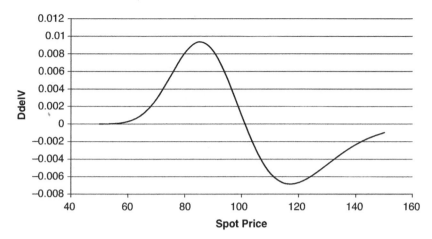

FIGURE 5.18 DdelV as a Function of the Underlying Price
Parameters are the same as those for Figure 5.6.

DdelV This is the sensitivity of an options delta with respect to a change
of volatility. It is given by

$$\frac{\partial^2 c}{\partial \sigma \, \partial S} = -\frac{\exp((b - r)\, t)\, d_2 n\, (d_1)}{\sigma} \tag{5.36}$$

It is normally expressed as the change for a one-point move in volatility. Because we can reverse the order that we take the derivatives, this is
identical to the derivative of vega with respect to the underlying price. As
vega is the same for calls and puts, so is DdelV. This is shown in Figure 5.18
as a function of the underlying price.

This greek often causes traders to pick up delta positions if they do
not correctly account for the correlation between the direction of the underlying and the implied volatility. For example, assume a trader has a position in some 30-delta calls on an equity index. As the underlying rallies,
we expect the options gamma to cause the delta to rise. But as we rally the
implied volatility drops (this is a very strong tendency in equity indices).
Lower volatility means that the DdelV reduces the option delta (informally
we can also think of the situation as saying a lower volatility means these
options have a lower chance of expiring in the money and hence a lower
delta). Sometimes this effect is so pronounced that the option delta can
actually be reduced.

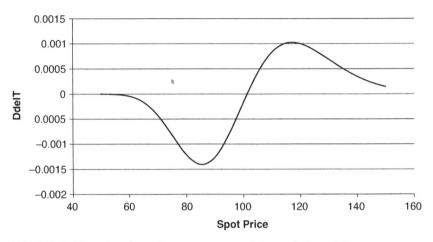

FIGURE 5.19 DdelT for Calls as a Function of the Underlying Price
Parameters are the same as those for Figure 5.6.

DdelT This is the sensitivity of an options delta with respect to a change of time. It is mathematically equivalent to the derivative of theta with respect to the underlying. It is given by

$$\frac{\partial^2 c}{\partial t \partial S} = -\exp((b - r)t)\left[n(d_1)\left(\frac{b}{\sigma\sqrt{t}} - \frac{d_2}{2t}\right) + (b - r)N(d_1)\right] \quad (5.37a)$$

$$\frac{\partial^2 p}{\partial t \partial S} = \exp((b - r)t)\left[n(d_1)\left(\frac{b}{\sigma\sqrt{t}} - \frac{d_2}{2t}\right) - (b - r)N(-d_1)\right] \quad (5.37b)$$

It is normally expressed as the change for a one-day move in time. This is shown above in Figure 5.19 as a function of the underlying price.

As time passes, the optionality of the option becomes less important. Out-of-the-money options see their delta go to zero and in-the-money options see their delta approach that of an equivalent position in the underlying, so call deltas approach one and put deltas approach negative one.

This gets a special mention even though we discussed it in the section on delta, because it is one of the few higher order greeks whose numerical value a trader must know. If an option has a 0.30 delta but has a DdelT of 0.03 then tomorrow its delta will be 0.33. If a trader does not account for this, there is a good chance that when he arrives the next day he will be unhedged. Obviously other things will also have happened. The underlying will also have moved, so gamma would also have changed the options delta. However, time is the one deterministic change we have to deal with, so becoming unhedged purely due to the passing of time is ridiculous.

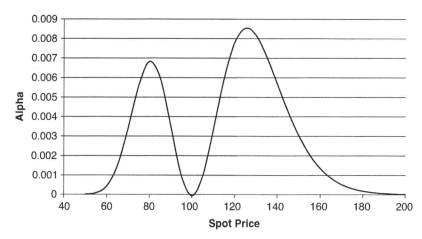

FIGURE 5.20 Alpha as a Function of the Underlying Price
Parameters are the same as those for Figure 5.6.

Alpha This is the sensitivity of an options vega with respect to a change of volatility. It is given by

$$\frac{\partial^2 c}{\partial \sigma^2} = S \exp((b - r) t) \, n(d_1) \sqrt{t} \left(\frac{d_1 d_2}{\sigma} \right) = Vega \left(\frac{d_1 d_2}{\sigma} \right) \qquad (5.38)$$

This is the same for puts.

It is normally expressed as the change for a one volatility point move. This is an exceptionally important quantity. The effects of movement in the underlying are easy to see as the trader normally spends a considerable amount of time examining risk slides that are designed expressly for this purpose If we are not careful the effect of volatility changes can sneak up on us.

The relationship between Alpha and the underlying is shown in Figure 5.20.

For at-the-money options this is very slightly negative. That is, the vega of an at-the-money option decreases slightly as the volatility increases. However, this effect is very small and a good rule of thumb is that the vega of an at-the-money option is constant with respect to volatility.

Alpha has double local maxima in the out-of-the-money options. I do not know of a closed form for the location of these maxima. Generally the options with the highest alpha will be between 5 and 10 delta. We can see this dependence by plotting alpha as a function of delta. This is shown below in Figure 5.21.

The shape of this curve is reasonably constant for a wide range of parameters and can be a useful guide for traders.

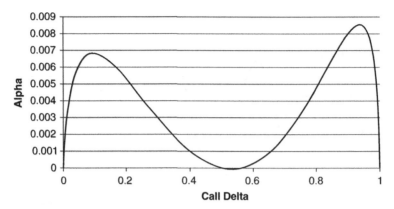

FIGURE 5.21 Alpha as a Function of the Call Delta
Parameters are the same as those for Figure 5.6.

SUMMARY

- As an option approaches expiration, its value converges to the intrinsic value. In the money options more closely begin to resemble the underlying. Out of the money options become worthless.
- Delta is the partial derivative of the option price with respect to the underlying. It is also the hedge ratio.
- Gamma is the partial derivative of the delta with respect to the underlying. It is also a good measure of the amount of optionality present. Gamma is maximized for short-dated, at-the-money options.
- Theta is the partial derivative of the option price with respect to time. Theta is maximized for short-dated, at-the-money options.
- If an option is fairly priced, the decay due to theta is compensated for by the profit due to gamma.
- Vega is the partial derivative of the delta with respect to the implied volatility. Vega is maximized for long-dated, at-the-money options.
- Options are usually referred to by their dominant greek. Short-dated options are called "gamma options." Long-dated options are called "vega options."
- Rho is the partial derivative of the delta with respect to the interest rate.
- The greeks are themselves functions of the underlying, time, and volatility. Traders need to be aware not only of their current greeks, but also how these will change.

CHAPTER 6

Option Strategies

One of the appealing features of options is that we can use them to create positions that reflect specific views of the underlying market. If we were limited to trading the underlying we could only express straightforward views such as being bullish (buying the underlying) or bearish (shorting the underlying). With options we can do much more. In this chapter we see how to do this.

When looking for an options strategy, there are three main things to consider:

1. Our forecast of the direction of the underlying.
2. Our forecast of the volatility of the underlying.
3. The amount of risk we are willing to take.

These are not the only considerations. As we have seen, option values also depend on interest rates and dividends, so these should also be considered. However these will generally be of far less importance than the three factors listed so can be taken into account last.

FORECASTING AND STRATEGY SELECTION

Bullish Underlying Forecast

If we are bullish we expect the underlying to rise. In this case we want to select an option strategy that profits when the market rises. So these strategies need to be long delta.

Bearish Underlying Forecast

If we are bearish we expect the underlying to fall. In this case we want to select an option strategy that profits when the market declines. So these strategies need to be short delta.

Neutral Underlying Forecast

In this case we either expect the underlying to remain in a tight range or we could have no opinion about the underlying at all. So we either design an option position that profits when the underlying remains range-bound or we are using options for a different purpose altogether. This could be trading volatility, hedging another exposure or implementing an arbitrage.

Volatility Forecast

As we briefly mention (in Chapter 4) and also discuss at some length (in Chapters 8 and 11), there are two types of volatility that options traders need to consider: realized volatility and implied volatility. A realized volatility forecast means that we are expecting the underlying's volatility to behave in a certain way. This forecast is expressed through a gamma position. An implied volatility forecast is a statement about the value of the options we are trading. This forecast is expressed through a vega position. A simple option position will generally have the same sign in gamma and vega, but this is not always true and the difference between implied and realized volatilities is a crucial one and should never be ignored.

Increasing Realized Volatility

Here we either expect the underlying's volatility to rise or at least that the underlying will be more volatile than is predicted by the option market. In this case we want to select an option strategy that profits from increased choppiness. These strategies should be long gamma.

Increasing Implied Volatility

Here we expect the implied volatility to rise. In this case we want to select an option strategy that increases in value when implied volatility increases. These strategies should be long vega.

Decreasing Realized Volatility

Here we either expect the underlying's volatility to fall or at least that the underlying will be less volatile than is predicted by the option market.

In this case we want to select an option strategy that profits from a range-bound market, or when the underlying becomes less choppy ("quieter"). These strategies should be short gamma.

Decreasing Implied Volatility

Here we expect the implied volatility to fall. In this case we want to select an option strategy that increases in value when implied volatility falls. These strategies should be short vega.

Neutral Volatility

In this case we either have no opinion about future volatility, implied or realized, or we are actively of the opinion that it will remain unchanged. These strategies will be both gamma- and vega-neutral.

Risk Tolerance

One of the great appeals (and traps) of option trading is that positions can be tailored to almost any level of risk. However this topic is too nuanced to split into two or three categories. As we introduce each strategy we will discuss the risks associated with it. More generally most of option trading comes down to managing risk, so it would not be an exaggeration to say that this entire book is about balancing the risks and rewards of various option trades and strategies.

ASIDE: OPTION NOMENCLATURE

Outside of the basic greeks and strategies, there is no such thing as standard-option nomenclature. Given the amount of money and risk involved, never assume that another trader, broker, or customer knows what you mean. Names vary between countries, exchanges, and even trading firms. For example, the same strategy of buying puts and selling calls with a different strike, can be referred to as a risk reversal, a combo, or a tunnel. Even more confusingly, the same name can mean different things in different places (e.g., a combo or a roll), so always check. In slow moments traders have even been known to invent strategies solely to confuse brokers. It can be amusing to ask for a price in a "put antelope." It can be even more amusing when a broker manages to find one....

It is tempting at this point to introduce some sort of strategy selection matrix, which categorizes strategies by where they fit on the direction/

volatility grid. In some cases this is obvious. If you are bullish on direction and volatility you might want to purchase a call. However there are also a number of other factors to consider when selecting a strategy, such as risk tolerance, the correlation of volatility and the underlying and the term structure of volatility. This can make a mockery of any simple classification scheme.

While generally it is a good thing to have an organizing framework, this is not always possible. For example, biology became a hard science after the discovery of evolution, but before then a lot of good work was done in classifying animals into various families. This chapter does not really have an organizing idea. It is more like a list that an ornithologist might make, categorizing various birds by their coloration, habits, and range. This is messy but also a more realistic approach. It lets us consider many of the common strategies and discuss the strengths, weaknesses, and uses of each.

We are also now going to remind the reader of our statement in the introduction that parts of this book "will require work and thought." If there is only a trivial difference between a long and a short position, we will not explicitly go though both. Having said that, we must always be cognizant that any strategy that contains short options is always subject to the risk of early exercise. This can turn your carefully constructed spread into an outright long position literally overnight.

We also expect the reader to be able to understand the implications of put-call parity. You should understand that any call position can be replicated with puts and vice versa.

These two points are interrelated. If a put strategy can be synthetically replicated by using calls, then why bother with puts at all? First, out-of-the-money strikes are typically more liquid and hence have smaller transaction costs associated with them. Second, put-call parity strictly holds for European options. For American options the put and call of a given strike will be subject to early exercise at different times and prices. This means that out-of-the-money strikes are far more popular for the implementation of directional- or volatility-related strategies, as exercise is less of an issue.

It is also important to note that practically none of these strategies is used in the same way by option market makers and other option traders. Market makers, and most other professional option traders, will be primarily more interested in a strategy's volatility characteristics (gamma, theta, and vega) rather than in constructing directional bets. Nonetheless, all traders must know what these strategies are. There are several reasons for this.

- The basic strategies are an important part of the common language spoken by option traders. All professions need a basic set of defined terms. This is ours. An option trader who was unaware of the term "butterfly" would be as marginalized as a doctor who did not know the word "aorta." This is true even if both were aware of all the other properties and characteristics of the entity.

- Market makers often have to quote prices for complete strategies, not just individual puts and calls. This is still true in the electronic marketplace. Puts and calls are now continuously quoted on computer systems, but the technology for providing prices for strategies is still in its infancy, so these are generally priced by brokers contacting market makers by phone or IM.

THE STRATEGIES

Now we go through the strategies in detail. For each one we will give the following characteristics.

- **Definition and description.** The type, class, and series of options needed to implement the strategy are given.
- **Profit and loss diagram.** This shows the profit of the position as a function of the underlying price. Unless stated otherwise we assume that the underlying is initially at $100.
- **The profit and loss breakdown.** This analysis gives the best case, worst case, and breakeven scenarios, the general dependence of the profit on the final underlying price, how the profit evolves through time (and hence how we might select the maturity of the options), and the effect of varying the strikes and implied volatility of the options.
- **General discussion of the risks involved.**

Constructing a Profit and Loss Graph

Knowing the profit and loss profile of an option position must be second nature to a trader. From this graph we can begin to understand how all the greeks will evolve through time, where we would ideally like the underlying to go, and at what points we might have trouble hedging.

The following rules help us to construct such a graph.

- The graph consists of straight lines between the strikes.
- Calculate the net outlay for the position. This will be negative if we have paid for options and positive if we have been a seller of option premium.
- Calculate the profit or loss of the position if the underlying expires in the regions defined by the intervals between each strike.

- Calculate the profit or loss of the position if the underlying expires at zero or infinity.
- In each region the profit or loss of the portfolio will be the value at expiry plus the original net outlay for the portfolio (we should really discount the option premium as this money could be invested, but we will ignore this so that we do not have to carry around discounting terms).
- Connect these points.

Example 1   We buy a 95 call for 6.6 and sell a 100 call for 3.1. What does the profit and loss graph look like?

Underlying Below 95

Value of 95 call $= 0$
Value of 100 call $= 0$
Position value $= 0$
Position P/L $= -3.5$

Between 95 and 100

Value of 95 call $= S - 95$
Value of 100 call $= 0$
Value of Position $= S - 95$
Position P/L $= S - 95 - 3.5$

Above 100

Value of 95 call $= S - 95$
Value of 100 call $= S - 100$
Value of Position $= S - 95 - S + 100 = 5$
Position P/L $= 5 - 3.5 = 1.5$

We can check our analysis by noting that there should be no discontinuities at the vertices of our graph. This is shown in Figure 6.1.

This method can be used to construct expiration profiles for far more complex positions.

Example 2   We have the following position. We are long two of the 95 puts from 2.1 each, short a 100 put at 4.4, short a 100 call at 4.5, long 3 110 calls from 0.8, and long one share of stock from 100.

The strikes of interest are 95, 100, and 110, and the net premium for this position is

$$-2 \times 2.1 + 4.4 + 4.5 - 3 \times 0.8 - 100 = -98.7$$

FIGURE 6.1 The Profit and Loss Diagram for the 95 100 Call Spread

Underlying Below 95

Value of 95 puts $= 2\,(95 - S)$
Value of 100 put $= -(100 - S)$
Value of 100 call $= 0$
Value of 110 calls $= 0$
Value of stock $= S$
Value of position $= 2\,(95 - S) - 100 + S + S = 90$
Position P/L $= 90 - 98.7 = -8.7$

Between 95 and 100

Value of 95 puts $= 0$
Value of 100 put $= -(100 - S)$
Value of 100 call $= 0$
Value of 110 calls $= 0$
Value of stock $= S$
Value of position $= -100 + S + S = -100 + 2S$
Position P/L $= -100 + 2S - 98.7 = -198.7 + 2S$

Between 100 and 110

Value of 95 puts $= 0$
Value of 100 put $= 0$
Value of 100 call $= -(S - 100)$
Value of 110 calls $= 0$
Value of stock $= S$
Value of position $= 100$
Position P/L $= 100 - 98.7 = 1.3$

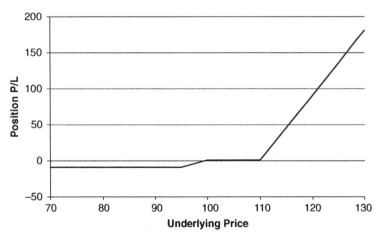

FIGURE 6.2 The Profit and Loss Diagram for a More Complex Strategy

Above 110

Value of 95 puts $= 0$
Value of 100 put $= 0$
Value of 100 call $= -(S - 100)$
Value of 110 calls $= 3\,(S - 110)$
Value of stock $= S$
Value of position $= -S + 100 + 3S - 330 + S = 3S - 230$
Position P/L $= 3S - 328.7$

This is shown in Figure 6.2.

A related diagram is the "payoff diagram." This has the same shape as the profit and loss diagram but the initial option premium is not included. Always make sure what you are looking at.

Now we can examine some common strategies.

Long Call

We buy a call. The profit and loss for this strategy is shown in Figure 6.3.

Maximum profit: Unlimited
Maximum loss: The call premium, C.
Breakeven price: The market must rally above the strike by the amount it cost to put on the position; therefore the breakeven price is $X + C$.
Profit at expiry: $-C$ if $S < X$
    $S - X - C$ if $S > X$

Profit as a function of time: This position has negative theta and as we approach expiration the call loses value. This is shown in Figure 6.4, where

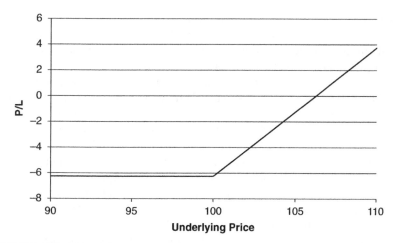

FIGURE 6.3 The Profit and Loss of a Long Call Position

The strike is equal to 100, so the call is initially at-the-money. In this case we have chosen the parameters to be such that the initial call premium is 6.25. In the Black-Scholes-Merton model this corresponds to a volatility of 30 percent, interest rates of zero, and 100 days to expiry.

we see that the current value of the call "collapses" toward its terminal value as we get closer to expiry.

Profit as a function of volatility: This position has positive vega and as implied volatility increases the position increases in value.

Note also that an increase in realized volatility is good for this position, because increased volatility means there is a greater chance that the

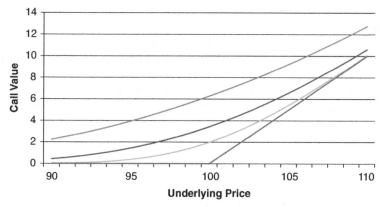

FIGURE 6.4 The Value of a Long Call Position as It Approaches Expiry

The uppermost line shows the value of the option with 100 days until expiry. The lower lines show its value with 30 days, then ten days, remaining.

underlying moves further in-the-money (to the right in Figure 6.3). This also means that there is a greater chance that the underlying moves further out-of-the-money (to the left) but as our loss is limited, this is not a problem. If we are long a call, increased volatility can only help us.

The strike and the initial underlying price only have meaning relative to each other. So when we speak of choosing a lower strike, we will be examining the same situation as if the underlying increased.

A long call underperforms the underlying by the amount $X - S_0 + C$ if the option expires in-the-money, that is, if $S > X$. This can be viewed as a penalty because our losses are limited. As this is a function of strike, we can see that if we choose a lower strike the underperformance becomes smaller. However, in this case the call premium will be greater so the risk is also greater. Also, as the strike gets smaller the strategy becomes more bullish because the position now more closely resembles the underlying. This is also reflected in the increasing delta as the strike decreases.

The comment above should indicate that a long call is equivalent to a long put and a long stock position. This was shown more formally when we derived the put-call parity relationship.

A long call position could be used as a direct stock substitute. This can be very effective in low volatility environments. Investors can take advantage of this to buy long-dated calls on stocks that they are bullish on. They benefit from price appreciation and also if volatility subsequently increases.

Investors can also take advantage of the leverage offered by calls. By purchasing call options they can obtain a bigger exposure to the underlying than they could if they spent an equal amount of money on the stock itself. If they are right about direction they can make a lot more money. They also have the benefit of limited losses. Leverage is a decreasing function of strike, so to gain the most leverage we should buy options that are as far out-of-the-money as possible. Naturally this increases the risk that they will expire worthless. This is a seductive trap.

Note that "limited losses" does not mean it is impossible to go broke buying options. It is quite possible to lose all of your investment, and if you trade big enough this could result in bankruptcy. Further, the portfolio margining given to market makers means that it is possible for them to be long options through leverage. These traders can also be bankrupted if implied volatility moves far enough against them.

Short Call

We sell a call. The profit and loss for this strategy is shown in Figure 6.5.

Maximum profit: The call premium, C.
Maximum loss: Unlimited.

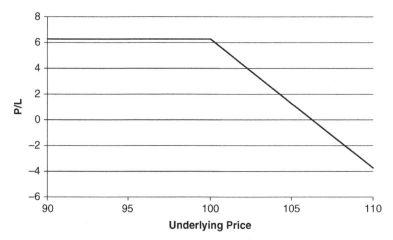

FIGURE 6.5 The Profit and Loss of a Short Call Position

The strike is equal to 100, so the call is initially at-the-money. In this case we have chosen the parameters to be such that the initial call premium is 6.25. In the Black-Scholes-Merton model this corresponds to a volatility of 30 percent, interest rates of zero, and 100 days to expiry.

Breakeven price: The market must rally above the strike by the amount
of premium we initially received. So the breakeven price is $X + C$.
Profit at expiry: C if $S < X$
$$X - S + C \text{ if } S > X$$

Profit as a function of volatility: This position has negative vega and as implied volatility increases the position loses value.

So far this should be obvious: a short call behaves exactly opposite to a long call position. The interesting thing is not what the position does; the interesting thing is why we might choose to do it.

The best reason to sell a call is to take advantage of a high implied volatility when we also want to take a short position in the underlying. This way, we will also collect a significant premium for selling the option. Of course the implied volatility will be high for a reason. Generally if the implied volatility is high, the underlying volatility will also be high, and a short option position can rapidly become a large loser. However there are times when this is not the case. Before earnings announcements or important news, implied volatility can often increase significantly even when the underlying volatility does not move. In these situations selling the call can be less risky than shorting the stock, as the call premium we receive gives us a margin of error over shorting the stock (this assumes that the implied volatility will drop after the news, so that even if we have to cover the call with the underlying higher, we can still somewhat mitigate our losses or even make a little money).

Another short call strategy is the covered call. Here we own a stock and sell calls against it, on the assumption that if the stock rallies through the strike and our stock is called away we would be happy to sell at that level anyway. If it does not rally, we will just collect the premium and we would be better off than if we had not sold the call. This last feature is sometimes referred to as "creating a dividend stream." There are a number of things wrong with this strategy.

- A short call and a long position in the underlying is synthetically a short put. So all this strategy does is use two instruments, and hence two sets of transaction costs, to do something that could be done with one.
- How do you know that you would still be willing to sell if the price did rise through the strike? This decision was made before the stock rallied. The rally may well have been caused by new information, and this new information could well have altered your decision.
- You have not created a dividend. A company pays a dividend from cash generated from its operations. This strategy is nothing like this. You may actually want to sell a put, but at least be smart enough to know that is what you are doing and honest enough to admit it.

Short Put

We sell a put. The profit and loss for this strategy is shown in Figure 6.6.

Maximum profit: P, the initial premium
Maximum loss: $P - X$
Breakeven price: The market must drop below the strike by the amount of premium we initially received. So the breakeven price is $X - P$.
Profit at expiry: P if $S > X$
$\qquad S - X + P$ if $S < X$

Profit as a function of time: This position has positive theta and as we approach expiration the position makes money. The option again coalesces towards its intrinsic value, as we saw with the example of a long call. However, this time it approaches from below.

Profit as a function of volatility: This position has negative vega and as implied volatility increases the position loses value.

This strategy has a payoff that outperforms owning the underlying by the amount $S_0 - X + P$ when the option expires in-the-money, that is when $S < X$. The disadvantage of this strategy is that profits are capped at P if $S > X$. As X gets larger the put will become more in-the-money.

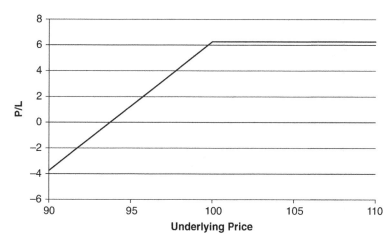

FIGURE 6.6 The Profit and Loss of a Short Put Position
Parameters are the same as in Figure 6.5.

As this happens, the maximum profit increases. The strategy becomes more bullish (it's delta increases). The strategy also becomes riskier as losses are greater if the underlying moves down (this is just another way of saying that the magnitude of the delta has increased).

A short put position is equivalent to selling insurance. Just like an insurance company, in carrying out this trade we take in money initially (the premium received when we sell the put) and hope not to pay out later. Sometimes our losses will greatly exceed the premium.

A short put is equivalent to a short call and a long stock position. Our knowledge of synthetically creating calls from puts and the underlying (or any one from a combination of the other two) should by now be sufficiently ingrained that we will no longer mention this point every time.

Selling puts is a strategy that should be implemented with caution. Many markets have underlying moves that are much faster when traveling downward than upward. So this position can become troublesome quickly. However, good traders should not completely ignore this strategy. There should always be a price at which you are willing to do a trade. There are times when selling a put is a good trade.

One example in which a short put can be a low-risk trade is when we actually want to purchase the underlying. Selling a put gives us a chance to acquire the stock for less than the market price. Let's say that we want to buy the stock of ABC Corporation. We have been following its business plan and we are confident in the company's long-term prospects. However, it is currently trading at $100 and we are willing to pay only $92. If we sell the $95 put for $3.50 and the stock is below $95 at expiry, we will have to

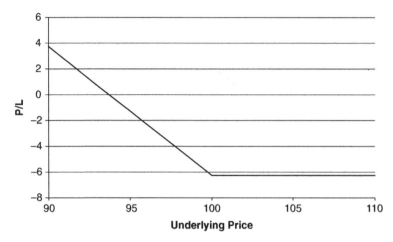

FIGURE 6.7 The Profit and Loss of a Long Put Position
Parameters are the same as in Figure 6.5.

pay $95 for the stock. But we have already collected the option premium, so our actual purchase price will be $95 − $3.5 = $91.5, which, based on our previous analysis, is a bargain price. Conversely if the options expire above $95 we still collect the option premium of $3.5.

This strategy also has risks. The first is that some news causes the stock to drop below the strike price, but also causes us to reevaluate our fundamental view of the stock so that we would no longer want to buy the stock. By selling the option we have lost our right to reevaluate. The second risk is that we were too correct with our opinion on the direction of the stock. If the stock rallies to $200, we will still only collect our $3.50 premium. This will be scant consolation for missing a 100 percent price increase in the underlying because our initial valuation was too low by $8.00.

Long Put

We buy a put. The profit and loss for this strategy is shown in Figure 6.7.

Maximum profit: $X − P$
Maximum loss: $−P$, the initial premium
Breakeven price: The market must drop below the strike by the amount it cost to put on the position. So the breakeven price is $X − P$
Profit at expiry: $−P$ if $S > X$
$\quad -S + X - P$ if $S < X$

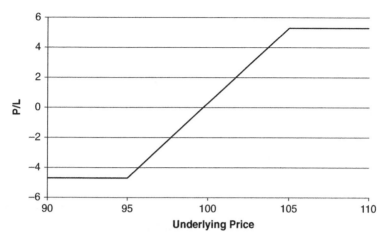

FIGURE 6.8 The Profit and Loss of the 95 105 Call Spread

Profit as a function of time: This position has negative theta and as we approach expiration the position loses money.

Profit as a function of volatility: This position has positive vega and as implied volatility increases the position gains value.

A long put position is equivalent to buying insurance. The further out-of-the-money the put is struck, the lower the premium we need to pay, and correspondingly the movement in the underlying will need to be more extreme for the insurance to have value.

Call Spread

A long call spread is when we buy a call and sell another call with a higher strike. It is "long" because it is long option premium. The profit and loss for this strategy is shown in Figure 6.8.

Maximum profit: The difference between the strikes minus the premium paid, $X_2 - X_1 - C(X_1) + C(X_2)$.

Maximum loss: The call spread premium, $C(X_1) - C(X_2)$.

Breakeven price: The market must rally above the lower strike by the amount it cost to put on the position. So the breakeven price is $X_1 + C(X_1) - C(X_2)$.

Profit at expiry: $-C(X_1) + C(X_2)$ if $S < X_1$
$\quad\quad S - X_1 - C(X_1) + C(X_2)$ if $X_1 < S < X_2$
$\quad\quad X_2 - X_1 - C(X_1) + C(X_2)$ if $S > X_2$

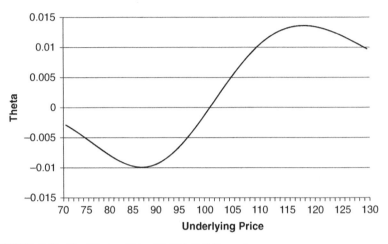

FIGURE 6.9 The Theta of the 95 105 Call Spread

Profit as a function of time: This is highly dependent on the choice of strikes. Normally a call spread is constructed by either choosing two strikes that are out-of-the-money or one that is at-the-money and one that is out-of-the-money. In these cases the call spread will lose value as it approaches expiration. But in general the theta of a call spread changes sign. When the underlying is close to the long strike the theta will be negative and the strategy will lose money with the passing of time. When the underlying is close to the short strike the theta will be positive and the position will make money as expiry nears. Obviously, there will be a point between the strikes where theta is zero. In this case, the single risk measure of theta fails to give a complete picture of the position's time dependence. The theta of a long call spread is shown in Figure 6.9.

An alternative way to state this is that the call spread value approaches its terminal value from different sides depending on whether the underlying is near the long or the short strike. This is shown in Figure 6.10.

Profit as a function of volatility: Again this depends on which strikes are chosen. If the strikes are both out-of-the-money, or if one is at-the-money and one is out-of-the-money, the position will be long vega, and hence gain from an increase in implied volatility. Again we see that the greek changes sign, so again a single number will fail to capture the volatility exposure of the position. We will need to be aware of vega as a function of the underlying. The vega profile is shown in Figure 6.11.

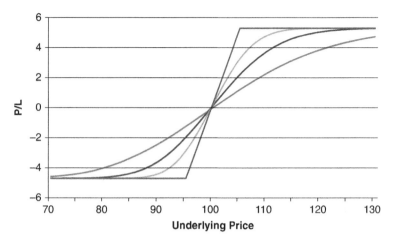

FIGURE 6.10 The Value of a Call Spread Position as It Approaches Expiry

The uppermost line shows the value of the option with 100 days until expiry. The lower lines show its value with 30 days, then ten days, remaining.

In many ways, a long call spread is just a lower risk, lower reward version of an outright long call position. Our loss is still limited to the premium paid, but we have chosen to make this premium lower than if we had just bought a call. The cost for this premium reduction is that our maximum profit is now bounded. A call spread would be appropriate if we expect the underlying to rally, but not by too much (in this section words such as "small," "large," and "too much" must be understood in the context of the volatility of the underlying, rather than any absolute amount).

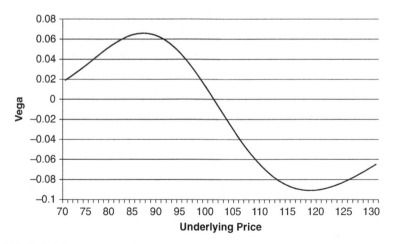

FIGURE 6.11 The Vega of the 95 105 Call Spread

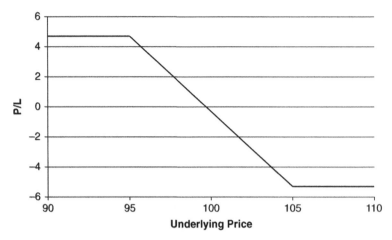

FIGURE 6.12   The Profit and Loss of the 95 105 Put Spread

Put Spread

A long put spread is when we buy a put and sell another put with a lower strike. It is "long" because it is long option premium. This is typical of option positions: it is quite possible to be long premium and short the underlying and volatility exposure. This is just another place where confusion is possible. The profit and loss for this strategy is shown in Figure 6.12.

> Maximum profit: The difference between the strikes minus the premium paid, $X_2 - X_1 - P(X_2) + P(X_1)$.
>
> Maximum loss: The put spread premium, $P(X_2) - P(X_1)$.
>
> Breakeven price: The market must drop below the higher strike by the amount it cost to put on the position. So the breakeven price is $X_2 - P(X_2) + P(X_1)$.
>
> Profit at expiry: $X_2 - X_1 - P(X_2) + P(X_1)$ if $S < X_1$
> $X_2 - S - P(X_2) + P(X_1)$ if $X_1 < S < X_2$
> $-P(X_2) + P(X_1)$ if $S > X_2$

Risk Reversal

We buy a put and sell a call with a higher strike. The profit and loss for this strategy is shown in Figure 6.13.

> Maximum profit: $X_1 - P(X_1) + C(X_2)$.
>
> Maximum loss: Infinite.

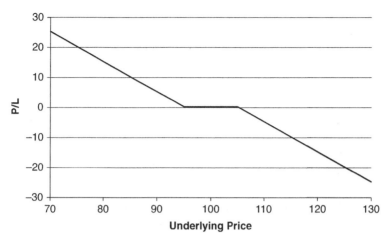

FIGURE 6.13 The Profit and Loss of the 95 105 Risk Reversal

Breakeven price: There is generally no single breakeven price because the payoff is horizontal between the two strikes and the strikes are often chosen so that the initial net cost of the strategy is zero.

Profit at expiry: $X_1 - S - P(X_1) + C(X_2)$ if $S < X_1$
$$-P(X_1) + C(X_2) \text{ if } X_1 < S < X_2$$
$$-S + X_2 - P(X_1) + C(X_2) \text{ if } S > X_2$$

Profit (time): This is again highly dependent on the choice of strikes. Often a risk reversal is constructed of options struck equally far from the current underlying price. In this case the position will often have a theta near zero. This situation changes as the underlying moves. If it drops towards the long put strike, the position will become one with negative theta, and as we approach expiration the position will lose money. Conversely, if the underlying rallies toward the short call position, it will become one with positive theta, and as we approach expiration the position will make money.

Profit (volatility): This is similar to the statement above on theta. A risk reversal that is symmetric around the underlying price will usually have a vega close to zero. If the underlying drops it will behave more like a long put and have positive vega. If the underlying rises it will behave more like a short call and have negative vega.

The risk reversal is a similar position to being short stock. We participate in big moves to the upside and downside and are indifferent to small moves. This position is often used to hedge a preexisting position in the underlying. Purchasing a put could do this, but if we also sell a call it reduces the overall cost of the position (at the expense of capping our upside

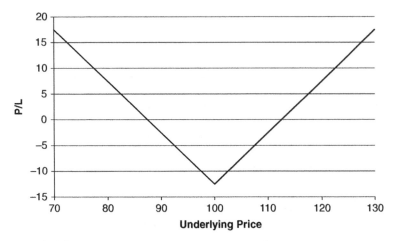

FIGURE 6.14   The Profit and Loss of the 100 Straddle

participation). A zero cost risk reversal is a common method used to hedge the restricted stock given to employees of companies as part of their compensation.

Long Straddle

We buy a put and a call with the same strike. The profit and loss for this strategy is shown in Figure 6.14.

> Maximum profit: Unlimited
> Maximum loss: The straddle premium, $C + P$
> Breakeven prices: The market must move away from the strike by the amount it cost to put on the position. So the breakeven prices are
> $X - (C + P)$
> $X + (C + P)$
> Profit $(S(T))$: $S - X - (C + P)$ if $S > X$
> $X - S - (C + P)$ if $S < X$
> Profit (time): A long straddle position has negative theta and as we approach expiration the position loses money. This is because we need movement, which takes time. As time passes we have less chance of getting enough movement. This dependency is shown in Figure 6.15.
> Profit (volatility): This position has positive vega and as implied volatility increases the position gains value.

The straddle is the simplest option strategy that is primarily a play on volatility. When we are long a straddle we do not care which way the underlying moves, only that it does move. This is the simplest version of volatility

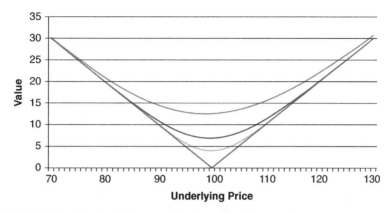

FIGURE 6.15 The Dependence of the Straddle Value on Time

The uppermost line shows the value of the option with 100 days until expiry. The lower lines show its value with 30 days, then ten days, remaining.

trading, but even for professional volatility traders the straddle is of huge importance. Indeed, in many interest-rate or commodity products the current value of the straddle is the most important thing a market maker needs to be aware of: It is the market's proxy for volatility.

The straddle is normally implemented using options that are initially struck at-the-money.

Long Strangle

We buy a put and a call with a higher strike. The profit and loss for this strategy is shown in Figure 6.16.

> Maximum profit: Unlimited
> Maximum loss: The strangle premium, $P(X_1) + C(X_2)$
> Breakeven prices: The market must move either below the lower strike or above the higher strike by the amount it cost to put on the position. So the breakeven prices are $X_1 - (C + P)$
> $X_2 + (C + P)$
> Profit $(S(T))$: $S - X_2 - (C + P)$ if $S > X_2$
> $-P(X_1) - C(X_2)$ if $X_1 < S < X_2$
> $X_1 - S - (C + P)$ if $S < X_1$

The profit as a function of both time and volatility is the same as for the long straddle position. The only difference is that we need a bigger move in the underlying for the position to profit. To compensate for this the premium paid for the position will be smaller than for a straddle.

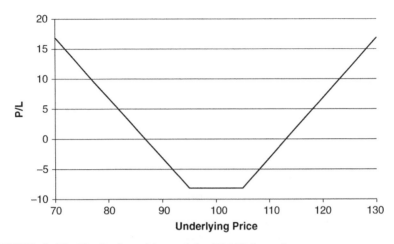

FIGURE 6.16 The Profit and Loss of the 95 105 Strangle

The strangle is normally implemented using an out-of-the-money put and an out-of-the-money call.

A related, if rarely used, strategy is the guts. This is a strangle implemented with an in-the-money call and an in-the-money put. Because in-the-money options are less liquid, this is normally a more expensive trade to put on in terms of transaction costs.

Long Butterfly

A call butterfly is a position where we buy a call, sell two calls with a higher strike, and buy another call with a still higher strike (we can also construct a put butterfly in an analogous fashion). Another way of saying this is that a butterfly is the difference between two call spreads. The strikes are generally equally spaced. The payoff for this strategy is shown in Figure 6.17.

Maximum profit: $X_2 - X_1 - (C(X_1) - 2C(X_2) + C(X_3))$
Maximum loss: The butterfly premium, $C(X_1) - 2C(X_2) + C(X_3)$
Breakeven prices: The market must either move above the lower strike
    or below the higher strike by an amount equal to the premium of
    the position. So the breakeven prices are
    $X_1 + C(X_1) - 2C(X_2) + C(X_3)$
    $X_3 - C(X_1) + 2C(X_2) - C(X_3)$
Profit $(S(T))$: $- (C(X_1) - 2C(X_2) + C(X_3))$ if $S > X_3$
    $S + X_3 -$ premium if $X_2 < S < X_3$
    $S - X_1 -$ premium if $X_1 < S < X_2$
    $-(C(X_1) - 2C(X_2) + C(X_3))$ if $S < X_1$

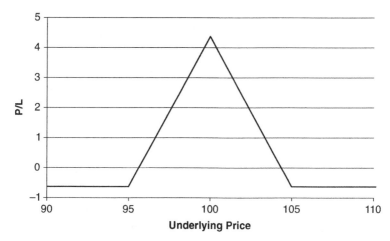

FIGURE 6.17 The Profit and Loss of the 95 100 105 Butterfly

Profit (time): A long butterfly position has theta that changes sign. If we are near one of the wings we will be negative theta and as we approach expiration the position loses money. If we are near the short strikes the position has positive theta and will collect money as we approach expiry.

Profit (volatility): This is again similar to the time situation. In the wings we will be long vega, and at-the-money we will be short vega.

The long butterfly is typically implemented as a short volatility position but unlike the short straddle it has limited downside. The disadvantages are:

- The potential profits are lower.
- Suitable strikes may not always be available.
- The transaction costs are higher as we need to trade more options.

Iron Butterfly

An iron butterfly is a position that has the same payoff profile of a butterfly but is constructed from out-of-the-money options. That is, we will be long an out-of-the-money put, short a straddle, and long an out-of-the-money call (equivalently this is long a strangle and short a straddle, or the difference between a call spread and a put spread). As this position is short premium it is a short iron butterfly. So a short iron butterfly has the same payoff as a long butterfly (more room for confusion). The iron butterfly

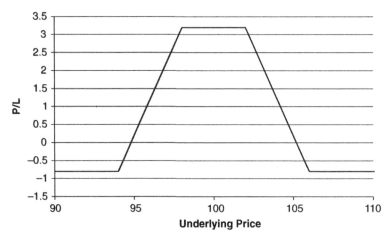

FIGURE 6.18   The Profit and Loss of the 94 98 102 106 Call Condor

may be more appealing, as the liquidity of out-of-the-money options is normally greater than that of the in-the-money option of the same strike. This also means that the transaction costs associated with position entry will be lower.

Long Condor

A call condor is a position where we buy a call, sell a call with a higher strike, sell a call with a still higher strike, and buy another call with an even higher strike (we can also construct a put condor in an analogous fashion). The strikes should be equally spaced. The profit and loss for this strategy is shown in Figure 6.18.

Maximum profit: $X_2 - X_1 - (C(X_1) - C(X_2) - C(X_3) + C(X_4))$
Maximum loss: The condor premium, $C(X_1) - C(X_2) - C(X_3) + C(X_4)$
Breakeven prices: The market must either move above the lower strike or below the higher strike by an amount equal to the premium of the position. So the breakeven prices are
  $X_1 + (C(X_1) - C(X_2) - C(X_3) + C(X_4))$
  $X_4 - (C(X_1) - C(X_2) - C(X_3) + C(X_4))$
Profit $(S(T))$: $-(C(X_1) - C(X_2) - C(X_3) + C(X_4))$ if $S > X_4$
  $S + X_4 -$ premium if $X_3 < S < X_4$
  $X_2 - X_1 -$ premium if $X_2 < S < X_3$
  $S - X_1 -$ premium if $X_1 < S < X_2$
  $-(C(X_1) - C(X_2) - C(X_3) + C(X_4))$ if $S < X_1$

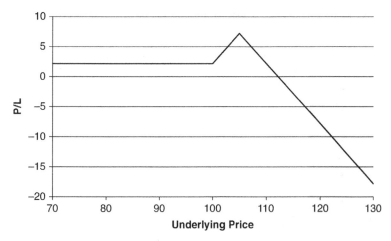

FIGURE 6.19   The Profit and Loss of the 100 105 One by Two Call Spread

The profile of the condor with respect to time and volatility is similar to the case of the butterfly. In most ways the relationship of the condor to the butterfly is the same as that of the strangle with respect to the straddle. It is the same basic strategy, just stretched out over more strikes.

We can also implement an iron condor using out-of-the-money options. This would consist of being long a put, short a higher strike put, short a higher strike call, and long a still higher strike call. Alternatively this could be stated as being short a put spread and short a call spread, or long a strangle and short a "tighter" strangle.

Ratio Spread

A ratio spread is a spread where the number of options bought and sold is not equal. Common ratios are one by two or one by three, and the strategy can be implemented with either calls or puts. Here we will look in detail at the 1 by 2 call spread, where we buy one call and sell two at a higher strike. The profit and loss for this strategy is shown in Figure 6.19.

Here, even more than usual, there is the possibility of confusion when labeling these spreads as "long" or "short." Depending on the choice of strikes and the volatility, buying one call and selling two could result in a credit or a debit.

This strategy can also be confusing as we can "buy" the strategy and become short vega. This is because we can become net short options even while paying premium. This can be used to take advantage of inexperienced traders. If volatility is rapidly rising, traders will be trying to buy anything they can. If they are not careful they can buy a ratio spread and find themselves short volatility (this is far more likely to occur in open out-cry environments than in electronic exchanges).

Maximum profit: The difference between the strikes plus the premium received, $X_2 - X_1 - C(X_1) + 2C(X_2)$.

Maximum loss: Unlimited

Breakeven price: This strategy can either have one or two breakeven prices. The lower breakeven is achieved when the market is above the lower strike by the cost of entering the position. If the position was entered for a credit there is no lower breakeven. This is the case for the example shown in Figure 7.20. The higher breakeven is given by

$2X_2 - X_1 - C(X_1) + 2C(X_2)$.

Profit at expiry: $-C(X_1) + 2C(X_2)$ if $S < X_1$

$S - X_1 - C(X_1) + 2C(X_2)$ if $< S < X_2$

$S - X_1 + 2X_2 - C(X_1) + 2C(X_2)$ if $S > X_2$

The profile of the ratio spread with respect to time and volatility is a potential source of confusion. Depending on the choice of strikes the strategy can be long or short vega and theta. The strategy is probably best thought of as a butterfly with a missing wing. It behaves much more like a butterfly than a call spread.

Ladder

A ladder is a spread where we buy an option, sell one that is more out-of-the-money, and sell another that is even further out-of-the-money. The profit and loss of a call ladder is shown in Figure 6.20.

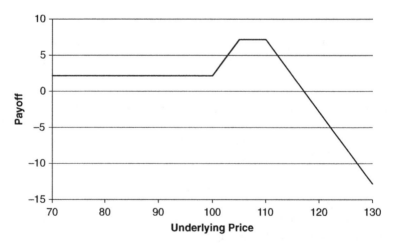

FIGURE 6.20 The Profit and Loss of the 100 105 110 Call Ladder

If the ratio spread is a butterfly with a missing wing, the ladder is a condor with a missing wing.

Calendar Spread

A calendar spread is any spread that consists of options in one month and an offsetting position in another month. For example, a straddle spread could consist of a long straddle in the front month and a short straddle in a later month. In this case the position would be implemented because the trader expects short-term volatility to be greater than long-term volatility.

Because the options expire at different times we cannot make a payoff diagram analogous to the other ones in this chapter. A trader who understands the characteristics of each month's position should, with experience, be able to work out how a calendar position will behave.

Calendars are dangerous for several reasons.

- It is difficult to make a forecast of volatility that is equally valid for different expirations. The relationship between options of different strikes in a single expiration month is far stronger than the relationship between any options in different expiration months.
- Different things happen in different months: different crops, dividend payments, economic news releases, weather patterns, and earnings announcements. These make it safer to think of different months as different things, rather than as elements of a spread.
- When the front month expires, you will not have a spread at all, just an outright position. Make sure you have planned for this.

Conversions and Reversals

A conversion consists of a synthetic short position and an offsetting long position in the underlying. A reversal is a synthetic long position and an offsetting short position in the underlying.

Conversion $= P - C + S$
Reversal $= C - P - S$

These positions have very little risk apart from the interest rate risk. Market makers generally implement them to make small arbitrage profits or to manage risk.

Another use would be if the stock were hard to borrow and short. Then a trader may be forced to enter a synthetic short position through the options instead.

SUMMARY

- Strategies are selected on the basis of the trader's forecast of the underlying's return and volatility.
- Be aware that an option strategy's characteristics can change dramatically as a function of both underlying price and time.
- A strategy can be both long premium and short (for example) vega. Never feel embarrassed to check.

CHAPTER 7

Volatility Estimation

Although it is always perilous to assume that the future will be like the past, it is at least instructive to find out what the past was like. Experience suggests that for predicting future values, historic data appear to be quite useful with respect to standard deviations, reasonably useful for correlations, and virtually useless for expected returns.

—William Sharpe, "Asset Allocation,"
in John L. Maginn and Donald L. Tuttle, eds.,
Managing Investment Portfolios:
A Dynamic Process, 2nd ed. (New York:
Warren, Gorham & Lamont, 1990)

I t is generally accepted by academics that asset returns are unpredictable. This is the basis for the efficient market theory. Here we will not get into the long-running and contentious arguments over the degree of correctness of this theory, except to note that they can quickly take on aspects of debates between atheists and religious fundamentalists.

My view is that the theory is correct in the same way that the theory that the earth is spherical is correct. The earth is not perfectly spheroid, but from a sufficient distance it looks spherical. The planet's bumps and irregularities are small and the idea of a spherical earth is a far better descriptive theory than the one it replaced, the idea that the earth was flat. Using the spherical earth theory has allowed us to do many useful things such as flying around the world. However, a pilot who blindly believed in the theory would put us in grave danger: his theory has no place for "anomalies" such as mountains. The efficient market theory is similar. Taking it as a starting point has allowed us to do many things, such as price futures and options using the principle of no arbitrage. But a good trader makes money by exploiting the small deviations from the theory without bothering to argue that markets are totally inefficient.

One reason that returns are so nearly perfectly unpredictable is that if there were exploitable patterns, smart traders would take advantage of these and soon the anomalies would be traded away. Imagine a stock is trading at $100, but smart traders know it will soon rise to $105. They will buy it. They will continue to buy it until it gets to $105. Acting on their prediction makes their prediction come true. Their action then renders the prediction worthless. In the limit of many traders acting quickly, knowing a stock will rise to a certain level will cause it to instantaneously be at that level. The profit motive eliminates predictability.

Why would the same argument not apply to the prediction of volatility?

The principal reason is that the linkage between a correct prediction of volatility movement and profitability is far weaker than with purely directional instruments and directional predictions. Indeed it is quite possible to predict realized volatility correctly and lose substantial amounts of money when trading options. So the smart trader argument for bringing about market efficiency is less persuasive. The availability of variance swaps should serve to make the volatility market more efficient, but as of the time of writing these are relatively illiquid and only available to the interbank market (even moderately large hedge funds will have trouble trading and clearing variance swaps). The VIX futures (futures on the CBOE implied volatility index) do not add anything significant to this debate, as these are futures on implied volatility, not on future realized volatility, which would be far more useful.

The next thing to consider is that volatility is not directly observable. An asset's price can be directly observed. At any time we can see its bid, ask, and last prices. These may be old, wide, or for small size, but at least they are real. Volatility is not like this. There is no such thing as *the* volatility. Volatility is defined in terms of the average deviation from another average. So we need to specify *what* averaging period we are using. There are many different ways to estimate volatility (using closing prices over different time periods, using daily ranges, using various combinations of opens, closes, highs and lows, etc.) but they are all just estimates. So much of the art of volatility prediction involves carefully measuring volatility. This is not an issue when trying to predict returns. This means that volatility prediction can be profitable because it is a hard problem

Once we have estimated current volatility, rough forecasts are surprisingly easy to make. Tomorrow's volatility will be the same as today's.

Very long-term volatility will be what it always has been. Anything between these two points is just a matter of interpolation.

DEFINING AND MEASURING VOLATILITY

Measuring volatility is not like measuring price. Price is something that can be directly observed. Instantaneous volatility is unobservable. Volatility needs time to manifest itself. Measuring it is something of an art form and we need to choose between various statistical estimators. But trying to find a definitive estimator is probably a fool's errand. Instead we will look at several different estimators, learn their strengths, deficiencies, and how each should best be applied.

The standard definition of volatility is as the square root of the variance. Variance is defined as

$$s^2 = \frac{1}{N} \sum_{i=1}^{N} (x_i - \overline{x})^2 \tag{7.1}$$

Where x_i are the logarithmic returns,

$$x_i = \ln\left(\frac{S_i}{S_{i-1}}\right) \tag{7.2}$$

WHY USE LOG RETURNS?

We have an asset that starts at $100 and moves to $99. There are a number of ways to characterize this $1 price change.

- As a simple return, $99 − $100= −$1.
- As a percentage return, −$1/$100= −1 percent
- As a logarithmic return, ln($99/$100) = −0.0100503

Which should we use? The choice becomes important when we consider the effect of compounding. The mean return is defined as

$$r = \frac{1}{N} \sum_{i=1}^{N} r_i$$

Imagine that our asset price series is $100, $99, $104.94, and $115.43. This corresponds to three successive daily returns of −1 percent, 6 percent, and 10 percent. The mean return is

$$r = \frac{1}{3}(-1\% + 6\% + 10\%) = 5\%$$

However, after three days we have accumulated $115.43, so the total return is 15.43 percent. Total return is defined by

$$r = \prod_{i=1}^{N} (1 + r_i) - 1$$

One of the great benefits of using the slightly less intuitive logarithmic returns is that compounding is much easier to handle. To get the N-period logarithmic return, we simply add the consecutive single-period log returns. Returning to our initial example, the daily logarithmic returns are -0.0100503, 0.0582689, and 0.0953101. The sum of these is 0.1435287. Inverting the logarithmic return equation we get a final price of

$$S = \$100 \exp (0.1435287) = \$115.43$$

So using log returns means we can easily construct the total return from the daily returns. For small returns logs are approximately equal to percentages but logs compound far more nicely.

$\overline{x}$ is the mean return in the sample and N is the sample size,

$$\overline{x} = \frac{1}{N} \sum_{i=1}^{N} x_i \tag{7.3}$$

Example: The daily closing price of Microsoft (MSFT) from the 1st of October, 2008 until the 31st of October 2008 is tabulated in Table 7.1. We also calculate the logarithmic returns, the mean and the squared difference of the log return and the mean.

So our estimate of the standard deviation is

$$\sqrt{\frac{1}{22} \times 0.71333} = 0.0569$$

When looking at financial time series, it is very difficult to distinguish mean returns (the drift or trend of the price) from variance, and estimates of the mean return are notoriously noisy, especially for small samples. So we generally set the mean return in equation 7.1 to zero. This increases accuracy of measurement by removing a source of noise. Note that we are not claiming that financial instruments have zero drift. We are merely

TABLE 7.1   MSFT Prices and Returns

Date	MSFT Price	Logarithmic Return	Mean Return	Squared Difference
10/1/2008	26.48			
10/2/2008	26.25	−0.00872	−0.00774818	9.44431E-07
10/3/2008	26.32	0.00266	−0.00774818	0.00010833
10/6/2008	24.91	−0.05506	−0.00774818	0.002238408
10/7/2008	23.23	−0.06982	−0.00774818	0.003852911
10/8/2008	23.01	−0.00952	−0.00774818	3.13934E-06
10/9/2008	22.3	−0.03134	−0.00774818	0.000556574
10/10/2008	21.5	−0.03653	−0.00774818	0.000828393
10/13/2008	25.5	0.17063	−0.00774818	0.031818776
10/14/2008	24.1	−0.05647	−0.00774818	0.002373816
10/15/2008	22.66	−0.06161	−0.00774818	0.002901095
10/16/2008	24.19	0.06534	−0.00774818	0.005341882
10/17/2008	23.93	−0.01081	−0.00774818	9.37473E-06
10/20/2008	24.72	0.03248	−0.00774818	0.001618307
10/21/2008	23.36	−0.05659	−0.00774818	0.002385523
10/22/2008	21.53	−0.08158	−0.00774818	0.005451137
10/23/2008	22.32	0.03604	−0.00774818	0.001917405
10/24/2008	21.96	−0.01626	−0.00774818	7.2451E-05
10/27/2008	21.18	−0.03617	−0.00774818	0.0008078
10/28/2008	23.1	0.08678	−0.00774818	0.008935577
10/29/2008	23	−0.00434	−0.00774818	1.16157E-05
10/30/2008	22.63	−0.01622	−0.00774818	7.17717E-05
10/31/2008	22.33	−0.01335	−0.00774818	3.13804E-05
			sum	*0.071336611*

acknowledging that trying to simultaneously estimate return and variance leads to unacceptably noisy results.

$$s^2 = \frac{1}{N} \sum_{i=1}^{N} (x_i)^2 \tag{7.4}$$

This is the sample variance. To estimate the population variance from this sample variance were need to make the conversion.

$$\sigma^2 = \frac{N}{N-1} s^2 \tag{7.5}$$

Unfortunately some authorities choose to avoid this step by directly defining the sample variance to be

$$s^2 = \frac{1}{N-1} \sum_{i=1}^{N} (x_i - \overline{x})^2 \tag{7.6}$$

so that is already an unbiased estimator for the population variance. It is very important to know exactly which definition you are dealing with and this seems to be a recurring source of confusion. Always check for the $N-1$ factor in the denominator. The Excel function, Var, uses this second convention.

If we choose not to incorporate the mean into our estimate of the MSFT volatility, we obtain 0.0575 instead. Further, if we apply the sample size adjustment of equation 7.5, we measure the volatility to be 0.0588.

This is our estimate of the daily volatility. We can also measure volatility over other time intervals. However, it is conventional to express all volatility estimates in terms of annualized volatility. To make this translation we multiply our estimated volatility by the square root of the number of periods in a year. For example, in the United States equities are generally open for trading 252 days in a year. (This need not be true for any given year. For example, the death of a president means the markets will be closed for a day.) So to convert our daily volatility to annualized volatility we would need to multiply by the square root of 252. If we had estimated the weekly volatility, we would use a factor of the square root of 52 to annualize.

So for our MSFT example, the annualized volatility would be

$$\sigma = 0.0588 \times \sqrt{252} = 0.933$$

(which would often be expressed as "93.3 percent").

If the historical price series includes the payment of a dividend (or a stock split), we must adjust the price series. The effect of a stock going ex-dividend makes it look like volatility existed even though there was none. It is true that the stock price changes by the amount of the dividend, but this is only because the dividend has been paid to the stockholder. The wealth of the stockholder has not changed. If this adjustment is not done our volatility estimate may well be wrong by a significant amount. For example, if we have a 3 percent price drop due to the stock going exdividend, it looks like a 48 percent move on an annualized basis (i.e., $0.03\sqrt{252}$). Obviously this is very significant.

There are several different ways of making this adjustment. The first is to simply subtract the dividend from the price before the exdividend date. This leaves the absolute values of the day-to-day changes before the exdividend date unchanged, but if we have enough dividends in the series this process can lead to negative stock "prices."

A better method is to multiply by an adjustment factor that leaves the percentage changes unaffected. This factor is

$$1 - \frac{\text{dividend}}{\text{price}}$$

Prices before the exdividend date are multiplied by this factor. This is "backward adjustment." Alternatively, it is possible to "forward adjust" prices, which would mean that the current price will not be the same as the adjusted price.

BIAS AND EFFICIENCY

As we have already mentioned, our measurement of volatility will be only an estimate. Estimates can clearly be good or bad to various degrees. We will chiefly be concerned with two ways of evaluating an estimate: *bias* and *efficiency*.

Bias

In normal useage it is a criticism to say something is biased. This is not necessarily true in statistics. Bias is defined as the difference between an estimator's expected value and the true value of the parameter being estimated. So if an estimator consistently over- or underestimates the parameter being measured it is biased. For example, most mechanical watches run a little fast, so they are biased estimators of duration.

Note however, that an unbiased statistic is not necessarily an accurate statistic. If the result of an estimator is sometimes far too high and sometimes far too low, it could still be unbiased. However it would still be fairly poor. Conversely, a slightly biased statistic that systematically results in very small overestimates could be far more useful. This leads us to our second criterion.

Efficiency

The efficiency of an estimator is the degree that it is stable from sample to sample. Alternatively, the less prone to sampling error an estimator is, the more efficient it is. We can also think of the efficiency of a statistic as the precision of the estimate. A more efficient estimator is more precise. It will require fewer data points to achieve the same degree of precision as a less efficient estimator.

The close-to-close estimator is the most commonly used; however, this estimator converges to the true volatility slowly. This is a very important concept to grasp. Figure 7.1 shows the dependence on the variance (of the sample variance) of various sample sizes.

Sampling error is not the same as measurement error. In a physics experiment we might only be able to measure a certain quantity to a limited degree of precision, due to the limitations of the measuring device or the experimental setup. But, at least if we ignore the bid/ask spread, the price of a stock is an exact number. So the historical volatility is an exact

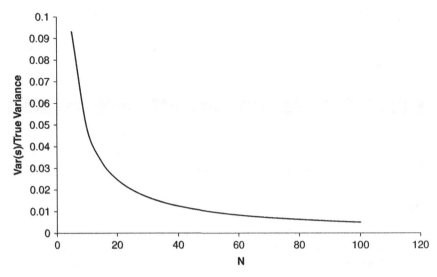

FIGURE 7.1 The Convergence of the Variance (of the Sample Variance) to the True Population Variance as a Function of the Sample Size, *N*

number. There is no uncertainty due to measurement. But there is uncertainty over whether the measure number is truly representative of the underlying reality. An analogous situation often occurs in sports. When a hitter in baseball goes five for five, he did hit 1.000. That is beyond dispute. But no one would claim he is truly a 1.000 hitter. We have just been lucky enough to see the portion of his career when he hit well. There will be other days when he goes hitless. Similarly we need to remember that like hitting ability, volatility is an unobservable quantity that we can only estimate. Our measurements are distorted reflections of the true volatility in the same way that a handful of plate appearances can only give a partial picture of a baseball player's true ability.

Many sports fans are now statistically educated enough to sneer at announcers who mention a player's statistics for the previous week as though they had anything more than very minor significance. However many option traders will still attach significance to the volatility of a stock measured over the last 30 days. How significant is this measurement?

A simple approximation for the rate of convergence is given by

$$\text{var}(s) \approx \frac{\sigma^2}{2N} \tag{7.7}$$

This gives an expression for levels of the confidence interval of the measured volatility. It is very important to remember this. Volatility measurements have significant uncertainty associated with them and for very small sample sizes this can overwhelm any information completely.

Equation 7.7 tells us that using more data (increasing N) will give us a smaller error. While this is no problem if we are measuring the volatility of an unchanging process, it is problematic for financial markets. If our data set is too small we will have a noisy measurement of volatility, which due to sampling error might not be close to the true volatility. Alternatively if we use too much data we will be using information that is no longer relevant to the current state of the market. Choosing the right compromise is something of an art and the most appropriate solution will be dependent on current market conditions.

However it should be obvious that the commonly used method of measuring volatility from the last 30 closing prices gives an unacceptably large sampling error. To see this, let's consider an example. Assume that the true volatility is 30 percent. Equation 7.7 then tells us that the variance of the sample standard deviation is $0.3^2/60$ or 0.0015. So the standard deviation is approximately 0.039. The usual 95 percent confidence interval of two standard deviations means that we could be off by as much as 0.078. As the actual volatility was 0.3, this error is about 26 percent of the quantity we are attempting to measure.

Most traders are completely unaware that this is even a problem. The fact that they do not know it is a problem is compounded by the fact that many commonly used systems calculate historical volatility using either 20 or 30 observations. This means the issue the traders are unaware of is quite large.

A "QUICK AND DIRTY" VOLATILITY ESTIMATOR

Option traders often have to estimate volatility quickly. A useful trick for doing this is to convert the close-to-close estimator to a form that relates the typical stock moves to volatility.

We have seen that the standard close-to-close volatility estimator for annualized volatility is

$$\sigma = \sqrt{252} \left(\frac{1}{N} \sum_{t=1}^{N} (x_t)^2 \right)^{\frac{1}{2}}$$

An estimator based on the "typical stock move" is

$$\sigma = \sqrt{126\pi} \left(\frac{1}{N} \sum_{t=1}^{N} |R_t| \right) \tag{7.8}$$

where R_t is the range on a given day, that is the logarithmic difference between the high and the low. This can be very closely approximated by the percentage difference.

This follows because

$$E\,[|\,R_t|] = \sqrt{\frac{2}{\pi}}\sigma \tag{7.9}$$

which means that

$$\text{average move} = \frac{\sigma\,S}{\sqrt{126\pi}} \approx \frac{\sigma\,S}{20} \tag{7.10}$$

This allows a simple translation between daily returns and annualized volatility.

Multiplying the daily return by 20 gives a useful "quick and dirty" estimate of annualized volatility.

Example: On the 31st of October 2008 MSFT had a low of 22.12 and a high of 22.91. The open was 22.53, so this range was 3.51 percent. According to equation 7.10 we estimate the annualized volatility to be 70 percent.

There are two basic ways of addressing the problem of the large sampling error. The first is to use the close-to-close estimator with higher frequency data. This allows us to increase the number of data points without including inappropriately old data. Alternatively, we can use another estimator that does not throw away all data points other than closing prices. Each method has limitations. However, using a better estimator is more generally applicable. If we can find such an estimator we could always apply this to higher-frequency data.

The first such estimator was developed by Parkinson. His estimator is

$$\sigma = \sqrt{\frac{1}{4N\ln 2}\sum_{i=1}^{N}\left(\ln\frac{h_i}{l_i}\right)^2} \tag{7.11}$$

Where h_i is the high price in the trading period and l_i is the low price. As before this would need to be annualized by multiplying it by the square root of the number of trading periods in a year.

The Parkinson estimator is very similar to our simple "rule of 20." This is because to first order

$$\ln\left(\frac{h}{l}\right) \approx 1 - \frac{l}{h} = \frac{h-l}{h} \tag{7.12}$$

So the logarithmic range is very close to the percentage range.

TABLE 7.2 Sampling Error in Parkinson Variance

Sample Size	Parkinson Variance/ True Variance
5	0.55
10	0.65
20	0.74
50	0.82
100	0.86
200	0.92

It intuitively makes sense that the range could give an estimate of volatility. That is generally what traders perceive volatility to be. It also seems likely that this estimate would need fewer time periods to converge to the true volatility as it uses two prices from each period instead of just one as with the close to close estimator. This is true. The Parkinson estimator is about five times more efficient at estimating volatility than the close-to-close estimator.

Unfortunately the Parkinson estimator has a significant amount of bias. Prices are only sampled discretely. This is true both because markets only trade in discrete units, but more importantly because markets are only open for part of the day. This means that the unobservable true price may not make a high or a low when we can actually measure it. So we will systematically underestimate volatility by using an estimator based on the observed range. It may seem strange to be speaking of an "unobservable true price" but we need to remember that volatility is also such an unobservable derived variable. Further, one of our assumptions is that markets are always open and trade continuously. This is a situation where these incorrect assumptions cause problems.

Table 7.2 gives the underestimation due to discrete sampling as a function of sample size.

Example If we measure the Parkinson volatility over the last 100 days to be 0.46, Table 7.2 says that the true volatility would be $0.46/0.86 = 0.535$.

The fact that this biases the estimates of volatility low, comes as a surprise to some. There is a pervasive misunderstanding that the Parkinson estimator is biased high, as it is impossible to actually trade at the extremes. The thought process goes something like this. "Using the high and low of the day the Parkinson estimator says volatility is 30 percent. But I can't trade at those prices, so real volatility must be lower than that." The inability to systematically trade at the extremes is true but irrelevant. Parkinson makes no claims about being able to trade at the extremes of the range, just that the range is related to the volatility. It is an estimator of volatility, not of tradability.

Many other estimators have been proposed. One could argue that we should spend time on each of these estimators, going through the benefits and drawbacks of each. I've chosen to present only two, because most of the others are based on either sampling the underlying at fixed time intervals (the close-to-close estimator is the canonical example of this type) or on using the range as a volatility proxy (the Parkinson estimator is the simplest of this type). As with most things, it is better to deeply understand a simple concept than to have a superficial grasp of a more complex model.

Surely one of these estimators must be "best"? Not really. All have weaknesses. All have slightly different strengths.

All of the estimators contain information. Given that we are unable to decide on purely mathematical grounds, we should consider what the various estimators are actually telling us and make our choice based on this criterion. For example, if the Parkinson volatility is 40 percent and the close-to-close volatility is 20 percent, we can reasonably conclude that much of the true volatility is being driven by large intraday ranges, and that the closing prices underrepresent the true volatility of the process. This is useful knowledge when deciding how best to hedge

Actually it *would* have been useful knowledge. How useful it will be going forward is another matter. But it seems reasonable that some classes of stocks such as ADRs or ETFs based on foreign stocks will have somewhat predictable Parkinson/close ratios, as much new information is revealed when these particular stocks are not trading.

It is also useful to remember that the close-to-close volatility is generally the industry standard. When a trader refers to the historical volatility, it is almost certainly the close-to-close version to which he is referring. This can create a trading opportunity if this estimator is significantly misestimating the true volatility as in the examples above.

Summary

Close-to-Close Estimator

Good Points

- It has well understood sampling properties.
- It is easy to correct bias.
- It is easy to convert to a form involving "typical daily moves."

Bad Points

- It is a very inefficient use of data and converges very slowly.

Parkinson Estimator

Good Points

- Using daily range seems sensible and provides completely separate information to using time-based sampling such as closing prices.

Bad Points

- It is really only appropriate for measuring the volatility of a Geometric Brownian Motion process. In particular it cannot handle trends and jumps.
- It systematically underestimates volatility.

Together, these two estimators work far better than they do individually. This is mainly because they use completely different information.

FORECASTING VOLATILITY

Now that we have seen how to measure what volatility currently is, we need to forecast what it will be over the lifetime of the option. This will obviously be more difficult. We need to always remember that forecasts are speculative at best, and our degree of confidence in our forecast is as important as the actual forecast itself.

Practical forecasting is an art rather than a science. There is no single correct way to approach the problem. This is the sort of issue that we deal with in life all the time. How would you estimate the time to make an unfamiliar journey? Or the length of a home run? Or decide which brand of car to buy? Statistical and scientific methods can certainly help, but we would also use the recommendations and opinions of friends, information in specialist publications and blogs, and finally experience and intuition. Financial forecasting is the same. Do not become so attached to mathematics that you forget this basic fact of life.

Before we do any formal forecasting, let's look at some of the characteristics of what we are trying to forecast. How does realized volatility behave? Figure 7.2 shows the volatility of the S&P 500 estimated using a rolling 50-day window from March 1990 until the end of August 2009.

There are some things that seem fairly evident.

- The volatility of the volatility is positively related to the level: volatility moves around more at higher levels.
- There are more large moves up than down. Volatility tends to spike higher then slowly relax back down. This is opposite to the behavior

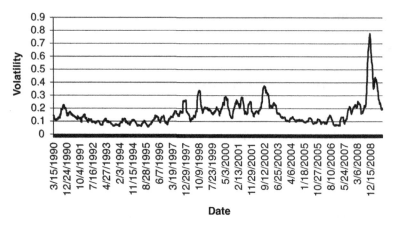

FIGURE 7.2   S&P 500 Volatility

that we expect from the underlying market, where in most cases we expect moves down to be sharp and moves upward to be more gradual.
- Volatility appears to be mean reverting: the further we get from the mean value the more we are likely to be pulled back towards it.

These general features need to be kept in mind as we try to make volatility forecasts.

The simplest forecasting method is to simply assume that the next N days will be like the last N. So if we have measured the volatility (using whatever estimator) over the last 30 days to be 20 percent, we will use this as our forecast for the next 30. This is not a bad place to start and it is the default forecast for most traders. This is sometimes known as the moving window method. The obvious problem with this forecast is that a big move in the stock's price, for example a jump due to good earnings, will stay in the volatility estimate for N days, then drop out abruptly. This effect is shown in Figure 7.3.

This is an artifact of the forecast procedure. Clearly the volatility forecast after the jump should not be 100 percent. The jump, a huge event, has already happened and is very atypical. Obviously it is biasing the forecast (note that it is *not* biasing the measurement of what volatility actually *was*. Volatility over the previous 30 days was indeed 100 percent). A standard way to address this is to use the exponentially weighted moving average model. This takes the form

$$\sigma_t^2 = \lambda \sigma_{t-1}^2 + (1 - \lambda) r^2 \tag{7.13}$$

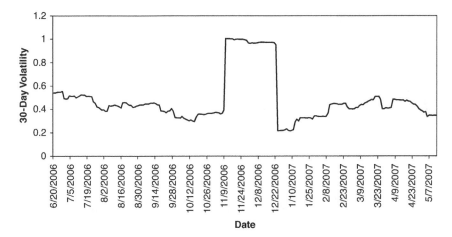

FIGURE 7.3 The 30-Day Moving Window Close-to-Close Volatility for True Religion Apparel, Inc. (TRLG), between June 20,th 2006, and May 7, 2007

where λ is a parameter between zero and one. This models the variance as a weighted average between the most recent squared returns and the previous variance. A lower value of λ means less emphasis is placed on the more distant past and more on the most recent observation. Generally values of between 0.9 and 0.99 are used.

This method has the virtues of being simple to use and understand. It is useful for smoothing volatility estimates during normal times. However it is a stupid way to deal with large one-off events. If the event truly was an outlier we would be better off completely excluding it from our data set when we forecast what volatility will be in the future. An exponential weighting may smooth the jumps in our volatility forecast, but it does so purely to make things look pretty: a better solution is for the trader to decide if the event really was an outlier and if it was to then exclude it or to treat it as a somewhat special case that could occur again and weight its contribution accordingly. To postulate that its effect decays exponentially really just dodges the issue. For example, a jump due to earnings is clearly an abnormal event. It would be good trading practice to exclude this from future forecasts (unless they include future earnings dates). Why would it make sense to use an exponential decay? The earnings announcement was a single event. There will not be a lesser earnings announcement the next day as well, and an even smaller one the day after that. Figure 7.4 shows the volatility of TRLG over the earnings period calculated using both the EWMA (exponentially weighted moving average) and using a simple rolling window with the earning date excluded. I would argue that in this situation simply throwing out the earnings day is a better approach.

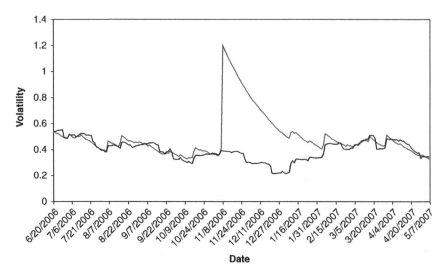

FIGURE 7.4 The 30-Day Moving Window "Jump Excluded" Close-to-Close Volatility and the EWMA Volatility for True Religion Apparel, Inc. (TRLG), between June 20, 2006, and May 7, 2007

A problem with these methods is that they do not take into account the context of the most recent measurement. Context is always of utmost importance to traders. Simply put: the same measurement can mean very different things at different times. We have already stated that volatility is a mean reverting process; high volatility is likely to be followed by periods of lower volatility and vice versa. The EWMA forecast ignores this. The forecast variance tomorrow is the same as the forecast variance for the day after and for all days after that.

The famous GARCH (Generalized Auto-Regressive Conditional Heteroskedasticity) family of models addresses this by adding a long-term average variance that we expect variance to revert to, so that if variance is currently high we may expect it to stay high in the near term (as in the EWMA model), but that it will eventually revert to normality. This has been extensively studied but is somewhat beyond the scope of this text.

VOLATILITY IN CONTEXT

Much work has been done trying to predict volatility. The 2003 Nobel Prize for economics was given for work in this area. However for a trader this work probably is not very useful. Traders need a forecast of the volatility distribution. Selling one-month implied volatility at 15 percent might seem like a good idea if we have a forecast of 12 percent. It will seem like less of a good idea if we know that in the previous two years the one-month realized volatility has had a range of 11 percent to 35 percent, so you will be selling volatility when it is already very close to the low of its range. It is not just the forecast that is necessary. It is putting the forecast into the context of a volatility range. A simple way to do this is through the use of volatility cones.

As stated by Burghart and Lane in their seminal paper on the subject, "The purpose of a volatility cone is to illustrate the ranges of volatility experience for different trading horizons." Let's look at the example of MSFT volatility for the two years ending December 30, 2009.

We calculate volatility (here we use the close-to-close estimator, but there is no reason another estimator could not be used) over (non-overlapping) periods of 20 trading days, 40 trading days, 60 trading days, and 120 trading days. These correspond closely to one calendar month, two months, three months, and six months. The results are tabulated in Table 7.3 and displayed in Figure 7.5.

When displayed graphically we can see why this method was called a volatility cone. The cone shows the tendency for short-term volatilities to fluctuate more widely than longer-dated volatilities. This is due to the effects of increased sampling errors for short-term estimates and the fact that big moves will be averaged away in the longer term.

In order to gain the most information from a given price series it would generally be necessary to use overlapping data. This will induce an artificial degree of correlation in the estimates of volatility and will bias our results somewhat. This is because if I am using a 30-day volatility and roll this forward by one day, I will still have 29 data points in common with the first data set. The two volatilities I calculate will be highly correlated because they are almost the same. Hodges and Tompkins found that

TABLE 7.3 The Volatility Cone for MSFT, Generated from the Two Years of Closing Prices Ending on December 31, 2008

	20-Day Volatility	40-Day Volatility	60-Day Volatility	120-Day Volatility
Maximum	0.969	0.887	0.807	0.620
75 percent	0.370	0.350	0.335	0.327
Median	0.271	0.306	0.312	0.309
25 percent	0.205	0.206	0.201	0.250
Minimum	0.123	0.147	0.155	0.178

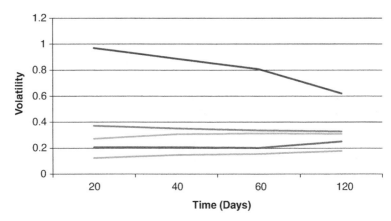

FIGURE 7.5 The Volatility Cone for MSFT, Generated from the Two Years of Closing Prices Ending on December 31, 2008

variance measured from overlapping return series needs to be multiplied by the adjustment factor,

$$m = \frac{1}{1 - \dfrac{h}{n} + \dfrac{h^2 - 1}{3n^2}} \qquad (7.14)$$

Where h is the length of each sub-series (e.g., 30 days) and $n = T - h + 1$ is the number of distinct subseries available for a total number of observations, T. Using this adjustment factor means we can use rolling windows for estimating volatility, which makes volatility cones a very useful trading tool.

Sadly, volatility cones are often not very helpful to market makers or other very active traders. This is because whenever the volatility cone tells you that implied volatility is historically high, these traders will already be short it. Generally they will have been selling it all the way up, and will now be sitting on a losing position. But at least they will now know that implied volatility is at an all-time high, and now might not be the best time to cover.

Few underlying markets trade completely independently of all others. When trading equity options in particular, we need to be aware of not just the stocks we have positions in but also the entire stock market.

The volatility cone is very useful for placing current information from a stock (realized volatility, implied volatility, and the spread between them) into historical context. But it does not place this information in the context of the current overall market. This is also something to monitor. If we had a choice of selling the MSFT implied volatility at 100 percent when realized volatility is 80 percent, or selling the S&P 500 implied volatility at 60 percent when its realized was 50 percent, we should think carefully. We are not getting much more edge (in percentage terms) for selling the single stock than we are for the index. You need to use the implied/realized spread of the index as a benchmark for the amount of edge you look for in all of your trades.

When making forecasts we will generally find that the implied volatility is equal to or significantly above our forecast volatility. For example, it is not uncommon for our forecasts to be 30 percent below current implied volatilities, but we practically never see the converse. There are a number of obvious reasons for this.

- By selling implied volatility we are selling insurance. Thus there is a risk premium associated with this.
- Market microstructure encourages implied volatility to be biased high. Market makers make the bulk of their money by collecting the bid-ask spread in the options. They will willingly bias their quotes a little too high to protect their business. In essence they are buying insurance (they want to be slightly long volatility exposure), as any prudent business owner will do.
- Perfectly reasonable things could happen that have never happened in the past. These things will not be taken into account if we base our forecast only on past data.

BAD THINGS HAPPEN

At 9:54 CT on September 8, 2008, a story hit the news wires that said United Airlines (UAUA) had filed for Chapter 11 bankruptcy. The stock, which had been trading around $11.80, plummeted. In four minutes it had dropped to as low as $3.00. In the next seven minutes it rallied back to $7.99, before the stock was halted. At this point the implied volatility of the September 12.5 straddle had increased from 135 percent to over 600 percent.

Could a trader have planned for this? To a certain extent all equity options have the bankruptcy event as part of their risks, but these events do not typically occur with no warning at all, and typically not without the stock being halted beforehand.

What happened in this case? The *South Florida Sun Sentinel* web site somehow posted a six-year-old story from the *Chicago Tribune* with the date changed. This was e-mailed to Bloomberg by a staffer for the investment advisory firm Income Securities Advisors. This is when the market noticed (apparently *The Florida Sun Sentinel* is not read by many traders). It then took time for United to issue a denial and for the stock to be halted. At 11:30 the stock reopened at a price of $11.3.

In the confusion, American Airlines had 20 percent wiped from its market capitalization. So did Continental, Northwest Airlines, and Delta. Even the S&P 500 dropped over 1 percent.

This was not a case of a stock dropping because of bad news. Obviously that happens. This was a case of a stock dropping because of a "bad" news story delivered by a reputable news source in the normal way. This was not the malicious lie of a clearly biased blogger, but a real newspaper. The increasingly automated nature of digital news services means such events will probably become more common, but to my knowledge this was the first time such an event had moved the market to this degree.

No matter how experienced you become, no matter how careful you are, no matter the depth of your research, at some point an event will occur that you have not anticipated. It could well be an event that neither you nor anyone else could have possibly anticipated. It could be an event that has never occurred before and will never occur again. These events are one reason the implied volatility will seem to be biased high.

For a position trader, context adjusted volatility cones can be very useful as these traders can monitor volatility without having to continuously make markets. They can wait to establish a position as it reaches the highs (and the market-makers will generally be eager to lighten up their positions at this point). Position traders have to take advantage of the fact that they can be selective. They can, indeed they must, wait until an opportunity appears.

SUMMARY

- Estimate volatility using a variety of methods, keeping in mind the strengths and weaknesses of each.
- Try to choose a sample length that achieves a balance between including data from periods that are no longer relevant and using too little data so that sampling error dominates.
- Place the forecast in context by using a volatility cone.
- Further consider the state of the entire market to determine if the particular implied volatility under examination is at an extreme level or whether this is just an appropriate level given the state of the broad market.
- Be selective. Wait for an edge that is clear, measurable and understandable.

CHAPTER 8

Implied Volatility

O ption traders need to be aware of two types of volatility. The first is *realized volatility,* the actual volatility of the underlying over the lifetime of the option. We looked at how to measure and forecast this quantity in the previous chapter. The second type of volatility is implied volatility, the volatility input to an option-pricing model that gives the market price of the option. A simple gambling example might make this clear.

Let's say that we have studied a baseball game. We have examined each side's hitters and forecast their batting averages, number of walks, and chances of hitting a home run. We have also forecast the performance of the pitchers, and then combined these results to arrive at a forecast for the game. We decide that the Cubs have a 55 percent chance of beating the Cardinals. This is *our* forecast of the result. It is analogous to an option trader's forecast of the realized volatility.

Now we find that the bookmakers have the Cubs at even money, so if we bet on them we stand to win $100 for each $100 we wager. This means that they think the Cubs have a 50 percent chance of winning. This is *the market's* forecast of the result. It is analogous to an option's implied volatility.

Neither one of these forecasts are particularly interesting on their own. What is interesting is the relationship between the two. When our opinion is different from that of the rest of the market we have a chance to trade and profit.

THE IMPLIED VOLATILITY CURVE

For any given underlying there is no single implied volatility. Options at each different strike and maturity have their own implied volatility. (Note that for put call parity to hold, European calls and puts of the same strike and maturity need to have the same implied volatility. This relationship need not hold for American options, but in practice it generally does.) This gives rise to the volatility surface. Figure 8.1 shows the shape of volatility curves (implied volatility as a function of strike) that we would expect for an equity index and a stock.

Some features of the curves are

- Lower strikes tend to have higher implied volatilities than higher strikes.
- The implied curve is convex
- The lowest part of the curve is either at-the-money or slightly above it.
- Also, but not obvious from the pictures below
- Options with less time to expiration have steeper and more convex implied volatility curves as a function of strike.

In order to deduce why each of these has the shape it does, we need to look at the reasons why the curve exists at all. Why don't all options have the same implied volatility?

Model Misspecification

In Chapter 4 we develop two option pricing models, the Black-Scholes-Merton (BSM) model and the Binomial Tree model. In both of these we assume that the distribution of returns followed a normal distribution. After hedging away the return, the only other parameter needed is the volatility (see Appendix A for a discussion of statistical distributions).

But we know that volatility is not constant. In many instruments it has a relationship to the level of the underlying. For example, in equity indices volatility tends to increase as the underlying falls. So options with strike prices below the at-the-money are given a higher implied volatility, because if they become the at-the-money strikes we expect volatility to be higher.

Further, the assumption of normal returns is wrong. Returns display both skewness and excess kurtosis. For example, from 1979 to the end of 2008 the Dow Jones Industrial Index had a skewness of negative 1.74 and a kurtosis of 42. To see how this leads to an implied volatility curve, let's just consider kurtosis (the same basic argument applies to skewness, but in that case we would think only about outsize returns of one sign).

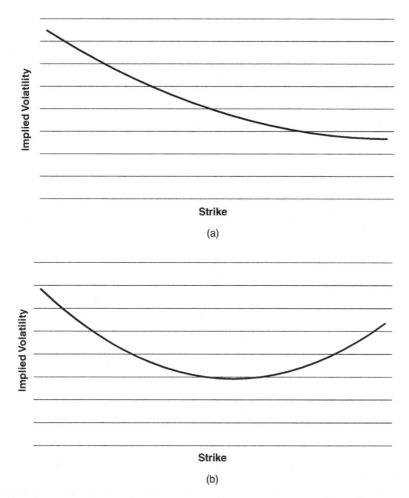

FIGURE 8.1 (a) A Typical Implied Volatility Curve for an Index and (b) a Typical Implied Volatility Curve for a Stock

Kurtosis is caused by the presence of large moves. When we include these large deviations with the rest of the data set they inflate the measured standard deviation, thus making a higher proportion of the data fall within one standard deviation of the mean than would be expected under a normal distribution. This causes the "peakiness" of the distribution, while the large outliers themselves make up the "fat tails."

The presence of these fat tails means that far out-of-the-money options are a lot more likely to pay off than would be the case if the distribution were normal. So they are more valuable. The only way our simple model can account for this is to put in a higher implied volatility. This creates the "smile." A similar argument concerning outsize down moves leads to the slope present in indices.

It is sometimes said that implied volatility is the wrong number that you put into the wrong model to give the right option price.

Supply and Demand

The idea that prices are set by the interaction of supply and demand is fundamental in economics, but this was never mentioned in our derivation of option pricing models. The fact that we have the ability to use different implied volatilities for different strikes allows us to incorporate supply-and-demand effects in the prices we charge for each option. Options that are in more demand will command higher relative values.

In many products the typical "end user" is long and will naturally buy downside protection. We see in Chapter 2 that someone who owns stocks may want to purchase out-of-the-money puts as insurance. This drives up their prices, and hence their implied volatility. This is a *static* cause: it would exist even if the underlying didn't trade. It is basically driven by the need of people to buy insurance for what they own.

Also, people who own stocks may decide to sell calls. This creates selling pressure that lowers the implied volatility of strikes above the at-the-money.

There is also a dynamic cause: the realized volatility of the underlying is strongly linked to the movement of the underlying. In equities, volatility generally increases when the underlying drops and decreases when it rallies. This is reflected in the implied curve where lower strikes have higher implied volatilities than higher ones. However, this effect is opposite in many commodities where panic and higher volatility is associated with higher prices. This applies in energy products, most agricultural products, and metals.

These features cause the slope of the curve. Convexity is caused by excess demand for out-of-the-money options relative to at-the-money options. Again there are several causes.

- Far out-of-the-money options are normally thought of in tick or price terms rather than in volatility terms (this is somewhat inconsistent with the rest of option trading practice, but it is reality nonetheless). Many traders will be overwilling to pay a few cents for options, buying them even after they represent statistically poor bets, just because the potential payoff is so vast. Even more traders will never short these options. This creates an asymmetric supply-and-demand scenario and drives up the implied volatilities.
- In equities, upside strikes often trade at a premium to the at-the-money strike due to the implied chance of a takeover.

- Mortgages generally contain an embedded prepayment option. This means that if rates drop many mortgages will be refinanced and the original loans paid off. This is bad for the mortgage issuers. If rates drop, bond prices will rise so mortgage issuers will often buy bond option calls to hedge this. This raises their implied volatilities.

If the implied curve starts to change shape dramatically it is often because of a new source of supply or demand of this type. For this reason, it is important for a trader to stay aware of what types of structured products are currently fashionable.

Dynamic Hedging

If supply and demand is such that customers are long puts and short calls then of course the market makers will be short puts and long calls. Most customers don't hedge (more accurately, the options *are* their hedge) and the market makers do. At least some of their hedging is dynamic. If the market drops toward their shorts the market makers will become short gamma and will be forced to sell the underlying. This selling pressure will tend to exaggerate the move and increase volatility. The opposite occurs if the market rallies towards their longs. In this sense the smile is a self-fulfilling prophecy of the dependency of volatility on the level of the underlying.

Implied Correlation

In equity indices the slope of the implied volatility curve is more pronounced than in the individual stocks that make up the index. This is because of implied correlation.

The volatility of an index, σ, is related to the volatility of the components, σ_i, by

$$\sigma^2 = \sum_{i=1}^{N} w_i^2 \sigma_i^2 + 2 \sum_{i=1}^{N} \sum_{j=i+1}^{N} w_i w_j \rho_{ij} \sigma_i \sigma_j \tag{8.1}$$

Where w_i are the component weights and ρ_{ij} are the correlations between the components.

So we can see that there are two ways the index volatility can increase, either the component volatilities can increase or the correlation can increase. Equation 8.1 is equally applicable to realized volatility and correlation or implied volatility and correlation. So the implied volatility of an index also contains an implied correlation effect. Even if all the components have flat implied volatility surfaces, the index can exhibit a smile if correlation is expected to increase as the underlying moves. And it is a generally held belief that correlation between stocks increase in crashes or sharp downward moves.

PARAMETERIZING AND MEASURING THE IMPLIED VOLATILITY CURVE

Now that we have seen why the implied volatility curve exists, we need to find a way to parameterize it so we can sensibly compare skews across products and among expirations in the same product. If we merely want to visually inspect the curve then using the forms of Figure 8.1, where we just plot volatility as a function of strike, is fine, but this fails as a comparison tool.

Along the Y-axis of the implied volatility curve, we can just use the implied volatility or at least the relative implied volatility (the strike's implied volatility divided by the volatility of the at-the-money strike). There is another opportunity for confusion here if we aren't careful with nomenclature. If we say "this strike is 10 percent higher than the at-the-money strike," do we mean it is 0.5 and the at-the-money is 0.4 because we know implied volatility is measured in percentages? Or do we mean it is 0.44 and the at-the-money is 0.4 because we mean 10 percent higher than the at-the-money volatility? To avoid this confusion I always try to refer to implied volatility levels in the units of "vols" rather than in percentages.

The bigger problem is what to do with the X-axis. Clearly it makes no sense to just use strikes. If a stock is trading at $20 the relationship between the 15 and 20 strikes will be very different from the situation where a stock is trading $100 and we need to compare the 95 and 100 strikes. Using percentages to parameterize is also bad. A 5 percent move is very different if the underlying has a volatility of 10 percent from the situation in which it has a volatility of 100 percent.

The easiest sensible measure for a trader to use is the delta of the option.

Plotting the volatility as a function of delta has several good points.

- Delta is a function of strike and expiration, so we can directly compare volatilities with different maturities as a function of a single variable.
- Delta is related to the risk-neutral probability of finishing in the money, so it is a sensible measure of "moneyness."
- Traders often informally use delta as a moneyness parameter, for example referring to the 10-delta put instead of to any specific strike.
- One bad aspect is that delta is a function of volatility, so the X-axis is not independent of the Y-axis.

TABLE 8.1 The Raw and Scaled Implied Volatilities of the QQQQ Options as a Function of the Out-of-the-Money Delta from the Morning of September 13, 2007

Delta	Oct. Raw Vol.	Nov. Raw Vol.	Dec. Raw Vol.	Mar. Raw Vol.	Oct. Scale Vol.	Nov. Scale Vol.	Dec. Scale Vol.	Mar. Scale Vol.
10	35.8	35.5	33	32	1.47	1.47	1.46	1.44
20	31.2	30.4	29.2	28	1.28	1.26	1.29	1.26
30	28.8	27.8	26.5	25.7	1.18	1.15	1.17	1.16
40	26.3	26	24	23.5	1.08	1.07	1.06	1.06
50	24.4	24.2	22.6	22.2	1	1	1	1
40	23.5	23.4	22.2	21.8	0.96	0.97	0.98	0.98
30	22	21.8	20.7	20.3	0.9	0.9	0.92	0.91
20	20.8	20.2	19.2	18.9	0.85	0.83	0.85	0.85
10	18.7	18.6	17.8	17.6	0.77	0.77	0.79	0.79

We have to be a little careful here to use call delta or put delta across the entire curve. If we choose to use the out-of-the-money options we will get into trouble around the at-the-moneys because the 50-delta call will not have the same strike as the 50-delta put, so we will have two possible implied volatilites for this part of the delta curve.

We parameterize the smile by the delta of the option, and then divide all of the volatilities in a given month by the at-the-money volatility of that month. This gives a curve that is remarkably constant across expirations. This has long been a trick market makers have used to compare volatilities. This is quite possibly the only reason it has any validity: another self-fulfilling prophecy. Table 8.1 shows this method using the example of the QQQQ options.

Note than in delta terms the curves are relatively constant across time even though in strike terms the shorter expirations have much steeper curves.

We see in Chapter 3 that call spreads cannot have negative values. In the limit of small strike differences, this can be written as

$$\frac{\partial C}{\partial X} \leq 0 \tag{8.2}$$

But in the situation where implied volatility is a function of strike this leads to

$$\frac{\partial C}{\partial X} + \frac{\partial C}{\partial \sigma} \frac{\partial \sigma}{\partial X} \leq 0 \tag{8.3}$$

This form of the delta, one that takes the volatility curve into account, is known as shadow delta. It is the correct hedge ratio when a volatility curve is present.

Using this inequality, we can obtain an upper bound on the volatility slope of

$$\frac{\partial \sigma}{\partial X} \leq -\frac{\dfrac{\partial C}{\partial X}}{\dfrac{\partial C}{\partial \sigma}} \tag{8.4}$$

and we know that

$$\frac{\partial C}{\partial \sigma} = X \exp\left(-rT\right) \sqrt{T} n(d_2) \tag{8.5}$$

and

$$\frac{\partial C}{\partial X} = -\exp\left(-rT\right) N\left(d_2\right) \tag{8.6}$$

So we get

$$\frac{\partial \sigma}{\partial X} \leq \frac{N\left(d_2\right)}{X\sqrt{T} n(d_2)} \tag{8.7}$$

similarly the condition

$$\frac{\partial P}{\partial X} \geq 0 \tag{8.8}$$

leads to the lower bound

$$\frac{\partial \sigma}{\partial X} \geq -\frac{N\left(-d_2\right)}{X\sqrt{T} n(d_2)} \tag{8.9}$$

And finally, we can recast the butterfly no-arbitrage condition (equation 3.35) in volatility terms to get the somewhat more complicated bound on the convexity

$$\frac{\partial^2 \sigma}{\partial X^2} \geq -\frac{1}{X^2 \sigma} - \frac{2 d_1}{X \sigma \sqrt{T}} \frac{\partial \sigma}{\partial X} - \frac{d_1 d_2}{\sigma} \left(\frac{\partial \sigma}{\partial X}\right)^2 \tag{8.10}$$

It is rare, but not unheard of, for these limits to be approached. This generally happens in periods of extreme panic. One notable example occurred on October 27, 1997, when Victor Niederhoffer's S&P 500 option positions were liquidated by his clearing firm. Market makers were able to pay negative amounts for put spreads.

Generally, traders will notice this arbitrage by observing option prices rather than the volatilities but the volatility form of the no arbitrage condition is also useful as a safety condition for automated volatility trading and market making systems.

THE IMPLIED VOLATILITY CURVE AS A FUNCTION OF EXPIRATION

The relative behavior of the level of the at-the-money implied volatility in different months is less consistent than the shape of the smile. There are several reasons for this.

The arbitrage-based constraints on the spread between volatility in different months is far looser than across different strikes. The implied volatility between time T_1 and T_2 is given by

$$\sigma_{12} = \sqrt{\frac{\sigma_2^2 T_2 - \sigma_1^2 T_1}{T_2 - T_1}} \tag{8.11}$$

Example

If the far expiry has a time until expiry of six months ($T_2 = 0.5$) and a volatility of 30 percent and the front expiry has a time until expiry of three months ($T_2 = 0.25$) and a volatility of 15 percent, then the forward volatility is 39.69 percent.

Because the argument of the square root function cannot be negative equation 8.11 gives a lower bound for the second month's volatility. Specifically

$$\sigma_{2,\text{min}} = \sigma_1 \sqrt{\frac{T_1}{T_2}} \tag{8.12}$$

So in this case the minimum possible volatility for the second expiration is 10.61 percent.

Sometimes the different months can actually have different underlyings. This is the case in many commodities where, for example, the later months are options on an entirely different crop, or on oil that has yet to be extracted. But it is also true for stocks, where later months are options on a stock expected to pay a dividend, which in itself is an uncertain payout (although we generally do not model it as such).

The front part of the curve is much more volatile than the back. The front is mainly driven by the short-term fluctuations of the underlying

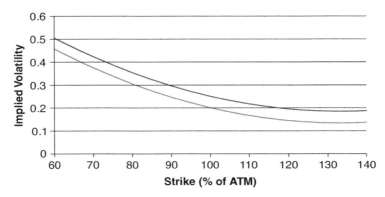

FIGURE 8.2 Two Volatility Curves That Differ by a Shift in the Level

whereas the back part of the curve stays close to the long term volatility which, as we saw in the section on volatility cones, is much more stable.

IMPLIED VOLATILITY DYNAMICS

Now that we have some idea what the curve looks like, we need to know how it moves. The first thing to emphasize is that most of the movement of the curve is a simple shift of the level of the curve. In fact studies have shown that about 75 percent of the volatility changes can be described by a shift and a further 15 percent by a twist. The remainder is due to a convexity shift and higher order effects. Figures 8.2 to 8.4 show what we mean by these movements.

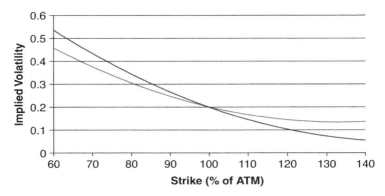

FIGURE 8.3 Two Volatility Curves That Differ by a Twist

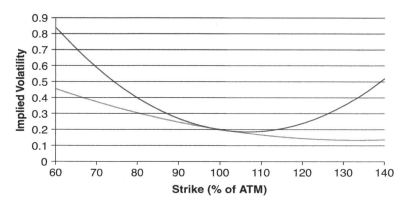

FIGURE 8.4 Two Volatility Curves That Differ in Convexity

The relative strength of these types of move sometimes surprises option traders. This is probably due to the fact that the effects of the nonlinear shifts are reasonably significant for them, even if the magnitude of the shift is small. Nonetheless the most important feature to study is the dynamics of the overall level of implied volatility. To study this we will use the VIX index. This is a model-free implied volatility index for the S&P 500 published by the Chicago Board Options Exchange (CBOE). This uses all the options, not just the at-the-money options, but its level is strongly correlated to the at-the-money implied volatility. Certainly it is close enough that we can make some broadly correct statements. Figure 8.5 shows the VIX from its inception at the start of 1990 until the end of May, 2009.

A couple of important features can be seen immediately.

- There are more large moves up than down; volatility tends to spike abruptly higher, then relax lower over a longer period.
- It looks to be mean reverting.

A commonly accepted idea among traders is that the volatility of volatility increases along with the level of volatility. This is true, but the relationship is far weaker than many believe. Figure 8.6 shows the rolling 30-day volatility of the VIX. Comparing this to Figure 8.5, it is difficult to see much of a relationship at all. The correlation is positive, but at around 45 percent it is certainly not what one would consider strong. In the absence of anything else, we expect implied volatility to become more volatile as it increases, but there is almost always something else happening. This is why volatility increases in the first place.

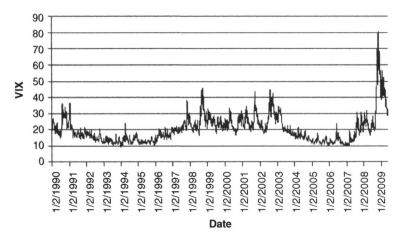

FIGURE 8.5 The VIX Implied Volatility Index

But we can say a few things about the volatility of implied volatility. Equation 7.7 gives the uncertainty in measured realized volatility due to sampling error.

$$\text{var}(s) \approx \frac{\sigma^2}{2N} \tag{8.7.7}$$

This gives an expression for the confidence interval of the measured volatility. This can also be used as the basis for relating implied volatilities of different maturities to each other (we state this result without any justification in Chapter 5). Let's assume that the movement in implied volatilities

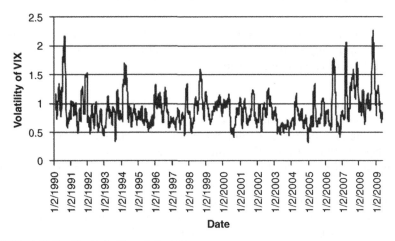

FIGURE 8.6 The Volatility of the VIX

is driven by fluctuations in the realized volatility, and that both maturities have the same true unobserved volatility.

The volatility beta of the maturity T_1 to the reference month T_{ref} is given by

$$\beta = \rho_{1,ref} \frac{\Sigma_1}{\Sigma_{ref}} \qquad (8.13)$$

where these volatilities, Σ, are the standard deviations of the implied volatilities.

Now we assume that the implied volatilities are perfectly correlated, so

$$\beta = \frac{\Sigma_1}{\Sigma_{ref}} \qquad (8.14)$$

using equation 7.7 as a proxy for the volatility of volatility and equating the sample size to the time until expiration, we get

$$\beta = \frac{\sigma / \sqrt{2T_1}}{\sigma / \sqrt{2T_{ref}}} = \sqrt{\frac{T_{ref}}{T_1}} \qquad (8.15)$$

This is the theoretical volatility beta. We have assumed:

- The true unobservable volatility is the same in all months.
- Implied volatility changes are driven only by realized volatility changes.
- Implied volatilities are perfectly correlated.

In many cases these assumptions will not hold. It is up to the trader to decide to use this theoretical volatility beta or to use a beta derived from historical data. This will have the same problems associated with it as calculating volatility or correlation from historical data, that is, sampling errors, data availability issues, and the fact that the past may not be a good predictor of the future.

If we plot the S&P 500 price on the same graph as the VIX, as we do in Figure 8.7, we can see another very important feature of implied volatility.

- When the underlying drops, the implied volatility is high and vice versa.

Again it is important not to overstate this fact. Other factors are always present, but generally large downward moves in the underlying will lead to a rise in implied volatility.

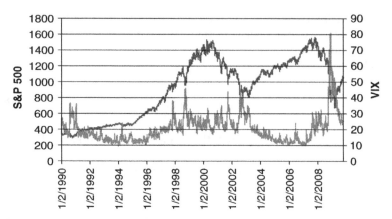

FIGURE 8.7 The VIX and the S&P 500

A trader needs to have a view on what happens to the implied volatility curve when the underlying moves. There are two major schools of thought here.

- The curve remains fixed in strike space, so that the volatility of a given strike is constant. This is sometimes known as a fixed strike model.
- The curve "floats" so that the at-the-money volatility stays anchored to the current underlying price. This is sometimes known as a fixed-delta model.

As is usually the case where there are two competing views that have persisted for a while, neither is correct. Sometimes markets float and sometimes they stay fixed. This isn't a very satisfying conclusion but it is just the way markets are. Remember that the implied curve is really just the consensus view of a particular option market and so it can vary as the participants change their views.

A fixed curve means that the at-the-money straddle is priced at a higher volatility if the underlying drops. This corresponds to reality. However, a fixed curve doesn't correctly reflect the behavior of the risk reversal, it often looks like out-of-the-money puts become cheap on a break when using a fixed curve. In contrast, a floating model works well for the shape of the curve (the risk reversals) but doesn't correctly reflect price straddles. One way to combine these features is to float the volatility curve on a "path": a line that gives the relationship between ATM volatility and the underlying price.

Estimating the slope of the path can be tricky. As we showed above, the statistical relationship between the level of volatility and the movement in the underlying is difficult to measure. Many traders like to use a slope that is equal to the at-the-money tangent of the implied volatility curve. This seems to fit many markets reasonably well.

SUMMARY

- The most important implied volatility for a trader is the at-the-money level. Most of the implied volatility movement is a shift in the level of volatility. The slope and curvature of the implied curve are of diminishing variability (and hence importance).
- Implied volatility is mean reverting.
- The shape of the implied volatility curve tends to be relatively stable in a given product, although the actual reason for the smile can vary dramatically between products.

CHAPTER 9

General Principles of Trading and Hedging

To be a good option trader, one must first be a good trader. Sometimes the particular complexities of managing an option position can blind us to this fact. In order to be successful, we have to put ourselves in situations where we can buy low and sell high.

Humans have been trading forever. Despite this, there is no consensus about what good trading practices are. Perhaps when it comes to specifics this is to be expected. By its nature successful trading can destroy the anomalies that make it possible. However, at a more general level we can state the essential characteristics that all successful trades must have. Further, it is almost certainly a better idea to improve upon a method that others have found to be successful than to try to find something completely new.

I want to emphasize the place of this chapter. This is meant to complement innate trading skill, which I certainly believe exists. I do think that a solid grasp of the quantitative analysis of probability and strategies can benefit any trader, but knowing all of these things is not enough to make a good trader. Traders already do a lot of quantitative analyses, often subconsciously. Good traders can read patterns and prices in ways that statistical analysis still finds too hard. As I have stated several times, measurements in markets are very context-dependent, and a good trader often has keen insight into what variables are currently important. Too many quantitatively driven traders dismiss the decisions of intuitive traders as merely arbitrary and little more than guesswork. But at least some intuitive traders make very thorough analyses of the situations they see. That this is subjective is generally because it is the best or only way to quickly amalgamate the data, place it into context and produce a conclusion. Granted, many more traders think they have this skill than actually do, but we should never totally dismiss the idea. Some intuitive traders, like some statisticians or some scientists, are not very good. They are irrational or even just stupid. But for those who are not, I hope this chapter helps them a little.

This chapter is about general trading principles. We may use option examples in places, but the concepts are more broadly applicable. The specifics of trading options will be covered in later chapters.

EDGE

You must have a definite source of edge. This is something that gives your trades positive expected value. Very loosely speaking, for something to be a source of edge it must be correct and not widely known. This second part is often forgotten. If you know only what others know, this is valueless. It will already be priced into the market. This is why, even if I was so inclined, it would be impossible for me to give you a recipe for profitable trades. The publishing of the recipe would render the trades generated from it almost immediately useless.

Looking for positive expected value is not the same as making only trades that we expect to win. This flawed thinking leads to the nonsense, "You only have to win more often than you lose." This is simply wrong. The winning percentage of a trader is not enough to know if he has been, let alone will be, successful. A similar error is perpetrated by those who refuse to buy options, on the basis that most expire out-of-the-money. This is a mistake made by even the most experienced traders. Jim Rogers, commodity trader extraordinaire and cofounder of the Quantum fund with George Soros, is quoted as follows in *Market Wizards* by Jack Schwager:

> *I don't buy options. Buying options is another fast way to the poorhouse. Someone did a study for the SEC and discovered that 90 percent of all options expire as losses. Well, I figured out that if 90 percent of all long option positions lose money, that meant that 90 percent of all short option positions make money.*[*]

I do not know what SEC study Rogers refers to. The 90 percent figure he gives may be true, but it is irrelevant. Profitability is the important thing to consider, not winning percentage. The 10 percent of winning trades

---

[*]Jim Rogers, In Jack D. Schwager, *Market Wizards: Interviews with Top Traders*, New York: HarperBusiness (1993).

might have won so much that they made more money than the 90 percent of losing trades lost. Similarly, when considering a potential trade, expected value is the crucial metric, not the percentage of winning trades.

Equally incorrect is the adage, "Let your profits run and cut your losses short." This is based on the flawed idea that if your winners are bigger than your losers, all will be well. But this is not true if your losses sufficiently outnumber your winners.

The important metric is expected value. Expected value is defined as the probability-weighted value of the payoffs, summed over all possible outcomes. For example, in the case of a trade that can have only two outcomes,

$$EV = \Pr(win) \times payoff(win) + \Pr(loss) \times payoff(loss) \qquad (9.1)$$

So if someone has offered us a bet on the toss of a fair coin, where he will pay us $1.10 if we win and we pay only $1.00 if we lose, our expected value is $0.5 \times 1.1 - 0.5 \times 1 = 0.05$. So we expect to win 5 cents, on average, when we play this game. As this is greater than zero this is a good trade for us. Note that in no single playing of the game will we win 5 cents. We will either win $1.10 or lose $1. Expected value is an average.

This is the essence of good trading: finding, making, and managing trades with positive expectancy. Everything else: news, business conditions, macroeconomics, technical analysis, psychology, and so on, must be subservient to this concept. A good trade is identical to one with positive expected value. Further, a good trader should be prepared to put on any trade if the price is good enough. For example, even if you think volatility will increase, you should be prepared to sell options if you get enough edge.

- If your trades have positive expectancy you will succeed. If not, you will not.

You must have some idea why a particular trade has positive expected value. Back-testing an idea will show you that something has worked in the past, but there are an infinite number of combinations of trade ideas, parameters, and products. Obviously some of these will have produced successful trades in the past. We need to know why they will do so in the future. This gives us confidence, but also tells us when to stop a particular trade. If you have no knowledge of why something worked in the first place, it is very tough to know that it has stopped working. Evaluating its diminishing effectiveness just from watching the results can be expensive and is also often difficult, as all trades will go through bad stretches.

How can you distinguish between a broken trade and a temporary bad run if you never really understood why the trade worked?

For example, let's consider market making. As we see in Chapter 10, this is a very complex trading operation where every trade's attractiveness will be contingent on the market maker's position. One market maker may be desperate to do a particular trade while another (equally good) market maker may be totally uninterested. This alone makes market making a very difficult thing to back test. It is also hard to estimate if a particular trade would have gone to a given trader. Just because you want to buy at the bid does not mean you can.

However, there is a very clear theoretical reason why market making should be successful. If the mid-market price of a liquid option is 10 and the bid is 9, then if we can buy at the bid we are buying below what the market thinks is its value. Similarly by selling at the offer we are getting a slight edge to the market's idea of fair value. So every trade we do should have a clearly identifiable value: the mid-market price.

So when the minimum tick size for SPY options decreased from $0.05 to $0.01, this was a very clear sign to market makers that their fundamental source of edge had changed, possibly even disappeared.

Most situations are not this clear cut. Generally, you gain confidence in your edge by using a combination of back-testing, seeking the reason for the trade and its realized profits.

Things become more complicated once a trade is made. Generally our trades are more nuanced than coin flips. We will have chances to modify our position as the trade plays out. This leads to the concept of hedging.

HEDGING

A hedge is a trade that we enter in order to somehow offset an existing position. For example, imagine that we buy the 100 call because its implied volatility is cheap. However, this makes us synthetically long the underlying, so we sell some of the underlying short in order to mitigate our directional exposure. This is a hedge. We see in Chapter 4 that this idea is at the core of option pricing, but when should we hedge trades in general? We need to have an understanding of hedging concepts, so we can deal with the complexities that will occur in real trading situations.

Ideally, we hedge all of the risks except those that we explicitly want to be exposed to. In practice this is seldom possible. Even most trades that we think of as arbitrages will have some minor difference in contact specifications. This exposes us to risk. Also common is the situation where a hedging instrument is available, but we have to weigh the benefits of hedging a risk against the costs of executing and managing another instrument.

There are a few situations where we should always at least consider hedging.

- We enter a trade that has multiple sources of risk and we only have positive expectation with respect to one of these. Directionally hedging an option trade to isolate the volatility exposure is an example of this situation.
- Our exposure has grown too big. This could happen as a result of losses in other parts of your portfolio, or it could occur when one position performs unexpectedly well. If you originally wanted a position to account for a certain percentage of your risk, you should consider rebalancing when it significantly exceeds this.
- We can enter a hedge for no cost. For example, in times of market turmoil, it has sometimes been possible to enter long put or call spreads for zero cost or even a credit. This is a great situation. These spreads will probably be a long way out of the money. They have a low probability of making money. But they could pay off, and they cost nothing. It is like being given free lottery tickets. Such situations happen less often than they used to, but they still occur, particularly in pit-traded products.
- The hedge was part of the original trade plan. Sometimes we do certain trades because we are reasonably confident that an offsetting trade will present itself before expiration. In 1997, around 11 A.M. London time, a customer would buy several thousand 20 delta DAX puts in clips of one hundred. Once we had noticed this pattern we would have a few hours each morning to work at buying puts on the bid, knowing that our hedge would appear later. These situations occur frequently, and give market makers a significant source of profit.

All hedging decisions need to be made on the basis of a risk-reward tradeoff. And as soon as risk is introduced to a situation, personal preferences matter. What is seen as an unwanted risk by some traders will be welcomed by others. For a market maker, inventory is a source of risk that he will pay to remove, but for a position trader inventory is necessary to make money.

But sometimes we just have a bad position. Part of the art of trading is recognizing this case and knowing when it is time to start again. In some types of trading this is all that position management is: merely a matter of knowing when to take profits and when to stop ourselves out of a bad position. Option positions are far more complex as they present us with multiple risks. In fact the flexibility they offer us in being able to tailor our position to exact views of the market (for example, we might forecast that the underlying will rally slowly, both implied and realized volatilities will decrease, interest rates will remain stable, but a special dividend will be declared) can mean that we are complicit in getting ourselves into overly complex situations. Keeping things as simple as possible is a good idea in most situations. Option traders in particular have a tendency to fall into the trap of overcomplication.

So, no matter what our views are and how certain we are in their correctness, we need always to be absolutely clear what it is we are trying to achieve, when we will admit we are wrong and what we will look to do to adjust our position as circumstances change. By definition, unforeseen circumstances cannot be predicted, however some contingency planning is always possible and the more it is done, the more effective it will become.

TRADE SIZING AND LEVERAGE

Volatility of a P/L is bad for several reasons. First, high volatility can make it much harder to know the real amount of edge we have as results will have more randomness associated with them. Secondly, high volatility leads to larger drawdowns. This gives a limit to the amount of leverage that we can safely employ. We may think that a positive expected return will eventually overwhelm any negative effects due to volatility, but quite the opposite is true. Volatility is dangerous. If we do not correctly account for the effect of volatility we will lose all of our bankroll, regardless of long-term expectation. This issue is known as Gambler's Ruin.

Gambler's Ruin

How much should we bet on a game of chance? This is a very old question and asking it has led to the development of much of probability theory. We will work our way into the general problem by considering a very simple game.

Our model game is one where we win one dollar with probability, p, and lose one dollar with probability, $1 - p$. As we saw above, the expected value of a single play is given by the probability weighted average of the outcomes.

$$EV = p \times \$1 - (1 - p) \times \$1 \qquad (9.2)$$

For example, in a game where $p = 0.55$, our expected value is ten cents. Each time we play with a dollar we can expect to win ten cents. In the absence of any other more compelling opportunities this is a game that we will want to play. And we will want even more to be able to play the game repeatedly. But what proportion of our fortune should we bet on each play?

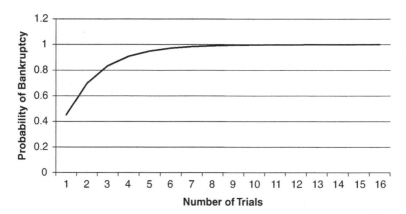

FIGURE 9.1 The Probability of Going Bankrupt, When We Have a 55 Percent Chance of Winning and Are Betting Our Entire Bankroll

If we risk our entire fortune we could make a lot of money. But we also will be bankrupted by a single loss. In N trials, our chance of being bankrupted is

$$P \text{ (bankrupt)} = 1 - p^N \qquad (9.3)$$

This is shown in Figure 9.1.

So even though we can have positive expected value, the fact that we can lose any particular game means we will eventually lose. The volatility has beaten the edge. This prospect is not particularly appealing, but if we bet very small we will not make any money at all. Clearly the best fraction is somewhere in the middle. So we imagine that we bet some fraction, f, of our bankroll on each bet. We also generalize our game to one where we increase our bankroll by W percent after a win and decrease it by L percent after a loss. Now our single-play expected value is given by

$$EV = fpW - f (1 - p) L \qquad (9.4)$$

It is clear from equation 9.4 that the expected value of the bet is increasing with f. That is, the larger the proportion of our wealth we bet, the higher our expected value. But this takes no account of risk. Expected value is not the same thing as the expected growth of our wealth. Expected value is a good metric for determining the desirability of any single bet, but it does not tell us how our wealth will grow. This is our real object of interest: the growth of our bankroll. This distinction is important.

A problem with expected value is that it ignores the relative likelihood of the bet outcomes. The game above where we win a dollar 55 percent of the time and lose a dollar 45 percent of the time, has an expected value of ten cents. A game where we win $999,999,999, 0.00000011 percent of the time and lose a dollar 99.99999989 percent of the time also has an expected value of ten cents. Would anyone really be indifferent to these two games? The first game is a slightly biased coin flip. In the second case, if you won you would be one of the richest people on earth, but the chances of winning are infinitesimal. The expected outcome of the second game would be for your bankroll to shrink by a dollar each time you played. If your bankroll was $100 and you played 100 times, you would expect to be broke even though your expected value was $0.1 \times \$100 = \$10$.

The fact that maximizing expected value might not be appropriate was first considered by Nicholas Bernoulli in 1713, and was solved independently by his brother Daniel in 1738, and by Gabriel Cramer in 1728. It is referred to as the St. Petersburg Paradox and is posed in the form of a proposition bet.

We play a game where we toss a fair coin until a head appears. If it appears on the Nth toss we win 2^N dollars. How much should we pay to play this game?

The expected value of this game can be calculated simply by considering the two possibilities at each time step.

$$E[B] = \frac{1}{2} \times 2 + \frac{1}{4} \times 4 + \frac{1}{8} \times 8 + \frac{1}{16} \times 16 + \ldots = 1 + 1 + 1 + 1 + \ldots = \infty$$

(9.5)

But in the real world it is highly unlikely that anyone would pay an infinite amount of money to play a game that pays 2 dollars about half the time. It is clear that much of the value of the game comes from exceedingly unlikely scenarios that pay off enormous amounts. The probability distribution of the payoffs is shown in Figure 9.2.

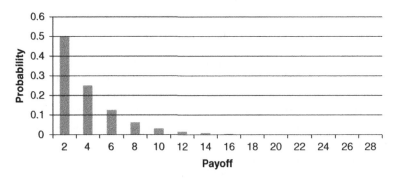

FIGURE 9.2 The Probability Distribution of Results of the St. Petersburg Game

The paradox challenges the idea that people evaluate risky propositions in terms of expected value. Instead we will explicitly consider the growth of our bankroll after repeated iterations of the game. (This isn't exactly the Bernoulli solution. He introduced the idea of utility. What we do is equivalent to choosing a utility function that maximizes growth, which is the outcome we were looking for.) Considering bankroll growth to be the important variable, leads us to the famous (among gamblers, at least) Kelly Criterion.

Let's return to our game above where at each play we stand to lose L percent or win W percent. So if our initial wealth is B_0, after a win this increases to

$$B = B_0 (1 + fW) \tag{9.6}$$

and after a loss it drops to

$$B = B_0 (1 - fL) \tag{9.7}$$

More simply, each time we win we multiply our bankroll by $(1 + fW)$ and when we lose we multiply our bankroll by $(1 - fL)$. So for n wins and m losses the gain factor (the factor we multiply our starting bankroll by) is

$$G(f) = (1 + fW)^n (1 - fL)^m \tag{9.8}$$

Or per trade we get

$$G(f)^{\frac{1}{n+m}} \equiv g(f) = (1 + fW)^p (1 - fL)^q \tag{9.9}$$

where $p = n/(n + m)$ is the probability of a win and $q = m/(n + m)$ is the probability of a loss. As $n + m$ tends toward infinity, this becomes the geometric mean of the gain. For this value of g, the value of our bankroll after $n + m$ games is given by

$$B = B_0 g^{n+m} \tag{9.10}$$

To find the value of f such that we maximize g, we differentiate with respect to f and set this equal to zero.

$$\frac{\partial g}{\partial f} = pW (1 + fW)^{p-1} (1 - fL)^q - qL (1 + fW)^p (1 - fL)^{q-1} \tag{9.11}$$

So at the maximum

$$0 = pW (1 - fL) - qL (1 + fW) \tag{9.12}$$

which has the solution

$$f = \frac{pW - qL}{WL} \tag{9.13}$$

This is the proportion of our bankroll that increases our wealth the most and the fastest. (We could also work with the gain directly and show that the same result occurs from trying to maximize the mean of the logarithm of the gain.). Trading more than this amount will reduce the expected bankroll and if we trade more than twice the Kelly fraction our growth rate will turn negative.

Example of Kelly Sizing

Consider the two examples above, which both had an expected value of ten cents. In the first we had a 55 percent chance of winning a dollar and a 45 percent chance of losing a dollar. Let's assume an initial bankroll of $100 (there is a slightly different form of the Kelly criterion if gains and losses are expressed in absolute dollar terms). Now equation 9.13 implies

$$f = \frac{0.55 \times 1 - 0.45 \times 1}{1 \times 1} = 0.1$$

In the second case we had a 0.00000011 percent chance of winning $999,999,999 and a 99.99999989 percent chance of losing a dollar. Here equation 10.13 implies

$$f = \frac{0.0000000011 \times 999999999 - 0.9999999989 \times 1}{999999999 \times 1} \approx 1 \times 10^{-10}$$

The concept of expected value might not be able to differentiate between these bets, but the Kelly criterion can, as the expected growth of the portfolio will be very different in these cases.

Generally in finance, the results of our trades will not be as simple as the "bets" we have looked at so far. However this analysis can be easily extended to cover trades with continuous outcomes.

The Kelly criterion is not the only possible scheme for trade sizing. As it involves a utility choice (a specification of risk appetite), it is quite possible that a trader might not be comfortable with certain aspects of Kelly sizing. For example, the results might be uncomfortably volatile. It is also possible that a trader might not be interested in making the most money in the long run. Perhaps short-term results are of more relevance.

But a reason often given for dissent is that using Kelly requires accurate estimates of trade win probabilities and win amounts, and that these numbers are never correct. This objection is irrelevant for several reasons.

- All trading requires these estimates. To make a trade at all means that the trader thinks it has positive expected value. How can he reach this conclusion without estimates for win probabilities and amounts? Equation 9.1 (expected value) needs the same inputs as equation 9.13 (the Kelly criterion). Even the most nonquantitative trader should be able to come up with some range of estimates if pushed hard enough.
- Even if a trader does not want to scale his trades by using the Kelly criterion, it still exists. It specifies an optimal leverage level. The mathematics is indisputable: if you trade more than this amount, then in the long run your growth rate will decline. This applies to any bankroll, not just one traded according to Kelly, just as the law of gravity applies to someone even if they have no idea of the mass of the earth.

SCALABILITY AND BREADTH

Some profitable trades just do not turn up often enough to be concerned about. A coin that turns up heads 51 percent of the time, and that can be tossed once a day, is much more valuable that one that shows 75 percent heads, but can be used only once a year. Look for small edges that can be applied across many products rather than specialized "killer" edges that have limited applicability across product class or time.

Scalability within Products

Some products are just not big enough to be worth trading. For example, the VIX futures only trade a few thousand contracts a day. It is very hard to make any serious money unless you can trade a decent amount of size. Obviously this amount will be dependent on your bankroll and some products may be appropriate for beginning traders or for those backing themselves, but not for larger firms.

This is often forgotten. Mark Cuban made this mistake when he proposed setting up a sports gambling hedge fund. On November 27, 2004, he stated in his blog (www.blogmaverick.com) that he intended to start a sports gambling hedge fund. He was convinced that there were some people who had the ability to profitably bet on sports. There are, but that misses a more important point. It is simply impossible to make a significant amount of money doing this. Even ignoring the fact that successful gamblers routinely have their bets refused or their accounts closed, the casinos and gambling web sites will not take enough money for a gambler to make a decent return.

Let's assume our hedge fund is running a baseball operation. The major leagues have 30 teams and they each play 162 regular season games. This gives 2,430 games (each team plays 162 games, but we need two teams to make a game, so the total is $162 \times 30/2$). Bets are widely available on the game winner and on the total, so we have 4,860 opportunities to find good bets. Let's be optimistic and say we bet on half of these games. Generally a casino would take a $5,000 bet on a regular season game. If we have a good system for placing bets, we might be able to place $20,000 on each bet by hitting several casinos at the same time. If we can make 5 cents profit for each dollar wagered we would make

$$\text{Profit} = 2,430 \times 2 \times 0.5 \times 0.05 \times \$20,000 = \$2.43 \text{ million}$$

Now consider that the hedge fund manager would receive only 20 percent of this money, or $486,000. This is certainly a nice income, but is there really any point starting a hedge fund that can only make this amount of money?

A lot of these numbers are not much better than wild guesses. The edge of 0.05 could easily be wrong. So could the percentage of games we bet on. This does not change the main point. It is not important that Mark Cuban was wrong here (he has been right enough that he has no reason to care what I think about him). The point is that breadth is as important as quality when we are assessing a strategy. Furthermore, this type of "back of the envelope" calculation is essential when contemplating whether to enter a new trade. Often we can do no better than provide rough estimates, but the process is essential. In this example, five minutes was enough to convince me not to go any further. The fact that Mr. Cuban has still not launched the fund may mean that he has reached the same conclusion.

SUMMARY

- Trades need to have positive expected value.
- The fundamental reason for the positive expected value must be understood.
- Hedging is designed to isolate risks.
- High volatility is more dangerous than low expected value.
- Correct trade size is a function of both edge and variance.
- A strategy's breadth is usually its ultimate limiting factor.

CHAPTER 10

Market Making Techniques

I n this chapter we will introduce and discuss the basic trading techniques that a high-frequency trader uses to extract value from his market. High frequency only makes sense as a relative term. It is the frequency where market microstructure is more important than any forecast of future market direction or volatility. This varies from product to product. If trading is analogous to a game of poker, high-frequency trading is the part of the game where we are playing our opponents rather than our cards.

Typically our aim in this type of trading is to capture the bid-ask spread. All traders try to buy low and sell high, but here "low" means on the bid and "high" means on the offer. This adds liquidity to the market. It is liquidity provision that these traders are paid for. Recently, this kind of trader has received a lot of bad press. Most of it was poorly informed and most of it was by people who do not have the ability to compete in this area. The disdain should not be too surprising. If the markets are an ecosystem, high frequency traders are the scavengers and decomposers. Their life is not glamorous or particularly noble, but they provide a service and markets would not function without them.

Some markets are far more amenable to the kind of techniques we describe here than others. There is no point attempting these maneuvers in a very illiquid product. In order to play games you need someone to play against. Liquid futures, where speculators and liquidity providers trade most of the volume, are ideal. You should also try to be aware if you are trading something that is typically used as part of a spread. This does not necessarily make the ideas useless, but it can change things. For example, it is only possible to move an index future so far before the index arbitrageurs trade and push it back. But we can also use this type of information. In fact we should try to take advantage of any consistent trading patterns.

MARKET STRUCTURE

Markets can be set up in a number of ways. As professional traders will be intimately involved with market structure and the price formation process, they need to have a good grasp of these differences. These differences can be significant, not only in the mechanics of placing an order, but also in the price series that result. There really is no such thing as *a* market, there are a number of different market types and they have different strengths and weaknesses. A trader should know the way orders are matched and prices are formed in his market. This knowledge is necessary for any theoretical analysis or analysis of price data.

There are two basic market structures:

- Order-driven markets, where traders submit a mix of market orders and limit orders. Here all traders can announce prices at which they are willing to buy or sell, possibly through brokers.
- Dealer-driven markets, where only market makers or specialists can give quotes and other traders must take them or leave them.

These two market types can also be combined to form a mixed market, where anyone can submit orders but there are also designated market makers or specialists to supply liquidity.

The dealer-driven market is now largely confined to some currency and OTC products. The greater flexibility and openness of the order-driven paradigm seems to be winning, and all American exchanges are now of this type.

The Order-Driven Market

The two basic order types are the limit order and the market order.

- A limit order specifies a price at which it is to be executed. An example would be "buy 1,000 shares up to a price of $100."
- A market order has no such price restriction. An example would be "buy 1,000 shares."

All limit orders, which have not been filled or cancelled, are collected together and form the order book. Thus the order book is the collection

TABLE 10.1 The Order Book for QQQQ, at 12:52 CST on February 25, 2009

Bid Size	Bid Price	Ask Price	Ask Size
5,947	28.68	28.69	1,320
1,686	28.67	28.70	1,172
1,796	28.66	28.71	1,854
1,409	28.65	28.72	1,631
1,225	28.64	28.73	1,648
1,136	28.63	28.74	1,136
9,960	28.62	28.75	1,090
1,033	28.61	28.76	1,042
1,028	28.60	28.77	9,440
9,390	28.59	28.78	1,020

of all the placed bids and offers for a given underlying. This is illustrated above in Table 10.1 for the QQQQ.

Pre-Opening Auction The trading day begins with a pre-opening process. Here the exchange or a specialist runs an opening auction process to determine the opening price. The exact details vary, but the important thing is that this is purely an algorithmic process; no discretion is applied.

"Everyone knows" that prices are created by supply and demand. Unfortunately, like most of the things that "everyone knows," this is too vague to help in anything more than a very general sense. I am unaware of any work that has rigorously applied the economists' concept of the intersection of a supply curve and a demand curve to calculate the correct price of a stock (some recent work in econophysics has studied the statistical properties of the buy and sell orders entering a marketplace with the aim of calculating a clearing price, but this work is different in spirit and practice from classical economics).

The one major exception to this is when we have an auction market. This is generally how stocks are opened each day and can be a fully automated process. Several European stock exchanges also operate a midday auction and a closing auction. A similar process is involved when an IPO price is being established.

The process works like this.

- The buy orders form the demand function.
- The sell orders form the supply function.
- The trading price is set to maximize the trading volume. The filled volume at any particular price is Min(Supply, Demand).
- All buy orders at or above this price are filled and all sell orders at or below this price are filled.

TABLE 10.2 A Pre-open Order Book

Price	Total Demand	Bid Size	Ask Size	Total Supply	Filled Volume
105	2	2	36	103	2
104	2	0	12	67	2
103	14	12	18	55	14
102	24	10	8	37	24
101	29	5	12	29	29
100	37	8	6	17	17
99	58	21	7	11	11
98	73	15	0	4	4
97	91	18	0	4	4
96	134	43	4	4	4
95	147	13	0	0	0

- Generally there will be a situation where the volume maximizing price does not have equal supply and demand. In this case not all orders will be filled and the earliest submitted orders will be filled first.

Consider the orders submitted in Table 10.2.

We can also display this graphically and see where the supply and demand curves intersect. This is shown in Figure 10.1.

Here we see that the price where supply and demand are equal is 101 and 29 shares trade at that price. All bids up to and including 101 are matched with all offers below and including 101. The market is left in the state shown in Table 10.3.

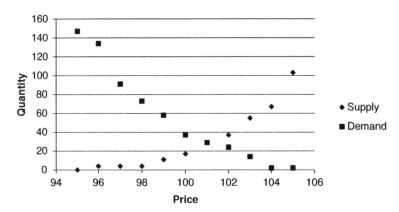

FIGURE 10.1 The Supply and Demand Curves Implied by the Pre-Open Order Book

TABLE 10.3 The Order Book Immediately After the Open

Price	Bid Size	Ask Size
105		36
104		12
103		18
102		8
101		
100	8	
99	21	
98	15	
97	18	
96	43	
95	13	

Normally the exchanges will publish indicative opening prices as the pre-opening period takes place. If traders see that a security is projected to open at an attractive price they will put in more orders until they drive the price to a point where they have no more interest.

The Trading Day   After the opening period the order book would look something like that of Table 10.1. It would contain bids below the current market price and offers above it. The difference between the best bid and the best offer is known as the bid-ask spread.

The supply demand curves meet in a characteristic V shape, called the *market depth*, which tells a trader how many shares can be executed up to a given price. The market depth for the order book of Table 10.1 is shown in Figure 10.2.

At this point any market participant can place an order. If they are a buyer, they might choose to lift an offer to assure a fill or they might join the bid. This could save them one cent per share, but there is also the risk that the market might move higher and they do not get filled at all. This issue is the main conundrum of execution that traders must face. Its existence leads to the presence of an entire class of traders and strategies: market making.

MARKET MAKING

Market making is a trading strategy where a trader tries to capture the bid-ask spread. Other traders willingly pay the spread so they can execute immediately. The market maker is paid to create liquidity. Each trade will

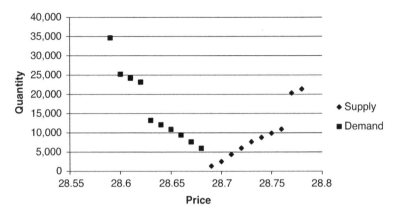

FIGURE 10.2 The Market Depth for QQQQ, at 12:52 CST on February 25, 2009

be an immediate winner when it is compared to the current midmarket price, but by trading he will accumulate inventory. Consequently, the most important part of his risk management is managing this inventory.

Let's first clear up some common misconceptions:

- Market making is not the same as being a broker. A broker executes a clients order. A market maker is someone whose principal trading method is to quote a two-sided market (a bid and an offer).
- Generally they are not guaranteed to be able to buy at the bid or sell at the offer: they try to but they are in competition with the rest of the market. In an order-driven market they are in competition with everyone, but even in a dealer-driven market they will have competing dealers.
- Market makers have very little power to manipulate or push a market. Usually they are far more at the mercy of the public than the other way around. (A good way to detect whether someone is really aware of market microstructure is to ask his opinion on why a certain move happened on expiration day. A popular conspiracy theory is that option market makers were moving the stock so that their shorts would expire worthless. This is as valid as most other conspiracy theories.)
- Making markets is not a risk-free way to make money. Managing inventory is crucial and not particularly easy.

As we have already said, the aim of market making is to collect the bid-ask spread. This is our compensation for the service of providing liquidity. Not only is the bid-ask spread what we are trying to get, it is the only thing in our favor. As we will see in this chapter, everything else will hurt us.

The spread is our only advantage, so the worst thing that can happen to a market maker is that he becomes unable or unwilling to make a market. It is partly due to machismo and a sense of professional pride, but mainly due to this simple fact of market microstructure that the best market makers will always make a market. During times of great turbulence it can be frightening to make a market, but these are also generally the best times to trade in. A market maker is running a shop. No good shopkeeper closes when his customers want to do business.

- Always be able to make a market.

Amadeo Giannini, the founder of the Bank of Italy in San Francisco, displayed a legendary example of this attitude. His bank was destroyed in the earthquake of 1906. The city was in tatters. His customers desperately needed a bank, both for security and to borrow funds for rebuilding. To keep his bank open he set up two barrels on the North Beach docks and laid a plank between them to make a desk. One barrel was labeled "deposits" and the other "withdrawals." He handwrote a sign, "Loans are available. The Bank of Italy is open for business."

He recognized the risks. He had four guards armed with shotguns. But he also recognized the need to keep trading. Mr. Giannini is a role model for all market makers and indeed all traders.

Market making in derivatives is a little different from market making in stocks or physical commodities. There is no need to maintain an inventory of product to fill demand, as contracts can be created as needed. However, the trader still has limits imposed on him by his clearing member, both on the long and short sides. So it is as if an inventory restriction existed.

With most trading strategies the crucial question is "How do I make money?," but with market making it is trivial to make money. It is just very hard to keep it. If a market maker is trading, he will be making money. Clearly this profit will be dependent on the width of the bid-ask spread and on the number of trades. Every time we complete a round-trip trade, a buy followed by a sell or vice versa, we collect the spread if the midmarket price has not changed.

For example, if we buy 100 shares at \$100 and sell them at \$101 we make \$1 times 100 = \$100. Even if we do not sell them, if the midmarket price (the midpoint of the bid price and the ask price) is \$100.5, we will have a marked-to-market profit of \$50.

In order to keep trading, we need to keep our inventory between our limits. The crucial issue for a market maker is not managing his strategy, it is managing his inventory.

The market maker's problem is this: When I do a trade, how do I adjust my bid and offer prices? In fact, if he does this well, his initial quote will not be particularly crucial to his success. He may make an opening bid that is too high and this will be hit, but now he will take this into account and lower subsequent bids (and offers).

There are two basic frameworks for addressing this issue. The first is to directly adjust on the basis of the accumulated inventory. In this paradigm we do whatever is necessary to minimize inventory. Having too much inventory is the ultimate risk because if that happens we can no longer trade.

The second idea is to adjust on the basis of information. If I quote a bid price and someone else hits that bid, it is obvious that the counterparty thought my price was too high. This should somehow be taken into account.

Of course in practice these methods are used in conjunction with each other. Also, both approaches cause us to move our quotes in the same direction, as a counterparty giving us inventory is correlated with his forecast of the price movement.

Inventory-Based Market-Making

Imagine that the underlying has an initial value of 100 (perhaps this value has been reached by an auction process like that described above). We will make markets using these rules.

- The initial price is 99/101.
- We always need to make a price that is no more than 2 ticks wide.
- All trades are in single units (this is not essential, but makes analysis easier).
- After a buy, we lower both the bid and the offer by one.
- After a sale, we raise both the bid and the offer by one.

Under these rules the inventory is the sole determinant of the quotes. We simulate this strategy assuming that buy-and-sell orders arrive randomly and with equal probability. Some sample paths for the midmarket price are shown in Figure 10.3.

Note that the underlying moves a considerable amount, just due to the fact that random orders are arriving and the market maker is doing his best to keep his inventory flat.

After running 10,000 simulations of 100 trades each we have the following distribution of market maker results. This is shown in Figure 10.4.

As we would expect, on average we make almost no money doing this. We make basically the bid-ask spread associated with one trade. After the initial trade, all we are doing is managing inventory. The average profit is actually 0.92, which is roughly as we would expect (we would expect to make half the bid-ask spread, or half of two ticks). What is far more

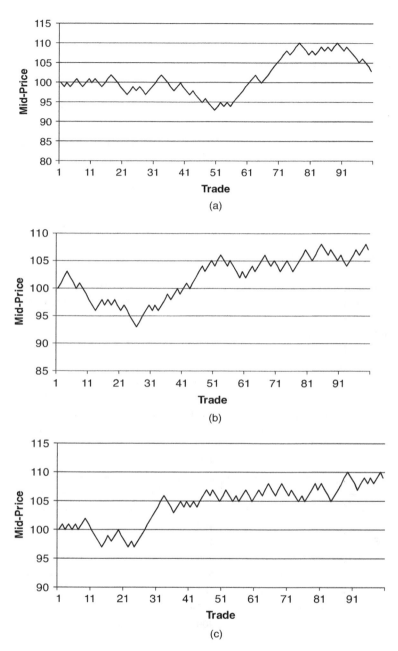

FIGURE 10.3 Some Underlying Price Paths in Our Market Maker Simulation

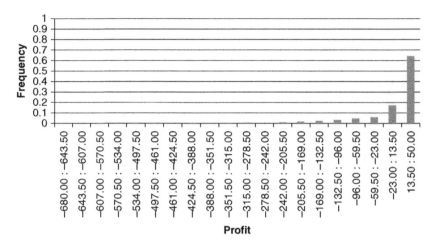

FIGURE 10.4   The Profit and Loss Distribution for the Market Maker

interesting is the *shape* of the distribution. Most of the time (69 percent) the market maker will show a profit, but the maximum profit is 50 while the largest loss is 680. This nasty skew is very typical of market maker profit distributions.

It is instructive to look at the relationship between the inventory size and the profit of the market maker. This is shown in Figure 10.5.

A market maker does far better when he has no inventory. This is because he accumulates inventory when the orders are all coming from one direction: either a preponderance of buys or sells. If orders alternate sign he will buy at 99, lower his bid, and offer then sell at thus 100 earning one

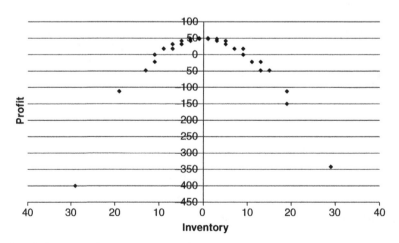

FIGURE 10.5   Profit as a Function of Inventory for the Market Maker

tick. But if two sell orders arrive in succession, he will also buy at 98. After lowering his bid and offer to 97 and 99, the midmarket price will be 98 so he will be sitting on a loss of one tick from his first trade (his buy at 99) and be long two units. This is the most important thing to remember.

Another way to look at this is through the lens of option theory. The market maker is paid a fee, the spread, but in turn is short two options: a put struck at the bid and a call struck at the offer. Figure 10.5 does indeed look a lot like the profit from a short strangle position (it may actually look more like a short straddle but this is just because the two "strikes," the bid and the ask, are so close together). The market maker wants the fee to be large, which means a large spread, and volatility to be low so that the value of his short options is low. This should seem sensible. A wide spread in a product that has a small range should provide good opportunities for market makers.

- Sequences of orders of the same sign hurt market makers.
  This leads to
- Trends in prices hurt market makers.
  and
- Accumulating inventory hurts market makers.

We can slightly change our simulations to explicitly demonstrate this. If we change the proportion of buy orders to 70 percent we obtain the profit distribution in Figure 10.6.

Clearly this is far worse than the case of Figure 10.4. In fact on average we lose 758 ticks here! We lose money in over 99 percent of cases.

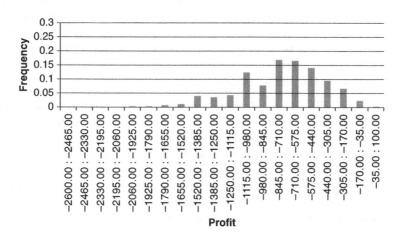

FIGURE 10.6 The Profit and Loss Distribution for the Market Maker When Orders Are Unbalanced

Obviously we cannot control the order in which trades are submitted. In the short term, we can avoid mark-to-market losses by "standing our ground" and hoping an offsetting order arrives, but in the long term market makers are fairly powerless to manipulate markets like this. "Defending a position" in this way is probably a waste of money.

At this point it may seem that being a market maker is a less than exciting proposition, in which any small trend can cause large losses. However, the bid-ask spread is a powerful ally and in most situations it is wide enough and the order flow uncorrelated enough for market makers to be profitable. This is exactly the case in many options markets.

A good market for a market maker is one in which

- Volume is high.
- The bid-ask spread is large.
- The daily range is low.
- Orders are uncorrelated.
- There are no persistent price trends.

I am reliably informed that the biggest single factor in whether or not a poker player is successful is his ability to find good games. Market making is the same. Some products are intrinsically much better to make markets in than others. As a successful trader once told me, "I do not want to be a famous trader in the biggest product. I want to be a good trader in a profitable product."

Information-Based Market-Making

Next we try to improve our market making by considering the information aspect of trades. We will try to construct a mathematical model of "optimal" market making. Like all of our models, this one will not be particularly realistic, but it will be a useful guide and can serve as a little framework around which to organize our thoughts.

Let's recap the market maker's problem:

- We start with an idea of the instrument's value, S, and also some uncertainty associated with this value, σ_S. That is, we have our best estimate, but we also do not claim that it is perfect.
- We quote bid and ask prices around this value, S_b and S_a.
- We do a trade at one of these prices. Let's assume we buy at S_b. This gives us information (someone thinks our price is too high), and of course inventory (we now have a long position).
- Now we need to update our estimate of value.

This problem is perfect for Bayesian analysis, in particular for a technique known as the Kalman filter.

BAYES'S THEOREM

Bayes's Theorem is a way to systematically update our knowledge of the world when we obtain new information. It combines the new information with our prior knowledge of an event's probability to give a new (posterior) probability. All good traders have a Bayesian model in their head. Traders constantly need to update their estimates of value as new information arrives.

The theorem is generally stated in terms of conditional probability and can rapidly become confusing. But the general principle is quite simple and can be illustrated with a basic example.

A patient goes to a doctor. The doctor performs a test that is 95 percent reliable. By this we mean that 95 percent of people who are sick will test positive and 95 percent of the healthy people will test negative. The doctor knows that only 5 percent of the people in the area are sick. If the patient tests positive, what are the chances that the patient is actually sick?

We may be tempted to guess 95 percent. But this is incorrect, as it does not take into account the fact that most people are not sick. We have neglected the base rate.

Imagine that we are dealing with the case of a town of 10,000 people. We know that only 5 percent, or 500 people, are sick, so 9,500 will be healthy. If we test everyone, the most probable result is that 95 percent of the 500 sick people test positive. But the test has a 5 percent error rate so it is also probable that 5 percent of the healthy people test positive. So if the doctor sends all those who tests positive to the national hospital, there will be an equal number of healthy and sick patients. So given a person who tested positive, there is only a 50 percent chance this person is sick!

As a slight aside, the basic problem here is that we are searching for something that is quite rare and using a test that really is not accurate enough to discriminate. A test needs to have an error rate that is lower than the incidence of the quality that we are searching for.

So given that intuition is a poor guide, how can we make this process systematic? This is where the conditional probabilities are necessary.

The short form of Bayes's Theorem says that for two events E and F

$$P(F|E) = \frac{P(E|F)\,P(F)}{P(E|F)\,P(F) + P(E|F')\,P(F')} \tag{10.1}$$

Where $P(F \mid E)$ means the probability of F happens, given that E has already occurred. In the example above we want to calculate the probability of a person being sick, F, given that they have tested positive, E.

So here $P(F) = 0.05$, $P(E \mid F) = 0.95$, $P(F') = 0.95$, and $P(E \mid F') = 0.05$ and equation 10.1 gives $P(F \mid E) = 0.5$ as we thought.

The Kalman filter is a method for optimally incorporating new information into an estimate of value. What exactly we mean by "optimal," and the proof that it is indeed optimal, are beyond this text. But we can look at a toy model and see that it passes a simple reasonability test.

How should we update our estimate of true value, and hence decide where to quote our new bid and offer prices?

$$S_{new} = S + k\,(S_b - S) \qquad (10.2)$$

where

$$k = \frac{\sigma_S^2}{\sigma_S^2 + \sigma_e^2} \qquad (10.3)$$

and

$$\sigma_{S,new} = \sqrt{1 - k}\,\sigma_S \qquad (10.4)$$

Equation 10.2 says that we update our estimate of value by adding to it a term proportional to the difference between our original value estimate and the traded price, in this case the bid price. The factor of proportionality is defined by equation 10.3. Equation 10.4 is our new estimate for our uncertainty. As we are learning from our new information, it makes sense that our estimate of value changes and also that we will become more confident in this value. This is a statement of the Kalman filter result.

σ_e is the uncertainty in the measurement. If the measurement was of a physical quantity, this could be obtained by considering how accurate our measuring device was, but here we know the bid price we traded exactly. Uncertainty means something different here. It encapsulates our degree of confidence that the new trade is meaningful. If we have no confidence that the trade is telling us anything, $\sigma_e \gg \sigma_S$ so $k = 0$ and we do not change our estimate of value at all. Conversely if we think the new trade is very significant, $\sigma_e \ll \sigma_S$ so $k = 1$ and we change our estimate of value to the traded price.

In order to make this at all useful, σ_e needs to be a function of all the variables the trader might be worried about. These could include trade size, current inventory level, and the counterparty's ability. Here we look at a very simple example where we judge the significance of a trade purely by its size. This simple model is surprisingly useful. This is possibly because it partially encompasses our inventory (we will always lower our price if we get hit on the bid and build up a long position), and the size of a trade has a positive correlation with the ability of the counterparty. We assume the following form for σ_e, as a function of trade size, T.

$$\sigma_e = \sigma_S \left(\frac{T_{\max}}{T} - 1 \right) \qquad (10.5)$$

where $T_{\max}$ is the trade size at which we think the size of the new trade will cause us to move our value to the last traded price. This form has the correct limits: at $T = T_{\max}$, $\sigma_e = 0$, and at $T = 0$, $\sigma_e = \infty$, so $k = 0$ and we do not move our price at all.

This type of thought process is useful for a trader when he has a theoretical value for a product. In our inventory-based model we did not assume this, but when dealing with options a trader will often feel that he has a decent idea of the true value, possibly based on his forecast of volatility.

The Kalman filter can be used as the basis of a completely automated market making system, but this is not why it is important. The Kalman filter is not a model of what a trader should do, it is a model that matches what good traders actually do.

- Adjust as new information arrives.
- Some trades should not cause you to adjust value much; others should cause you to move your value to the traded level.
- Information is strongly correlated to size, but other factors are also relevant.

Varying the Bid-Ask Spread in Practice

We have actually made things more difficult for ourselves than we had to. In each of these analyses we have kept the bid-ask spread at a constant width and adjusted the midmarket price, either on the basis on accumulated inventory or information. In practice we would also vary the bid-ask spread to reflect market conditions. Actually we can only vary *our* bid-ask spread, not the actual spread in the market. In an order-driven market, there is nothing to stop other traders posting bids and offers inside a market maker's prices.

To get an idea for how we would go about this, we need to understand the components of the spread. There are four main reasons why a spread exists.

- **Order-processing costs.** In order to make prices, a market maker needs to pay exchange fees, exchange membership costs, clearing fees, and interest charges. There is also an opportunity cost that he must pay. Being a market maker means he cannot be doing something else with his time.

- **Asymmetric information costs.** If the market maker is systematically trading against people who know more than he does, he will tend to make bad trades. Note that many traders *think* they have superior information or superior information processing skills. This is irrelevant. What matters is if they actually do. This tends to be more of an issue in thinly traded stocks and agricultural commodities, and less of an issue in broad stock indices and interest-rate products.
- **Inventory holding costs.** Having inventory exposes the market maker to risk, and he will want to be compensated for this. This risk is positively correlated to the volatility of the instrument being traded and the time that the trader expects to have to hold on to his inventory.
- **Competition.** The above reasons would exist even if the market maker were not looking to make a profit. He needs to charge a spread merely to break even. However, he also wants to make the spread as wide as he can in order to make as much money as possible. He is limited here by his competition: if he quotes too wide a spread another market maker will get the trade, and also by the willingness of his customers to trade: if his spread is too wide he will get fewer trades (and tend to trade only with informed customers). Remember that what is important is the spread times the number of trades. Increasing the first factor will decrease the second. In practice a market maker executes a difficult balancing act trying to maximize this product (in the presence of competition).

So in general, the quoted bid-ask spread will be an increasing function of direct trading costs, interest rates, asymmetric information, volatility, holding time, and the willingness of customers to pay for immediacy. The bid-ask will be a decreasing function of competition.

There is another piece of sociology that tends to keep the quoted bid-ask spread more constant than it should be if it were only a function of these factors. Brokers tend to become frustrated with traders who widen out their quotes "too much" (where this is defined by the brokers). This means these traders will not get given trades. And not just for the volatile period when the market maker felt compelled to widen his prices. Brokers have long memories.

The Ultimate Method: Mimicry

If a trader has no clue where to quote a market, a good trick is to identify a competent trader and post the same prices as him. This will work both in open outcry settings (holding up the same number of fingers) and in electronically quoted products (trading software often has a "join" setting which does just this). In fact, when floor trading was the industry standard many otherwise inept traders made a decent living using this method purely because brokers liked them enough to give them trades. This will still work in OTC markets.

The identification of the "competent" trader is not actually crucial either. This trick works purely because it keeps the trader on the general market and hence collecting the bid-ask spread. And as we saw in the Chapter on volatility trading, even hedging these trades at the current implied volatility gives as good a result as anything else.

This method is good for generating revenue, however it is poor for inventory management and traders using it will find themselves with problems as they approach expiration.

Now that we somewhat understand the idea and risk associated with market making, we can look at some of the tricks and techniques traders use to increase profits.

TRADING BASED ON ORDER-BOOK INFORMATION

The "Ratio" Trade

Consider the following state of the order book for a hypothetical future.

Bid Size	Bid Price	Ask Price	Ask Size
1,000	100	101	20,000

This means that to move the offer, 20,000 futures need to be bought at the market, whereas to move the bid, only 1,000 need to be sold. So if we assume for the moment that market orders arrive randomly, it is 20 times more likely for the bid to trade through before the offer. Based only on this, we should either hit the bid or (preferably) sell at the offer.

Selling the offer relies on establishing good order priority. We want to be able to be near the front of the order queue. If the order priority is established on the basis of "time stamp" priority or "first-in, first-out" (FIFO), then to take advantage of such a set-up, we would need to seed the order book by stacking it with bids and offers at all levels, then selectively canceling these until favorable unbalanced situations occur.

However, if orders are filled on a pro-rata basis (which, for example, is the case in Eurodollar futures), then we could take advantage of this order book by placing a large order on the offer. Then if anything traded at this price we would be filled proportionally. For example, if we offered 5,000 futures at 101 we would then make up 20 percent of the offered amount (5,000/(20,000 + 5,000)). So if 100 futures were bought at the offer price we would be allocated 20. This is the straightforward and obvious course of action. It is sometimes called the *ratio trade*.

In some markets the bid-ask spread will be wider than a tick and we can adopt a slightly different strategy. Let's assume the market order book was

Bid Size	Bid Price	Ask Price	Ask Size
1,000	100	105	20,000

Again, we expect the large order to cause the market to fall and we would like to sell. We can step in front of the offer by entering an offer for 100 at 104 so the inside of the order book will now look like

Bid Size	Bid Price	Ask Price	Ask Size
1,000	100	104	100

Note that in making the order book look unbalanced like this, with much larger size on the bid than the offer, we have made it more likely that we will be filled. Anyone who is only looking at the inside of the order book will think that this is a chance for them to benefit from the ratio trade. In not seeing the huge 105 offer, they are missing a vital piece of information. It costs money to get this information, as generally it is more expensive to access the entire order book. However, if you want to play these order book games, it is an essential cost of doing business.

This is sometimes known as "ticking" because we have improved the market by the minimum amount: a tick. This generally annoys other traders (actually it really only annoys those whom we have ticked). On the other hand, if they had really wanted to sell at 104 they could have been there in the first place.

If we get filled, we immediately enter a bid at 101 and hopefully make three ticks. Note that if we are wrong we hope to have a chance to buy some of the futures at 105 before the entire size there trades. This is known as leaning on an order.

This action is sometimes referred to as "front running." It is not. Front running is the situation where a trader has been asked to execute an order for a customer account that is big enough to move the market. To take advantage of this, he does a trade for his own account, and then executes the large order. After this has moved the market, he closes out his smaller trade for a profit. The problem with this situation is that he is acting on privileged information. This is unethical and generally illegal. In contrast, the ratio trade uses only public information. It is true that traders with faster computers or faster connections to the exchange are more easily able to benefit, but this does not make the situation wrong. This is simply a case where people are being rewarded for investment in infrastructure. People who do not like this situation are more than welcome to buy faster computers.

Flipping

Now we can bluff. Say we know that other traders are looking for these set ups. Assume the order book is in the state below and the market is one with a time-stamp priority system.

Bid Size	Bid Price	Ask Price	Ask Size
1,000	100	101	1,000

We place a large order at the offer to make it look like an unbalanced order book. For example, we could offer 9,000 at 101 to create the order book below.

Bid Size	Bid Price	Ask Price	Ask Size
1,000	100	101	10,000

Then we bid 100 for 50, so the book is in the state below.

Bid Size	Bid Price	Ask Price	Ask Size
1,050	100	101	10,000

At this point we hope that traders playing the ratio trade will sell the bid or at least that the bid trades out through random market action (remember we are last in the offer queue, so 1,000 futures need to trade before we get filled on the offer). If things go according to plan, we get filled on our bid because we have led other market participants to believe there is selling pressure. At this point we pull our offer. Hopefully other traders realize no genuine selling pressure ever existed and try to buy back the futures we sold. We can sell our 50 lots into this demand for a small profit.

Creating fake buying or selling pressure is sometimes known as "flipping" and was employed to great success in the German interest rate futures complex by Paul Rotter. He was immensely profitable. But many traders were outraged and thought this was disgraceful and dishonest behavior. It was not. It was simply good trading. There was nothing dishonest about it at all and failure to use all legally obtained information is not honorable. It is just stupid.

If we know someone is employing a certain strategy we can always profit. Let's assume that someone is flipping. What do we do? We call their bluff. Remember that in our example above we showed an offer of 9,000 futures but we did not really want to sell any. However, in modern electronic exchanges these orders are real. Someone can always trade them. We are at risk.

Let's expand the order book to see more than just the best bids and offers.

Bid Size	Bid Price	Ask Price	Ask Size
1,050	100	101	10,000
200	99	102	200
200	98	103	200
200	97	104	200
200	96	105	200
200	95	106	200

To call the bluff, buy 11,800 futures up to a price of 105. This leaves the order book looking like this.

Bid Size	Bid Price	Ask Price	Ask Size
1,000	105	106	200

Now the flipper (whom we assume had 9,000 futures at 101) is sitting on a marked-to-market loss of 9,000 times 4.5 ticks. Further, it looks like there is still further buying pressure. Hopefully this creates so much pain for him that he liquidates the position. We will be waiting for this and can sell our position into his liquidation.

Obviously real situations are never this clear. Real order books are in a constant state of flux. However, this cycle of trade, bluff, and counterbluff is used in the markets and is the basis for a number of successful high-frequency trading operations.

Stop Hunting

Market makers and other high-frequency day traders will often try to set off large stop orders. This is not a matter of inside information or collusion. Like the trading strategies described above, it is a legitimate way of gaming the structure of the market. Earlier we discussed the importance of not placing stops in places where other market participants may expect them. This is why.

Imagine that we are short the stock ABC. In the past week the stock has made several attempts to rally above $30 and each time it failed. This point has been established as a point of resistance. Market makers might think that there are stops above this point. Their reasoning would be that shorts think an upper limit has been placed at this point, but if the market rallies through it then their short position would be wrong. The market will have changed regimes. If the market gets close to this point, the market makers will buy stock to get a price print above 30 (remember that stops will be set off by a single price print). If large stop orders are triggered the price will sharply gap higher and the market makers can cover their long positions for a decent profit. If there are no stops they will look to sell as soon as possible. They are aiming to take a few cents of risk and are hoping to make ten or fifteen cents of profit. Microsqueezes like this can be a significant source of profit for market makers.

Trading Correlated Assets: The Implied Volatility Surface

Until now we have considered trading a single asset. Market making consisted entirely of trying to buy the bid then sell the offer (or vice versa) in this one product. When trading options this will not be the case. Here we will have a large number of put call pairs of various strikes and maturities. Market makers do not think of these as separate entities. While it would be ideal to buy one option and then be able to sell the same one, we cannot restrict ourselves to doing only this. Instead, market makers think of the entire implied volatility surface as a single element. Option market making really consists of working in and out of various spreads.

As we see in Chapter 3, there are many arbitrage relationships that hold amongst options. These would obviously be a market maker's first choice when he is looking to trade options against each other. For example, if he bought a call on the bid, he would be happy to sell a put of the same expiry and strike on the offer and create a reversal.

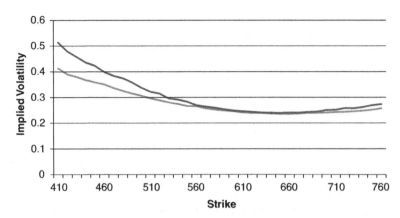

FIGURE 10.7 The Bid and Ask Implied Volatility Curves for the Google February Option Expiration at 2 P.M. CST on December 21, 2009 (Calls)

But this type of trade is not generally available. More generally, market makers need to enter volatility spreads. Instead of thinking about option prices, traders directly think in terms of the implied volatility surface. This surface also has a bid and an offer associated with it, corresponding to the bids and offers of the corresponding options. An example of this is shown in Figure 10.7.

Note that the bid-ask spread in volatility terms tends to be larger for far away from the money options. This is because the spread tends to stay relatively constant in price terms over all strikes, and strikes that are far from the at-the-money have smaller vega. This implies a larger spread in volatility terms.

Option market makers try to buy the bid of the implied volatility curve and sell the offer of the curve. They tacitly assume that the shape of the curve will stay relatively constant. Clearly this is not true. We see in Chapter 8, that the curve changes both level and shape. But we also saw that the majority of change was due to the level of the curve, so if a trader can sell options that are close together (so that the trade is vega neutral), most risk will have been neutralized. In this regard, a 50 delta, 45 delta spread is far more stable (and hence a sensible piece of hedging) than a 50 delta, 5 delta spread. Spreads across months are even more precarious.

When we were discussing making markets on a single instrument, we needed to decide how much to adjust our value after we had performed a trade. When we are trading options (or any other set of correlated securities) we need to decide how much to change the implied volatility of the traded point, then how much to change all of the other points. A given trade will not only change the implied volatility of the traded option but also all those around it, in degrees that depend on the *closeness* to the traded point.

The word "closeness" has been left purposely vague. Generally this means moneyness or delta, and the curve will move as we discuss in Chapter 8, but in some situations this simple approximation does not hold. Sometimes certain spreads have traded in such large size relative to the other strikes that their value is essentially constant. Implied volatility curves normally do have fairly smooth shapes, but beyond the limits implied by the no-arbitrage conditions they can take on a lot of strange, lumpy shapes. These will normally be due to abnormally high open interest in the strikes involved.

If a trade involves a single option it will generally be fairly obvious how the trader should adjust. Assume we sell some options that according to the inventory-based scheme is a big enough trade to completely adjust of theoretical to match the traded price. If this is the at-the-money option, we can just move the entire implied volatility curve up to this point.

If the option is not at-the-money we have to attribute some of the movement to a shift of the level of volatility but also some to a shift of the slope and some to a shift in the curvature. Typically most of the shift is attributed to the level, less to the slope, and a small amount to the curvature, but for a single trade this is very imprecise.

When trading a strategy that consists of multiple options, the problem is even more complex. If we trade a call spread consisting of the at-the-money call and a 5 delta call should we do all volatility adjustment to the at-the-money strike on the basis that it will have most of the vega? Or should we move both options' implied volatilities? Again, for a single trade we can make a lot of semiplausible arguments, none of which are completely convincing.

However, once we have started to accumulate an inventory, things become unambiguous. I can take one look at a market maker's position and tell him what adjustments he needs to make to his theoretical values. If he is long out-of-the-money puts and short out-of-the-money calls, then his implied curve is too steep. If he is short teeny calls and puts, then he is running the volatilities of the wings too low. A market maker's inventory will grow in direct proportion to how wrong his theoretical values are.

It might be tempting to think that a trader's forecast of the underlying's realized volatility could be useful when market-making options. It really is not. Only over the medium-to-long term is there a real relationship between realized and implied volatilities. A market-maker needs to be aware of realized volatility, but only for position management purposes. The bid-ask spread will generally be much too tight for forecasting to directly factor into the market making process.

The other important issue to consider when market-making options is that as we are trading a surface rather than a single option, we can be less reactive to each individual trade. If we buy an option we can look to sell any other option, not just the one we bought. Clearly selling the same option is best and then we will look to sell those close to it, becoming progressively less happy with the sale of options further away.

Option market-making can be summarized as

- Buy options below their theoretical value and sell options above their theoretical value.
- When you cannot do both, change your theoretical values so that you can.
- A good rule of thumb is that if you do more than three consecutive trades of the same sign (e.g., three trades that involve buying vega or three trades that involve taking on skew risk), you should adjust your theoretical values.

Practicing: The Trading Game

One of the reasons that trading is difficult is that the learning curve is so steep. There are no minor leagues to practice in. So it is a constant source of surprise to me that people starting out do not practice more.

In this section we look at a game that has been used for decades by market-making firms to help train people. In addition to improving the trading techniques discussed in this chapter it helps develop record keeping skills. Further, as the shouting gets louder, the game takes on a realistically stressful edge. It is important to play this game for money: Even contracts worth only a cent a tick vastly enhance the realism.

Let's assume we have five people playing.

- Take 30 pieces of index cards and number them from 1 to 30.
- Give a card to each person.
- The idea is to trade the total held by the participants, so if a trader thinks the total will be over 75 he might start out by shouting "75 bid!"
- When a trade occurs the two traders concerned each write down what they did. For example, the buyer would write, "Paid 75 for 2 from Joe."

The unconditional statistics of this game are simple. The mean value of any five cards chosen randomly will be $5 \times 15.5 = 77.5$, with a standard deviation of 17.97. However, each trader has a unique piece of information, his card. For example, if a trader is holding a 1, he knows the sum is expected to be lower than 77.5; specifically its new expected value is 65.

This is calculated as $1 + $ (new mean) $\times 4$, where the new mean is the average value of the 29 cards numbered from 2 to 30, which is 16.

After a few minutes, trading tends to converge to a market consensus. Now we give the entire group new information by turning over one or more of the 25 unused cards.

As a further wrinkle, we can introduce option trading. Players can ask for markets in calls, puts, and various combinations.

We repeat this process for a set time, then calculate the group's total to arrive at a settlement price. At this point all transactions can be settled in cash. For example, if the settlement price in the example we considered above were 82, Joe would need to pay 14 cents to the buyer. I would also strongly recommend that a fairly punitive fine be levied against any traders whose contracts did not clear correctly. A few trades that cannot be matched can turn a valuable training exercise into a joke. A $5 fine seems to work wonders in encouraging trade checking.

SUMMARY

- Most markets are order driven. Here market makers are distinguished primarily by their trading aims, rather than by any institutionalized advantage.
- A market maker must always be able to trade.
- His profit will be determined by the number of trades he makes and the size of the bid-ask spread.
- His biggest risk is the accumulation of inventory.

CHAPTER 11

Volatility Trading

Volatility trading, or the misnomer *volatility arbitrage*, is a trading strategy that aims to capture the difference between an option's implied volatility and the realized volatility of the underlying. Sometimes this is a stand-alone strategy, but the concepts behind it are important for all option traders, as every position they take will inescapably expose them to volatility risk. In this chapter we show how to hedge options to isolate the volatility component. We also look at how we can expect our profit and loss to evolve as a function of time.

We see in Chapter 4 that the fair price for an option is related to the standard deviation of the underlying's returns. But the option market is forward-looking: the volatility that is used in option pricing models is in some sense the option markets forecast of volatility over the lifetime of the option. We can also make a forecast using the historical statistics of the underlying.

If our estimate of volatility differs significantly from that implied by the option market then we could trade the option accordingly. If we forecast volatility to be higher than that implied by the option, we would buy the option and hedge in the underlying market. Our expected profit would depend on the difference between implied volatility and realized volatility. Equation 5.23 implies that instantaneously this profit would be proportional to

$$\frac{1}{2}S^2\Gamma\left(\sigma^2 - \sigma_{\text{implied}}^2\right) \tag{11.1}$$

But from the relationship between gamma and vega (equation 5.32) we can write this as

$$\frac{Vega}{\sigma T} \left(\sigma^2 - \sigma_{implied}^2 \right) \qquad (11.2)$$

This is the expected profit from trading the option, then hedging it. The other way we can make money is if the implied volatility changes. Vega is defined as the change in value of an option if implied volatility changes by one point (e.g., from 19 percent to 18 percent). This means that if we buy an option at $\sigma_{implied}$ and volatility immediately increases to σ, we would make a profit of

$$Vega \left(\sigma - \sigma_{implied} \right) \qquad (11.3)$$

However, the gamma is highly dependent on the moneyness of the option, which obviously changes as the underlying moves around. So the profit from a hedged option position is highly volatile and path dependent.

HEDGING

We see in Chapter 4 that the idea of hedging is central to the BSM framework. The concept of hedging was used in the derivation of the Black-Scholes-Merton (BSM) equation and it is necessary to hedge to remove exposure to the return of the underlying. To isolate our volatility exposure we need to hedge. As we state in Chapter 9, a hedge is designed to eliminate the risks we do not want and to give us exposure to the ones we do. Hedging should not be thought of as a way to make money by trading the direction of the underlying.

Even if a trader can profitably trade both volatility and the direction of the underlying, he should not forget the fact that these are two separate strategies. Further, even the best directional traders will not always have a view on the underlying, while an option trader always needs a hedging plan. In this chapter we devise such a plan. As always, when devising a plan we should keep our overall aim in mind.

The aim of hedging an option is to reduce directional risk. Good hedging is defined as reducing the most risk for the least cost.

If we could trade the underlying in any size we wanted and without incurring any costs, we should do so and continuously adjust our stock position to remain delta neutral. Equation 11.1 shows that this would make our profit a function of the difference between the implied volatility and the

TABLE 11.1	The Average Profit Realized When Rebalancing Hedges at Different Intervals (In a Perfect BSM World, We Would Make $10,000)	

Hedge Frequency	Average Realized Profit
Weekly hedge	$9,791
Daily hedge	$9,220
Twice faily	$8,830
Five times daily	$7,952

realized volatility. However, in the real world we can trade only in discrete size, and each trade costs us money in commissions and bid-ask spreads. This makes continuously adjusting delta impractical.

It is hard to overstate the importance of hedging cheaply and efficiently. Replication risks due to imperfect hedging can easily exceed the anticipated profits from the perceived implied volatility mispricing. Transaction costs from hedging can be large. They are also easy to ignore, as they accumulate progressively over the lifetime of the trade and are not easily perceived by traders, who tend to become focused on short-term results.

To see the extent of the issue, consider the following example. We are short $1,000 of vega of at-the-money options on a stock initially priced at $100. The options have one year until expiry. Volatility is 40 percent and we sold it at 50 percent. So according to equation 11.3, before any costs we expect to make a profit of $10,000 if we hold the position until expiry. However, the bid-ask spread in the underlying is $0.1, so each time we hedge we incur costs by crossing this. Table 11.1 shows the total expected profit for this position if we hedge to a delta-neutral position at various frequencies (these numbers were the results of a Monte Carlo simulation of this situation, where we looked at the average result of ten thousand realizations of this situation)

HEDGING IN PRACTICE

Hedging at Regular Time Intervals

A very common hedging strategy is to pick a time interval and at the end of each period do a trade in the underlying to make the net delta position zero. This has the advantage of being simple to understand and implement. It has the disadvantage of being totally arbitrary in the choice of time interval. Obviously, hedging more often decreases risk. Equally obviously, hedging less often decreases costs. This is merely replacing intuition with a fixed, arbitrary rule. It is not clear that we have gained anything by doing this.

Hedging to a Delta Band

This is a strategy commonly used by market makers or traders who trade only a few products. Here we choose a fixed delta that we are able to tolerate. When our delta exceeds this, we hedge. This is also arbitrary.

Hedging Based on Underlying Price Changes

When using this strategy, the trader rebalances the delta after the underlying has moved by a certain amount. This is based on the sensible idea that the risk in the portfolio is due to underlying moves, so these should form the basis for rebalancing decisions. However, we are still left searching for a method that tells us how to choose the appropriate price change. Traders also need to decide whether to calibrate the method based on percentage changes, dollar changes, technical levels of "importance," or implied or historical standard deviations.

Utility-Based Methods

Hedging is a tradeoff between reducing risk and incurring costs. The economic concept of utility gives us a way to quantify our risk aversion.

Stewart Hodges and Anthony Neuberger recognized that as BSM really prices the replication strategy rather than the option directly, they could do the same thing but incorporate transaction costs. The most important idea in their work is that there comes a point where the option trader is indifferent to holding the risk associated with the mishedged option and the cost associated with hedging it. If we incur more risk than this we rehedge until we are again indifferent. If we can specify our level of risk aversion this strategy is optimal.

The particular form of the utility function they worked with was exponential, although it was later shown that this choice was largely immaterial. This has the form

$$U(W) = -\exp(-\gamma W) \tag{11.4}$$

where U is utility, W is our wealth, and γ is the risk-aversion parameter. Examples of this utility function are shown in Figure 11.1.

The important things to understand about utility theory are

- The absolute value of the utility is not important.
- Utility rises (we prefer more to less).
- It is concave (we do not like risk).
- Higher-risk aversion (higher gamma in the case of the exponential utility function) gives a more concave utility.

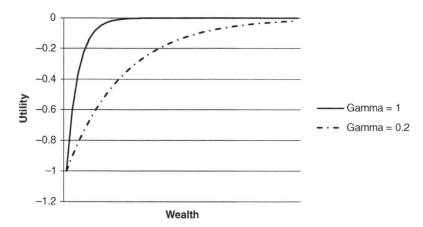

FIGURE 11.1 The Exponential Utility Function

The mathematics required to formulate and solve the hedging problem are complex and well beyond the scope of this book. Also the resulting valuation equation has no analytic solution and needs to be solved numerically. Even this is not easy. The required computations are prohibitively time consuming. There is no practical way to use this methodology as a real-time hedging guide.

But because it is the optimal solution, its properties are important to understand. Figures 11.2 a and b show the hedging bandwidth for a long call position and a short call position. When our position's delta moves outside the band, we hedge to bring our delta back to the edge of the band. The parameters chosen are not particularly realistic. They have been chosen to exaggerate the properties of the solution. We chose the case of a one-year option with volatility of 0.3, transaction costs of 2 percent, zero interest and carry rates, and a risk aversion of one.

Several points are immediately obvious.

- The short and long positions should be hedged differently. The band for the short position is narrower. So we hedge our short positions more defensively. We have time decay on our side so we take less chance with delta, whereas when we are hedging long positions we need to "let our deltas run." This is in complete accordance with trader folklore. Traders are generally more defensive with short gamma positions.
- The optimal delta band does not span the BSM delta. A perfectly hedged portfolio in the BSM world may need to be adjusted when transaction costs are present.

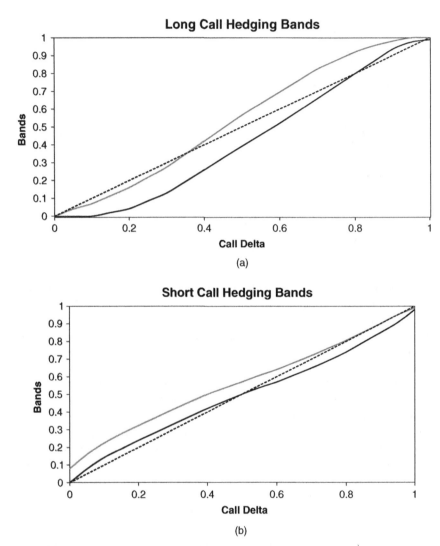

FIGURE 11.2 The Optimal Hedging Bands as Functions of the BSM Delta Which Is Shown as a Dashed Line

Not evident from the figure, but the essential feature of the model, is that the width of the hedging band is dependent on the risk aversion. A large risk aversion parameter means that the trader wants to accept little risk. So he wants tight hedging bands and will hedge often. Conversely a trader with a small risk aversion parameter will be prepared to hedge less frequently, accepting risk to reduce hedging costs. Neither of these choices is more correct than the other. As with all hedging methods we need to decide how risk averse we are. But given this choice, the HN formalism gives us the optimal balance between risk and reward.

Another important aspect of the model is that it is dependent on the magnitude of the gamma. More gamma means that we need to be prepared to hold more deltas. Another way of stating this is that what it means to be "flat" delta is dependent on how much gamma we have.

Choosing the Risk-Aversion Parameter

There are two ways of doing this. One way is to directly estimate the parameter from the trader's stated risk preferences. The other is to back out the parameter from the amount of delta risk he is comfortable with. This is a similar situation to the estimation of volatility, where we can either use time series methods or the option's implied value.

The Direct Method Suppose the distribution of future wealth has a mean, μ, and a standard deviation, σ. For example, $\mu = \$20,000$ and $\sigma = \$5,000$.

So

$$E[U] = E[-\exp(-\gamma W)] \tag{11.5}$$

$$\approx -\exp\left(-\gamma\left(\mu - \frac{1}{2}\gamma\sigma^2\right)\right) \tag{11.6}$$

So the certainty equivalent, W_0, is given by

$$W_0 = \mu - \frac{1}{2}\gamma\sigma^2 \tag{11.7}$$

This is the amount of utility that we would have to receive to be indifferent between that payoff and a uncertain future distribution.

This can be inverted to give an expression for the risk aversion, γ.

$$\gamma = \frac{2(\mu - W_0)}{\sigma^2} \tag{11.8}$$

Now suppose that the trader is indifferent between this distribution of wealth and a certain outcome of \$15,000, that is, $W_0 = \$8,000$.

Here

$$\gamma = \frac{2(20,000 - 15,000)}{5,000 \cdot 5,000} = 0.0004$$

The Implied Method   Here we solve the problem for a range of risk-aversion parameters and then compare the hedging bands that this gives us to what the trader would have done in a given situation. For example, we could ask "If you were long 1,000 one-year at-the-money calls on MSFT, how many deltas would you not bother to hedge?" We then compare his answer to the model-generated values and see what risk-aversion parameter it corresponds to.

If we are just going to replicate the trader's current method, have we even gained anything? Actually we have. While a trader might be able to answer a simple question like this, he will have trouble making his answers consistent across different situations. How many deltas should he hold if he has a six-month option? What if volatility changes? In this regard a hedging method is like a pricing model: it gives a consistent framework to think within (an astute reader will by now have realized that this is how we think of all financial models: they are frameworks not representations of reality).

The Asymptotic Solution of Whalley and Wilmott

We have already said that the optimal solution of Hodges and Neuberger (HN) is practically unusable. So now we try to find approximations that can be used that still retain most features of the ideal solution. To do this we assume that the transaction costs are small relative to the value of the option. Now it is possible to derive some approximate solutions to the full problem. This was first done by Elizabeth Whalley and Paul Wilmott (WW). They show that the boundaries of the no transaction regions are given by

$$\Delta = \frac{\partial V}{\partial S} \pm \left(\frac{3}{2} \frac{\exp\left(-r\left(T-t\right)\right) \lambda S \Gamma^2}{\gamma} \right)^{\frac{1}{3}} \qquad (11.9)$$

Where λ is the proportional transaction cost, that is, transaction costs are of the form

$$tc = \lambda \left| N \right| S \qquad (11.10)$$

Where N is the total number of shares traded.

This solution has a number of pleasingly sensible aspects. An example of the resulting hedging bands is shown in Figure 11.3. This was for the case of a one-year option with volatility of 0.3, transaction costs of 2 percent, zero interest and carry rates, and a risk aversion of one.

- As transaction costs decrease, the hedging bandwidth decreases. Indeed as costs go to zero, the BSM delta is recovered.

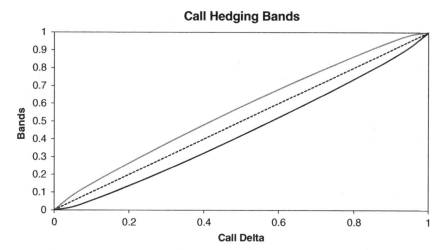

FIGURE 11.3 The Approximate Hedging Bands from the WW Asymptotic Method as Functions of the BSM Delta

- As risk aversion increases, the hedging bandwidth decreases as in the full HN theory.
- The method can also deal with transaction costs with different structures.

It also has some unfortunate aspects.

- The asymmetry of long and short gamma positions that came out of the full HN solution is lost. Only the magnitude of gamma is relevant to the asymptotic solution.
- The hedging band is now centered on the BSM delta, losing another feature of the full HN solution.

It can be difficult to estimate the parameters for this model. In particular, it can be difficult in practice to distinguish between volatility and transaction costs. To a trader these can look the same. They both make the underlying more "whippy" and hedging more difficult. However the impact in these models (HN and WW) is very different. For an at-the-money option, increasing the volatility will lower the gamma, which leads to a tighter hedging band. But increasing the bid-ask spread (the proportional transaction cost) leads to a wider hedging band. This is an important difference!

The discrepancy is caused by the fact that these models explicitly incorporate risk aversion. Volatility is a traded quantity and it provides both risk and reward. When volatility is high these models tell us to fear the worst and hedge often. But the bid-ask spread is purely a cost. It has no rewarding aspects. If the bid-ask spread is wide, the models tell us to avoid hedging to avoid multiple "whipsaw losses." The trader needs to consider this and think carefully about what aspect of the market is really changing. Volatility is not the same as transaction costs at all. This can be seen because even a perfect, frictionless market has volatility as a result of its movement. Volatility and trading costs might look the same at first glance but they are fundamentally different.

The Double-Asymptotic Method of Zakamouline

The WW approximation is very useful. It is simple enough for a trader to be able to remember its results for particular instances of interest. For example, he might know that if he is long 1,000 MSFT gamma he wants to hedge when he gets to a delta of more than 2,000, and if he is long 200 he will hedge at a delta of 700. However this model loses some of the appealing aspects of the full HN model. More crucially, numerical simulations show that the approximation can significantly underperform the full strategy, that is, for a given level of transaction costs a portfolio hedged with the WW model will experience more variance than one hedged according to the HN model.

Valeri Zakamouline examined the stylized facts of the nature of the utility based hedging strategies (essentially the bullet points above) and proposed a functional form for a hedging strategy that preserved the most important features. The hedging bands take the form

$$\Delta = \frac{\partial V(\sigma_m)}{\partial S} \pm (H_1 + H_0) \tag{11.11}$$

Immediately we can see that instead of being centered on the BSM delta, it is based on the BSM delta evaluated at the modified volatility, σ_m.

$$\sigma_m^2 = \sigma^2(1 - K) \tag{11.12}$$

H_1 will be a gamma-dependent term, similar in effect to that in the WW model. The exact numerical solution of the HN model shows that even for very far out-of-the-money options (with practically no gamma), the width of the hedging band does not go to zero. This feature is not captured by the WW model. This means that we need to introduce the H_0 term.

Zakamouline postulated the functional form of the solution and then used numerical analysis to fit the parameters. The results were

$$H_0 = \frac{\lambda}{\gamma S \sigma^2 T} \tag{11.13}$$

$$H_1 = 1.12 \lambda^{0.31} T^{0.05} \left(\frac{\exp(-rT)}{\sigma} \right)^{0.25} \left(\frac{|\Gamma|}{\gamma} \right)^{0.5} \tag{11.14}$$

$$K_\sigma = -4.76 \frac{\lambda^{0.78}}{T^{0.02}} \left(\frac{\exp(-rT)}{\sigma} \right)^{0.25} \left(\gamma S^2 |\Gamma| \right)^{0.15} \tag{11.15}$$

An example of the resulting hedging bands is shown in Figures 11.4a and b. These were for the case of a one-year option with volatility of 0.3, transaction costs of 2 percent, zero interest and carry rates, and a risk aversion of one.

As can be seen from Figures 11.4, Zakamouline's method gives results that look much closer to the HN result than those of WW. In particular, the middle of the no-transaction region does not coincide with the BSM delta. This comes about from using a modified hedging volatility.

Numerical simulations show that Zakamouline's approximation clearly dominates that of Whalley and Wilmott. By this we mean that for a given level of risk, the strategy costs the least to implement.

A further consideration when choosing a hedging strategy is that not all are equally easy to implement. The Hodges-Neuberger scheme is at one extreme, in that it is the optimal solution but practically impossible to use. The Zakamouline scheme is a better approximation to this ideal than is the Wilmott-Whalley method, but it is also more difficult to use in practice as some trading software does not easily facilitate its implementation (in particular the change in delta with respect to volatility is not calculated by many off-the-shelf trading systems).

Static Hedging

Another complication is that an option position will often have a gamma profile that changes sign as a function of the underlying. This can result in situations where we are better off not hedging in the underlying. For example, consider a long butterfly.

Imagine that we managed to somehow enter this position for zero cost. We are now in the fantastic situation of having a position that can only make money because a butterfly can never become negative in value. But dynamically hedging can ruin this situation. If the underlying fluctuates between the wing strikes, we will always be short gamma. So if we hedge the deltas that we accumulate, buying high and selling low, we can easily lose money.

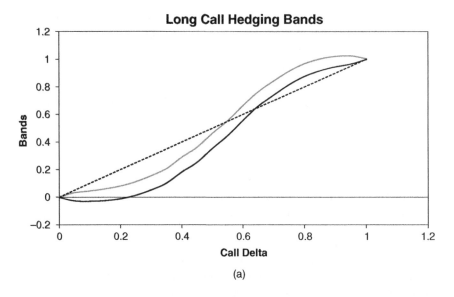

(a)

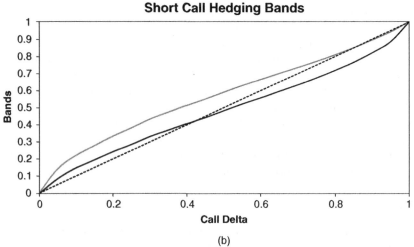

(b)

FIGURE 11.4 The Approximate Hedging Bands from the Zakamouline Asymptotic Method as Functions of the BSM Delta

This example tells us two very important things. First, the dynamic hedging strategy needs to take the global gamma profile into account. Second, if we can cheaply work into a static hedge with other options, this is vastly preferable to dynamic hedging with the underlying. In practice we aim to statically hedge as much as possible and dynamically hedge our residual risk.

There is a more important point that needs to be made here. As we emphasize throughout this book, it is vital to figure out exactly what one is trying to achieve at any point in the trading process. Specifically, what is the point of hedging? Superficially it is to remove exposure to the direction of the underlying market. More generally it is to remove exposure to risks we do not wish to accept while keeping exposure to those we do. If we are market-making options, our edge comes from collecting the bid-ask spread. To keep as much of this as possible, we should hedge as much of our volatility exposure as we can by trading other options (preferably by collecting the spread on these as well). However, if we are attempting positional volatility arbitrage and explicitly set out to take a position on the spread between realized and implied volatilities, then we will not want to remove volatility risk. Here that "risk" is actually our source of edge.

THE P/L DISTRIBUTION OF HEDGED OPTION POSITIONS

Now that we know how to hedge, we need to know what our profit-and-loss (P/L) distribution can be expected to look like. This is important for two reasons.

- We need to have an idea of the expected volatility of our profit, so we know how much leverage we can employ safely.
- It is important to understand what "normal" looks like. Many traders start to second-guess themselves and change their strategy because they think they are trading a losing strategy, when in actual fact they are just in a perfectly expected drawdown and their overall strategy is still sound.

Our expected profit is given by

$$P/L = Vega \left(\sigma_{\text{implied}} - \sigma_{\text{realized}}\right) \tag{11.16}$$

This is true only on average. There are wide fluctuations around this amount. In this section we look at the causes and magnitude of these, so we know exactly what we can expect as the results of our trades.

The central insight in the BSM argument is that an option can be replicated by trading the underlying. Figure 11.5 shows the results of 100 simulations, where we actually try to replicate this one-year option, where the

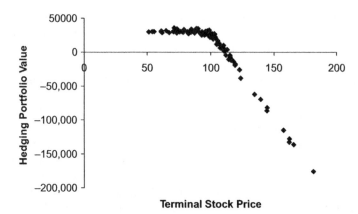

FIGURE 11.5 100 Realizations of the Hedging Strategy for the One-Year Option

underlying has a volatility of 30 percent, and we hedge once a day. As we are long a call, the replicating portfolio should look like a short call position.

So things are approximately what we expect. This indeed looks like the payoff from a short call position struck at 100. But the replication is not perfect. There is significant dispersion around the true value. The dispersion is dependent on the final underlying price, with the most variability occurring when we expire near the strike.

The first thing to note is that in this simulation (and indeed in real life) we are not hedging continuously. Discrete hedging makes our nondirectional strategy very path-dependent. Two sample paths with exactly the same realized volatility can lead to different P/Ls. Consider an extreme example where all the movement of the underlying is due to one jump. In the first path the jump happens on the first day. In the second path the jump happens right before expiration.

Path 1

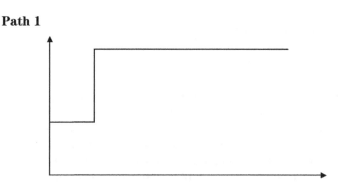

Path 2

In each case the position *P/L* is the change in the call price minus the change in the value of the hedge position.

$$P/L = C(T) - C(0) - \sum \Delta(t) \times (S(t) - S(t-1)) \qquad (11.17)$$

But in this special case we only need to evaluate the delta immediately before the jump. For the case of an at-the-money call

Case 1: $\Delta > 0.5$
Case 2: $\Delta = 0.5$

So the difference in *P/L* in these two instances is

$$\Delta(P/L) = (\Delta_1 - \Delta_2) \times (S(T) - S(0)) \qquad (11.18)$$

So if we are short this call, we do better in the first instance because we are long more stock as a hedge.

This is admittedly an extreme example but the general principle holds. The timing of a move is very important to the profitability of an option.

Let's now look in more detail at the size and nature of this effect when we have more realistic sample paths. Take a stock initially trading at $100. Assume that rates, dividends, and the drift of the underlying are zero. Again we buy one-year call options with a total vega of $1,000, at an implied volatility of 30 percent and simulate 100 paths where the realized volatility over their lifetime is in fact 30 percent. Specifically, we use Geometric Brownian Motion (GBM), so the stock path is given by

$$S(t + \Delta t) = S(t) \exp\left(-\frac{\sigma^2}{2}\Delta t + \sigma\sqrt{\Delta t}\varepsilon\right) \qquad (11.19)$$

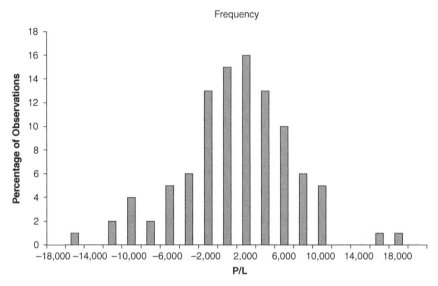

FIGURE 11.6 The P/L Distribution for $1,000 Vega of Initially At-the-Money Options When Hedged Once a Week

Where ε is drawn from a standard normal distribution with mean of zero and standard deviation of one. In Figure 11.6 we hedge weekly. The results are summarized in Table 11.2.

In Figure 11.7 we hedge daily.

From this crude experiment we can draw some tentative conclusions.

- The average P/L is roughly zero.
- The distribution of the P/L is roughly normal looking.
- The standard deviation is inversely proportional to the hedging frequency; more specifically, it is approximately proportional to $N^{-1/2}$ when N is the number of hedges (see Figure 11.8)

We previously state that "realized volatility over their lifetime is in fact 30 percent." This is not exactly true. The process that generated the underlying price DID have a volatility of 30 percent. But we were only

TABLE 11.2 Summary Statistics for the Hedging Experiment

Hedge Frequency	<P/L>	$\sigma_{P/L}$	Kurtosis	Skew
Daily	−107.19	2615.2	4.05	0.25
Weekly	−140.36	5714.6	3.66	0.16

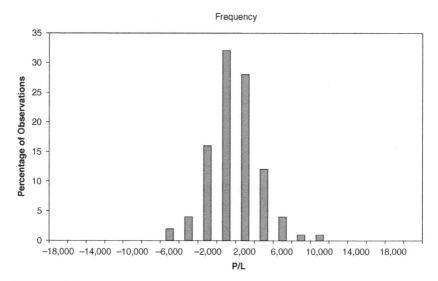

FIGURE 11.7 The P/L Distribution for $1,000 Vega of Initially At-the-Money Options When Hedged Once a Day

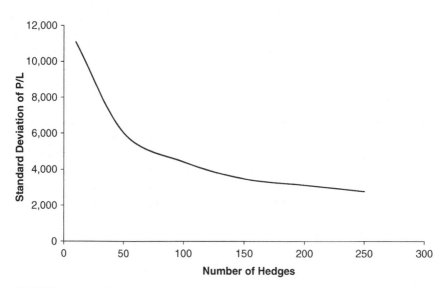

FIGURE 11.8 The Distribution of the Hedging Error as a Function of the Number of Rebalances

observing the process at discrete intervals. This introduces sampling error. From equation 7.7 we know that the sampling error is given by

$$\sigma_{\text{measured}} \approx \sigma \pm \frac{\sigma}{\sqrt{2N}} \qquad (11.20)$$

So the volatility of the P/L as a function of the initial option value will be approximated by

$$\sigma_{P/L} \approx Vega \frac{\sigma}{\sqrt{2N}} \qquad (11.21)$$

This argument is appealingly intuitive but is not really correct. The actual relationship, which does not have as simple an interpretation, is given by

$$\sigma_{P/L} \approx \sqrt{\frac{\pi}{4}} Vega \frac{\sigma}{\sqrt{N}} \qquad (11.22)$$

The important point, is that a trader can be correct about his assessment of realized volatility and still not make money. This is just the risk we take for not hedging infinitely often and running up an infinite amount of trading costs. This variability is unfortunate but we can always reduce it by hedging more frequently. Note that this is when the underlying follows a diffusive process. If there are jumps, we cannot alleviate the issue by hedging more often. In the real world there are simply some risks that cannot be hedged away.

Choosing a Hedging Volatility

In the same way that traders often have ill-considered and incorrect hedging methods, they can also be confused about what volatility to hedge their options at, and what the results of this choice are. Here we examine this.

The above analysis has assumed that we were hedging our options at the true volatility. In practice this is unknown and we need to choose a hedging volatility. There are two obvious candidates, σ_{forecast} and σ_{implied}.

A simple set of examples shows that the results of this choice are again very path dependent. Consider the two underlying price paths shown in Figure 11.9. These have exactly the same annualized volatility (23.44 percent) but in one case the price drifts higher and in the other case it does not.

When the underlying is drifting and we are long gamma, our hedges are going to be losers. We will be selling into a rising market. So we want to hedge less often. If we use a higher volatility, we see a lower gamma, so we hedge less.

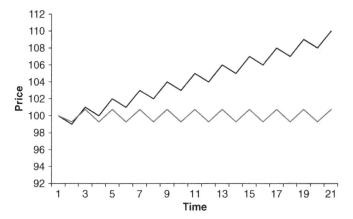

FIGURE 11.9 Two Price Paths with Identical Volatility

Conversely, in a choppy, trendless market our hedges will be winners. So we want to hedge more often. So if we use a lower volatility we can "gain" more gamma. The situation is obviously opposite if we are short options. Traders refer to this hedging trick as "letting their deltas run" if they are long in a trending market, or "hedging defensively" if they are short gamma in a trending market. This is summarized in the mnemonic table below, Table 11.3.

This is good as far as it goes, but in general we will not know if a market is trending until after the fact. As we state in Chapter 7, volatility is far more predictable than direction. This is really why trading options can be so lucrative. So we need to more generally examine the problem of choosing a hedging volatility. We assume we sell an option at an implied volatility, σ_i, and we then hedge at the realized volatility, σ_r. Let's examine how the P/L of this position evolves through time as we hedge it. This is really just the same argument we use in Chapter 4 when we derive BSM, but now we

TABLE 11.3 The Direction One Should Bias Volatility for Different Option Positions as a Function of Market Direction

Position	Market	Hedging Volatility Bias
Short gamma	Trending	Low
Short gamma	Range Bound	High
Long gamma	Trending	High
Long gamma	Range Bound	Low

need to be very careful whether we are evaluating quantities at the implied or realized volatilities.

Expression 4.28 gives the value of the hedged portfolio after the first time step. Note that we need to evaluate the option at σ_i because we are interested in the portfolio value as it is marked to market, but Δ needs to be evaluated at the realized volatility because that is how we have chosen to hedge. This is the P/L that hits our accounts at the end of each day.

$$C(S_{t+1}, \sigma_i) - C(S_t, \sigma_i) - \Delta(\sigma_r)(S_{t+1} - S_t) - r(C(\sigma_i) - \Delta(\sigma_r)S_t)$$

$$(11.23)$$

However, we also know that we can evaluate the portfolio at the realized volatility, σ_r, and here the option will be valued "correctly" (by definition) so that

$$C(S_{t+1}, \sigma_r) - C(S_t, \sigma_r) - \Delta(\sigma_r)(S_{t+1} - S_t) - r(C(\sigma_r) - \Delta(\sigma_r)S_t) = 0$$

$$(11.24)$$

So over one time step our marked to market profit is

$$dC(\sigma_i) - dC(\sigma_r) + r(C(\sigma_r) - \Delta(\sigma_r)S)dt - r(C(\sigma_i) - \Delta(\sigma_r)S)dt$$

$$(11.25)$$

Now using the BSM expression we could also write this one step profit as

$$\frac{1}{2}\left(\sigma_i^2 - \sigma_r^2\right)S^2\Gamma(\sigma_i)dt + (\Delta(\sigma_i) - \Delta(\sigma_r))((\mu - r)Sdt + \sigma SdX)$$

$$(11.26)$$

- Expression 11.25 tells us that we will make money if $\sigma_i > \sigma_r$ (leaving aside the issues associated with discrete rebalancing).
- Equation 11.26 tells us that this profit does not arrive smoothly. Equation 11.26 contains a random variable.
- The way the profit is realized depends on the drift term, μ.

Figure 11.10 shows five possible paths for the P/L evolution as a function of time for an option hedged at realized volatility. This was for the case of a short position consisting of 1,000 vega of one-year, at-the-money calls, sold at a volatility of 40 percent and hedged at the realized volatility of 30 percent until expiry. Drift, rates, and dividend yields were zero.

Traders should be familiar with this situation. These P/L swings essentially are due to other people (the market) marking options against our position. This is not a conspiracy theory. We traded the options because

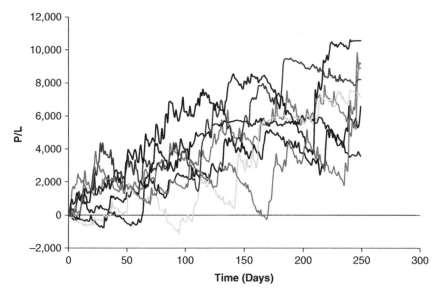

FIGURE 11.10 Profit as a Function of Time for a Short Position, Hedged at the Realized Volatility

they were mispriced. They still are. We end up carrying the wrong amount of stock against our position. We are hedged in our mind but not according to the market.

Next we look at what happens when we hedge at the implied volatility. We go through the same analysis as above, but now all the relevant variables are evaluated at the implied volatility. The one time step mark-to-market profit is given by

$$dC(\sigma_i) - \Delta(\sigma_i)dS + r(C(\sigma_i) - \Delta(\sigma_i)S)dt = \frac{1}{2}(\sigma_i^2 - \sigma_r^2)S^2\Gamma(\sigma_i)dt$$

(11.27)

- Equation 11.27 contains no stochastic terms. The profit arrives deterministically.
- There are no issues with the options being "marked against us." Whatever they are marked at, we hedge accordingly.
- This is a viable hedging method even if we do not know how to forecast volatility very well! If we sell options because our only opinion is that implied volatility is too high we can still make money.

If we take the present value of the one step profit, then sum over all time steps, we arrive at the total P/L for the position.

$$\frac{1}{2}\left(\sigma_i^2 - \sigma_r^2\right) \int \exp\left(-rt\right) S^2 \Gamma\left(\sigma_i\right) dt \tag{11.28}$$

We can now see the path dependence effect that we observed in the earlier example. Even if our option is initially struck at-the-money, the drift in the underlying will take it away from there until the option's gamma is small and hence the potential profit (equation 11.28) is small. This makes sense. We are putting on a volatility bet. We get paid only if we assume some volatility risk, and if an option is sufficiently far from the at-the-money point we have no volatility exposure left. This is why traders want to end up near the strike at expiration. The gamma is largest at that point in time and space. If you are correct in your volatility assessment, you make the most money there. This is also an argument for trading strangles or strips instead of straddles. We want to have a volatility position over a wide enough range of the underlying.

This path dependency is also a reason why different strikes should indeed trade at different implied volatilities. The path the underlying takes has different effects on options of different strikes because their gamma

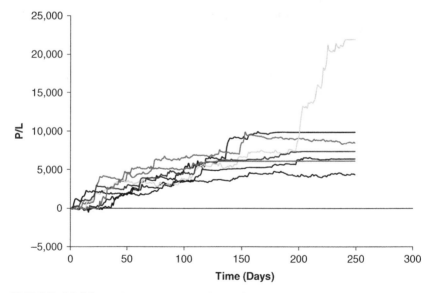

FIGURE 11.11 Profit as a Function of Time for a Short Position Hedged at Implied Volatility

profile will be very different. Equation 11.28 tells us that the fair implied volatility (the volatility that makes the P/L zero) is gamma dependent.

Figure 11.11 shows five possible paths for the P/L evolution as a function of time for an option hedged at implied volatility. This was for the case of a short position consisting of 1,000 vega of one year, at-the-money calls, sold at a volatility of 40 percent, and hedged at the implied volatility until expiry. Drift, rates, and dividend yields were zero.

Figure 11.11 shows that hedging at the implied volatility gives a "smoother" P/L, but the end result is far more variable than when we hedge at realized volatility. Most traders find this a far easier situation to deal with.

Some other things to note are

- Out-of-the-money option positions have far more variance than at-the-money options.
- We have less variance if we err on the high side when choosing a hedging volatility.

SUMMARY

- Successful hedging removes the most risk for the least cost.
- The Hodges-Neuberger formalism solves this problem in theory, but is too cumbersome to use in practice.
- The approximation of Zakamouline is a very good working solution that retains most of the desirable features of the HN method.
- The Whalley-Wilmott approximation is a good rough approximation that can be implemented within many commercially available pricing software solutions.
- Dynamic hedging should not be relied upon. It must be combined with static hedging using other options. Only this can offset the risks associated with jumps.
- Hedged option positions are very path dependent.
- Correctly predicting realized volatility is no guarantee of being profitable.
- Hedging more frequently can reduce variance in P/L.
- Hedging at realized volatility makes our final P/L more certain but very noisy.
- Hedging at implied volatility smoothes the P/L but makes the final amount more uncertain.

CHAPTER 12

Expiration Trading

There are some risks that are unique to expiration. The good news is that in addition to generating specific risks, expiration also leads to some new opportunities for making profitable trades.

Some traders mistakenly believe that the Black-Scholes-Merton (BSM) model "breaks down" around expiration. This isn't true. The model can only "break" if it ever "worked." Our point of view, that the model is a framework for organizing thoughts, still applies around expiration. However, it is more important than ever to understand the limitations of the assumptions underlying the model, as some of these assumptions are less applicable than usual.

PINNING

When the underlying settles at, or very close to, a strike at expiration it is said to have been pinned. This happens far more than we would expect if the price action were random and the strike prices were nothing special. For example, if strikes were $5 apart we would expect to be within 10 cents of a strike $0.2/5 = 0.04$ of the time.

I conducted a study of the 30 stocks currently in the Dow Jones Industrial Index and the 100 stocks in the NASDAQ 100. I looked at the number of times the stock settled within fixed distances of a strike. This was done from January 2002 until June 2009 (the start date was chosen so that all of the stocks were priced in decimals). The results are summarized in Table 12.1.

TABLE 12.1 Pinning in American Stocks

Dow

Distance to Strike	10 cents	20 cents
% of Stocks	5.65	9.97
Expected % if no pinning	4	8
T-score	3.62	3.50

NASDAQ

Distance to Strike	10 cents	20 cents
% of Stocks	5.35	9.48
Expected % if no pinning	4	8
T-score	4.26	3.22

As we can see, pinning is a real effect. A stock is about to expire within 10 cents of a strike more often than we would expect due to chance alone (the t-scores indicate that these results are statistically significant at the 5 percent level).

We also did the same study for all nonexpiration days. These results are shown in Table 12.2.

In each case the t-score is positive but less than two. This means that, while there might be a tendency for stocks to settle near strikes, we have less evidence for this than would normally be considered statistically

TABLE 12.2 Nonexpiration Days

Dow

Distance to Strike	10 cents	20 cents
% of Stocks	4.2	8.08
Expected % if no pinning	4	8
T-score	1.57	0.41

NASDAQ

Distance to Strike	10 cents	20 cents
% of Stocks	4.06	8.03
Expected % if no pinning	4	8
T-score	0.83	0.22

significant. Any pinning is certainly less than it is on expiration days. Finally, other studies have shown that no such pinning effect occurs with stocks that have no options listed on them.

This suggests that the pinning effect is unique to expiration, and is somehow affected by the option market. Something happens on this day that causes the stocks to be "pulled" toward the strike prices.

Pinning occurs often, but not always. Why does it occur at all and why does it not occur in every stock?

The first thing to state is that this effect is not the result of option market makers colluding in an effort to have their short option positions expire worthless. Deliberate manipulation of underlying prices certainly does occur, and this has been done around expiration. However, this is a costly exercise as a lot of stock needs to be traded. This generally puts this type of manipulation beyond the financial means of market makers. Also, pinning by deliberate manipulation would be easier in illiquid securities. But this is not where most pinning occurs. The pinning effect is indeed due to the activities of market makers but in a more complex way, and unless they are careful it can easily be to their detriment.

To make the situation as simple as possible, assume that the entire option market consists of a customer and a single market maker. Assume that the customer sells an option to the market maker. Many customers trade options to obtain directional exposure so they will not hedge, or will at least hedge less frequently than the market maker who will be actively delta hedging his position. If the underlying is below the strike, the market maker will be a buyer of the underlying, and if the underlying is above the strike, the market maker will be a seller. As we approach expiration the market maker's gamma will grow if we are close to a strike. His hedges will become larger. This creates pressure pulling the price toward the strike, and the effect becomes stronger as the time to expiry decreases.

Note that we will be pulled toward the strike purely from the dependence of delta on time. Assume we are long a 100 strike call and the market is trading 96. With five days until expiration and an implied volatility of 50 percent, these have a delta of 0.25, so we need to be short 25 shares as a hedge. With three days remaining, the delta is 0.19 so even if nothing else had happened we would need to buy six units of stock to rebalance our hedge. This pushes us towards the strike. Alternatively, if we are trading 104 with five days left, the call delta is 0.76 and so our hedge is to be short 76 shares. With three days remaining the delta has changed to 0.81. Again our hedging has exerted pressure toward the strike. A similar analysis shows that the same effect holds when we are long puts: the passing of time causes us to adjust our hedges in a way that moves us toward the strike.

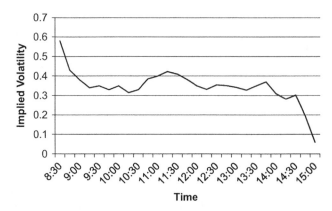

FIGURE 12.1 Implied Volatility on Expiration Day for Google
This is the implied volatility of the 550 strike on October 16, 2009.

A further factor is that as traders begin to sense which strike we will settle near, they aggressively sell those options. This causes implied volatility to collapse and the option holders to gain even more gamma. This implied volatility collapse is shown above in Figure 12.1.

We can see that this effect is due to the underlying price being pinned to the 550 strike in Figure 12.2. When it becomes obvious that the underlying will expire close to 550, the volatility collapses.

The dynamic hedging carried out by option holders causes pinning. So for pinning to occur we need large open interest in the option market in strikes near the underlying price. We also should look for stocks that are not hard to borrow. These two conditions mean that option holder will

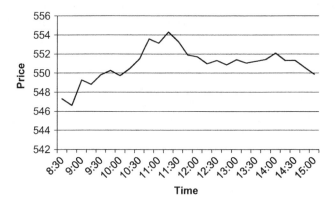

FIGURE 12.2 Google Price on October 16, 2009

want to hedge, and that they actually can. The conditions that lead to pinning are summarized below.

- Large open interest in options.
- Delta hedging market participants are long at the money options. The easiest way for a trader to decide that this is the case is to assume that his position is reflective of all of his type of traders. It is nearly impossible for an active market maker to have the opposite position from other market makers.
- An underlying that is not hard to borrow.
- A stock that is a popular vehicle for directional speculation.

There is also some evidence that stocks have a disproportionately large amount of small returns on expiration day. This would suggest that many stocks would end up pinned to the strikes that they closed near on Thursday evening.

However, it is also important to note that pinning isn't the only thing happening in the market. For example, Google (GOOG) releases earnings the night before expiration. This will cause a move in the stock price and it is well known that stocks do not instantaneously adjust to earnings data, creating post-earnings announcement drift. So Google may move significantly during the day and the strike it opens near may not be the one that it eventually settles near. However, the Google earnings announcement is a great catalyst for pinning because it means a lot of front-month options will have been bought for directional speculation. Google is often pinned (finishing within 10 cents of a strike about 12 percent of the time), although picking the pinning strike needs to be done well after the open. Normally the final resting strike begins to become apparent with a few hours of trading remaining. For many stocks this would be too late to be of direct interest, but because the price of Google shares is so high ($492.48 on September 25, 2009) the options can still have significant premium left with only a few hours left until they expire. This makes Google an excellent candidate for active expiration trading.

Once it has become apparent that a market is going to be pinned, it is easy to construct an option position with a good risk reward profile. A short straddle is often the only practical choice, but ideally we would cap our losses by using either a butterfly or a ratio spread.

PIN RISK

Pin risk occurs when the underlying settles close to an option's strike value at expiration. Anyone short these options is exposed to pin risk. The specific risk is that it is impossible to predict whether the option will be exercised or not. Let's consider some examples.

Example 1

We are short the 100 calls and the stock settles at 99.98. Theoretically the calls are not an exercise candidate, as they are two cents out-of-the-money. Also these calls will now have a delta of zero, so according to a standard pricing model they will be unhedged. However, at this point we need to make a purely probabilistic assessment of our chances of assignment. Is any news coming out? Why would anyone want to pay $100 for an underlying that was worth $99.98? There are actually plenty of reasons. Many of them come down to the fact that the call holder thinks the stock is going up and will be higher at the next opening. A further consideration is that by exercising, the call holders will be guaranteed a purchase price of $100 and will not have to take slippage into account.

Example 2

A large customer started buying slightly out-of-the-money bond options on the day of expiration. He paid a tick for many thousands of puts. After the bond option traders had sold all they could, traders from other pits were still begging to sell more. The puts expired out-of-the-money. Then the holder exercised them. Now the market makers owned the futures. True, the options were out-of-the-money, so the market makers owned the futures from slightly below the market. The problem was that they owned so many that their collective selling pressure would drive the price lower. The customer had determined that he could buy the puts for less than the market impact cost of liquidating the position. As always, if something looks too good to be true, it probably is.

Note that we are exposed to pin risk whenever we are short any options with a strike near the underlying price. For example, if we are long 20 calls and short 10 puts of the at-the-money strike we are still exposed because of the short puts, even though we are net long options. Put-call parity cannot save us from pin risk.

To gauge the magnitude of pin risk, we have to measure two things.

1. What is the average move from one close to the next open? This is the amount that the position we are given could go against us. Of course it could also go in our favor, but as we are talking here about risk (or uncertainty) we need to think about the average magnitude of the move.
2. What is the likely market impact of those with positions due to assignment having to unwind them? This will always go against us.

These costs can be significant and sensible traders will often try to remove the possibility of pin risk by paying to liquidate positions in the days before expiration. Traders should be very wary if the front-month conversions (or reversals) start to trade at what look to be silly prices. This is generally due to people trying to avoid pin risk.

Note that because pin risk is caused by the possibility of a trader receiving an unplanned position in the underlying that he then needs to liquidate, it is not an issue with cash-settled options. Here we receive cash for the intrinsic value of any expiring options. Cash does not need to be unwound or liquidated when the market reopens. However, cash-settled options have their own expiration wrinkle.

FORWARD RISK

With most options, when an in-the-money option expires we receive the corresponding position in the underlying (a long position for long calls, short position for long puts, short position for short calls, and a long position for short puts). As we will be holding an offsetting position in the underlying as a hedge, after expiry we will have no net position.

This is not the case with cash-settled options. Here we generally hedge with a future or another traded asset, but at expiry we receive cash. So our expiration position does not offset our hedge. If we don't want to have a directional position we need to flatten our option deltas in the expiring month.

Example

We are long 100 deep in-the-money April Eurostoxx (ESX) calls. Our best hedge is the June future, so we are short 100 of these. At April expiration, the calls will convert into cash and we will be short 100 futures. To avoid this, we will try to work out of the position by actively looking to sell calls and buy futures, or by using a broker to find a counterparty with the opposite position who is also looking to unwind. Note that, unlike pin risk, forward risk applies to any in-the-money options and it not confined to times when we are expiring near a strike.

EXERCISING THE WRONG OPTIONS

Failing to exercise options will lose money. Exercising options that shouldn't be exercised can lose you a lot more.

Example 1

Options on the DAX index did not always exercise automatically if they expired in-the-money. The trader had to actively exercise any options he wanted to have exercised. At one expiration, a trader (from a large and respected American market making firm) exercised all of his options, not just those that were in the money. To see the scale of this disaster, remember that at this time the DAX was trading around 2,000 and strikes were listed with a range from 600 to 3,000. A tick was 10 Deutschmarks, so each 3,000 call that was exercised would cost around 10,000 DM. Now remember that a typical option market maker would have large positions in such out-of-the-money options (often as parts of spreads). This was a multimillion dollar error.

Example 2

FTSE options also had to be manually exercised. Somewhat unusually for cash-settled index options, these had both American and European options listed on the exchange. One trader (from a not-so-large and not-so-respected market making firm) exercised not just his expiring in-the-money options but also those in the second month. This means he lost a month's worth of volatility value: an error costing several hundreds of thousands of pounds.

Example 3

On Friday, September 18, 2009, Lorillard (LO) was trading around $73.6. A few minutes before the market closed and the September options would expire, a buy order for 1.5 million shares hit the market and pushed the price to $75.3. This meant that the 75 calls were now in-the-money and would be automatically exercised. But would it really be a good idea to pay $75 for something that until a few minutes previously was worth $73.6? About 67 percent of the option holders exercised (or, more accurately, they failed to not exercise). As the options were so far out-of-the-money immediately prior to expiration, their delta would have been practically zero, so no one would have been carrying any hedge against them. So traders who were assigned on their short options were now short the stock. On Monday it opened at $74.66 and they could cover for a windfall profit.

Was it the trader who actually made these errors? This would be unlikely. Equity options expire on Fridays and traders are far too busy on Friday evenings to stay in the office doing bookkeeping. These were almost certainly errors by a junior trading assistant. But would either of these firms have allowed the same assistant to make trades that could possibly lose close to this amount? Again, risk management isn't very exciting. Much of it is boring and menial. But that doesn't mean it isn't important.

IRRELEVANCE OF THE GREEKS

As expiration approaches, the usefulness of most of the Greeks as risk measures diminishes. Vega and rho become irrelevant, as they tend toward zero as time to expiry tends toward zero. More crucially, gamma and theta become quite misleading.

At the moment of expiration, gamma is infinite if our option is at-the-money and zero elsewhere. This is because we are exactly at the point where the option changes from being equivalent to an underlying position to being worthless. Its delta will be flipping from one to zero as the underlying price crosses the strike. In order to avoid incurring enormous hedging costs, the trader should stop thinking in terms of continuous delta hedging and instead wait until he is reasonably sure the option delta has reached its expiring value and then hedge. This isn't as alarming as it sounds, as this will probably involve only a move of less than a dollar.

Theta also becomes misleading. The lessening of relevance of theta starts earlier than gamma, often producing fairly bizarre numbers several days before expiry. The major issue here is that theta has been normalized to show decay of option value over the period of a day. Normally this is a good thing as it converts theta into a directly relevant number, but close to expiry it becomes senseless as the theta changes too quickly over the period of a day.

Example

We are long the 100 call on a stock that is trading at $100, with an implied volatility of 50 percent and rates of zero. The theta of this option for the five days before expiration is shown in Figure 12.3.

This might not seem unreasonable, until we look at the value of the option on the same time scale. This is shown in Figure 12.4.

With one day left we have a theta of −1.17, but the entire value of the option is only 0.466. Clearly our decay cannot be more than the option value. This problem is caused by the fact that theta is the slope of the option value when it is a function of time, but it is generally expressed as the change over a period of a day. Near expiration, theta is changing so rapidly that this gives nonsensical answers. If we are pricing options using a numerical method, this should not be a problem, as the times step we use to calculate theta can be made arbitrarily small (no matter what time period we use to express theta).

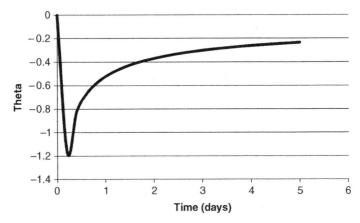

FIGURE 12.3 Theta as We Approach Expiry

EXPIRING AT A SHORT STRIKE

Option traders have always held that it was the ideal situation to expire at a short strike. Even more specifically, they want to move *through* longs *to* shorts. This is an interesting example of a situation where theoretically traders are incorrect but in the real world they have a point. Let's go through the idea.

The most naive expression of this idea is that by expiring at a short strike the trader will receive the entire option premium as the option expires worthless. This is certainly true, but it is equally true that if the underlying whips around while we are long options, we can make money.

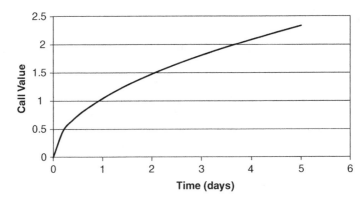

FIGURE 12.4 Option Value as We Approach Expiry

In fact, one of the central results of Chapter 11 is that, while expiring at a strike dramatically increases the volatility of P/L, we make money if we are long implied volatility and realized is higher, or if we are short implied volatility and realized is lower. This rule applies equally at expiration or at any other time.

However, in the real world things are more complicated. First, if we are long options we will dampen realized volatility with the market impact of our delta hedging. This makes it rare that we will be at a strike and realized volatility will be high: our presence in the market makes this so. But if we are at a short strike and we gently settle there, then clearly the implied volatility will have been higher than realized. Almost by definition this is a favorable outcome. This situation is also vastly simpler to hedge, and hence capture the volatility: we just wait and hope.

The situation can be summarized as follows.

- Near expiration the practicalities of hedging dominate the market.
- Hedging a long position where we are crossing a strike will dampen volatility.
- Hedging a short position where we are rapidly crossing a strike will increase volatility.
- Hedging a short position where we are slowly settling to a strike will not impact the market as it simply involves waiting and hoping.
- We want to be in a position where we don't need to hedge at all.
- This ideal is achieved by going through longs to shorts.

Experienced traders often have important information to convey. What they say may be true, but the reasons they give can be incorrect. This is a problem, but we have no choice but to persevere. If you were searching for water in a desert, would you listen to the advice of a Bushman who thought water was the tears of the gods, or a geologist who worked in a university in another country?

SUMMARY

- At expiration an option trader's hedging activity can dramatically alter the dynamics of the underlying.
- Generally, this will occur in a way that hurts the dynamic hedger.
- Pinning is a real effect.
- Remember what the option's underlying is, and what the options are hedged with. If these are not the same, work to unwind as many forwards as possible.

CHAPTER 13

Risk Management

You can't be perfect, but if you don't try you won't be good enough.
—Paul Halmos, *I Want to be a Mathematician*
(New York: Springer Verlag, 1985)
In preparing for battle I have always found that plans are useless, but planning is indispensable.
—General Dwight D. Eisenhower, quoted in
"Krushchev," in *Six Crises* by Richard Nixon
(New York: Doubleday, 1962)

M any professional option traders find that making money is relatively easy, but keeping it is much harder (this is characteristic of any trader who makes money principally as a liquidity provider). As we state in Chapter 10, a "me, too" strategy in which we simply mimic the quotes of another trader can be very successful. As anyone can do this, there must be another aspect to option trading that has been overlooked so far; otherwise, every trader would be successful. This aspect is risk management. Most of what professional option traders do is risk management; playing defense and trying to keep money. If a market maker can manage to keep a third of the bid-ask spread, he will be very successful in the long run. The stress on risk containment is a key differentiator between amateurs and professionals.

There are two things to remember when putting risk management into context.

- Sometimes it is good to "take a shot" when making a trade. This could be for a number of reasons. You might want to start trading a new strategy. You may have a hunch that you simply cannot get the hard evidence to confirm. Or you may need to do a trade to help out a broker. No one trade should hurt you (with the caveats involving appropriate sizing that we discuss in Chapter 9). However, it is never appropriate to "take a shot" when managing risk. Risk management is far too important to take chances with. You really need to have no tolerance for mistakes.
- Professional option trading is not about making big, memorable trades. It is about grinding out small, consistent profits and keeping risks under control.

In a general sense, this entire book is about risk management. The discipline that is normally referred to as risk management is really the process of risk *measurement*. Traders are the ones who actually manage risk. They do this by making trades to mitigate and lower the risks that earlier trades have led to. Many of the trades—both in the underlying and in options—which an option trader makes are of this type: not designed to make money, but designed to keep it.

What counts as "risk" is different for different types of traders. Generally speaking, risk is an unintended consequence of a trade. If a volatility position trader sells a straddle, his vega position is not really a risk: It is intended and he expects to make money from it. But by selling the straddle, he will also have an exposure to interest rate changes. This would properly be thought of as a risk. In contrast, an option market maker aims to make money by collecting the bid/ask spread, so any inventory at all is a risk. Consequently, most of the discussions in this chapter will be relevant to market makers, but all option traders will incur at least some risks. Position traders normally have an easier time than market makers with risk management. Normally their positions are quite simple, so to manage risk they can normally just trade out of the position or at least reduce its size. A slight exception to this is when the market has not quite gone according to plan, but neither is it a total disaster. In this case, we may just want to slightly modify the position. This is sometimes referred to as "position repair."

EXAMPLE OF POSITION REPAIR

Option trades more often than not are neither unqualified successes nor outright failures. Their outcomes tend to be more nuanced. Also, after the trade is initiated, we will have many opportunities to make adjustments. This is an example of how a trader might adapt to changing circumstances.

Imagine that the stock of ABC Corporation is trading $100. We sold 1,000 of the two-month 110 calls and bought 1,000 of the 90 puts. We hedged the position to become delta-neutral. We did this because we thought that the underlying would rally, and this would cause the implied volatility of the calls to drop. We would then profit from our short vega position and also collect theta each day. We bought the puts as insurance, because the biggest uncertainty in our forecast was over the direction of the underlying. Although we thought the most likely scenario was a slow, easy rally, we also could not definitively rule out a horrific crash.

We were right about the rally. Unfortunately, over the next few weeks we rallied too far and too fast. We went to a price of 120. The realized volatility in the underlying over this period was higher than we had forecast. Hedging our accumulated deltas on the close each day gave us a loss. Even worse, we are now above our call strike. We expect out of the money calls on an index to have a lower implied volatility than the at-the-money strike, but the 110 calls were now synthetically out-of-the-money puts and were hence priced at a higher implied volatility than the at-the-money strike. Finally, our long puts were too far away to serve as much protection.

In summary, despite being correct about our directional prediction, we were wrong with respect to both realized and implied volatility movements, and hence lost money both on gamma and vega. However, we still think the initial forecast of a slow move higher is most likely at this point.

What are our options?

- Do nothing. This is a bad idea because the current position does not reflect the market forecast. We still want to be short calls and long puts. If we rally further, we will be going further away from the short vega, so we will not benefit as much from a decline in volatility. Clearly, if volatility does not decline we will continue to lose money. And finally, if the underlying market declines we could lose money as well, because we would drop through the short call position and the puts are now so far away as to be useless as protection.
- Completely roll the position so that the current vega profile is the same as the one we wanted initially. This would involve trading a call spread and a put spread. We would buy back the short 110 calls and sell the 130 calls. We would also sell the 90 puts and buy some 110 puts. This plan involves trading a lot of options (four separate strikes) and we need to trade an in-the-money option that may have a relatively wide bid-ask spread.

- Exit the trade. But we still think the initial forecast is likely to be correct in the end. We've lost money, but not so much that we are scared of going bankrupt. The big problem is that the current position will not profit from the forecast. There is no reason to give up at this point. The initial forecast is basically still valid. We have not been proven wrong.
- Adjust the position. We look at the current available options and choose a trade that gets us close to where we want to be. We do not need perfection. We decide to buy the two-month 110 puts instead of the calls, because we could get a better price in these more liquid options. Next we sell some three-month 130 calls to reestablish our short upside vega position. We decide to just live with our two-month 90 puts and not buy any others. Now we return to delta hedging each day.

This is the type of scenario analysis that option traders do continually. You start with an idea and put on an option position to benefit from this idea. Then things start to evolve, never exactly as you foresaw, and you need to start adjusting. This cycle never ends. And the line between "trade" and "hedge" becomes increasingly blurred.

The correct way to think about the cost of repairing a position varies. If the position was intended to be a directional play (that is, the options were deliberately used to create a delta position), the cost of repair is the price of any options we need to purchase. However, if we are repairing a volatility position, the options will be hedged, so the cost is the bid-ask spread in the option: We do not expect to lose the entire premium.

Options depend on a number of variables and parameters and hence a single number cannot describe their risk. There is no single risk measure that captures all of the risk. Attempts have been made to do this, particularly within the VaR (value at risk) methodology. This technique attempts to give a threshold value that we expect to give a bound to our losses on a certain percentage of days. For example, if we have a one-day 5 percent VaR of $1 million, there is a 5 percent probability that we would lose more than $1 million on any given day. VaR has its uses, but it needs to make many distributional and relational assumptions to come up with this single number. An experienced option trader, who is willing to accept the need for many risk measures, should be able to do much better. In addition, VaR will not tell us how exactly to reduce risks. The approach we will outline is designed specifically to do this.

Note that it is not a bad thing that we cannot categorize risk by a single number. It is not really possible, in any situation complex enough to be interesting, to use a single measure. For example, how do you decide if a car is good? There is no single measure. Instead you need to consider speed, mileage, cost, reliability, depreciation, and expert opinion. Good option traders understand this concept and accept that options are multidimensional.

We should attend to risks in the order of their riskiness. We can split risks into three categories.

1. **Primary Risks**
   - Inventory
   - Delta
2. **Secondary Risks**
   - Gamma
   - Jump risk
   - Vega (including skew and calendar risk)
3. **Tertiary Risks**
   - Correlation risk
   - Rho
   - Dividend risk
   - "Buy-in" risk
   - Early exercise
   - Strike risk
   - Pin risk

The exact order of these risks is open to a little interpretation but this is basically how I view things. If anyone wants to make an argument that rho is less risky than dividend risk, I will not put up much of a fight.

Further, the importance of the risks changes over time. On the day of expiration, vega, rho, and skew become far less important, and strike risk and pin risk become far more important.

I have also assumed that the trades are denominated in the trader's currency of determination. If he is trading options denominated in another currency, he will also have to take the exchange rate risk into account. Foreign exchange can be hedged, so the overall effect on the trader's profitability will be somewhere around the level of interest rate risk.

A very important metarisk is *liquidity*. If markets for the underlying or the options become illiquid, a trader's options for reducing risk become correspondingly reduced. There is really not much that a trader can do about this. It is often said that traders should "be careful" or "not trade too big." Unfortunately, what these terms mean typically only becomes clear after the event. The threat of liquidity holes just seems to be something we need to accept. In fact, some have claimed that everything that happens in markets is due to liquidity and its creation. This seems too extreme, but it is an ever-present fact of trading. It is not always a bad thing either: in Chapter 10 we see how creating and manipulating small spots of illiquidity can be a source of edge in market-making and other forms of high-frequency trading.

Although it can be a source of their edge, liquidity risk is also most dangerous to market makers. They are paid to create liquidity. So when they need to exit a trade, liquidity will clearly be lower than normal as there will be one fewer liquidity provider than usual. Further, if one market maker is forced to liquidate his position it is likely that others are also in trouble. This can lead to situations where literally no one is willing to make a two-sided price.

Now we go through each of the enumerated risks in detail, showing why they are important and what a trader should look for when evaluating each one. But I'm also going to warn of an impending bait-and-switch. After I've told a few amusing warning stories about each of these risks, I'm going to say that we never really look at each in isolation. Option trading is about doing a lot of things at once. The risks can never be handled individually.

Of course none of these risks are dangerous in themselves. They are only risks in that they can cost us money. Having a position with a million dollars of vega is totally meaningless unless we know how much implied volatility can move.

In this chapter we will be using examples and we will need some sort of baseline for deciding what an acceptable amount of money to lose is. I am going to arbitrarily decide that we are traders looking to make an average of a thousand dollars a day, or roughly $250,000 a year. This is just to get a sense of scale. Generally a good rule of thumb is that taking risks that could cost you a week of profit is acceptable, but risks that could cost you a month are too big.

INVENTORY

You should always make sure the position at your clearing firm matches what you think it should be. You can always chase down errors in prices later, but if you have an option position that is different from what you think it is, things can get very ugly, very quickly.

This is the most vital part of option risk management, and it is nothing more than careful bookkeeping. It is fashionable to point out that derivatives are very complex and subject users to risks due to higher-order moments in the underlying return distribution. This may well be true, but most spectacular losses are not due to these effects.

Many of the catastrophic and infamous derivatives losses have been caused when an institution did not know what its position was. Granted, the ones that have become newsworthy have been due to a trader hiding his position, but there have also been many other smaller cases when individual traders have blown out because they were unaware of their position. Until a trader knows exactly what he has in his position, he is unable to do anything sensible to mitigate or even to measure risks.

Example 1: Barings Bank

The trader and risk manager, Nick Leeson, lost £827 million in 1995 by taking unauthorized positions in Nikkei and Japanese government bond futures and option straddles. Originally, he was trying to make back money lost due to other errors, but as he lost money he added to his losing positions.

This is an example of bad risk management for several reasons.

* It is bad business practice for a risk manager to also be a trader. While trading options is indeed largely a matter of risk management, any well-run firm will also have a separate risk management section to avoid conflict of interest.
* Barings had no way to manage the position because they did not know what it was.
* Leeson's trading strategy was a classic martingale, where he added to his losers. Chasing losses is practically never a good idea.

The fact derivatives were involved in this debacle was almost incidental.

Example 2: Sumitomo

In June 1996 Sumitomo announced that it had lost $2.6 billion due to unauthorized copper trades conducted by Yasuo Hamanaka. This was a simple case of fraud. Mr. Hamanaka forged the documents confirming the forward trades and did not submit them to the bank's risk department. Again, the loss was due to the bank being unaware of its position.

Example 3: Société Générale

In 2008 the French bank Société Générale announced losses of approximately €4.9 billion. This is currently the subject of a legal dispute. The bank alleges that Jerome Kerviel, who was employed to conduct index arbitrage, "had taken massive fraudulent directional positions" and used his knowledge of the bank's back-office control systems to hide these from management. He denies this.

This is an interesting case because the bank's defense is essentially an appeal to their own poor risk management. If the bank is found to be correct, they are still guilty of massive incompetence. They did not know what their position in the market was.

DELTA

When a trader loses a lot of money very quickly, it is almost inevitably because his delta position has gone against him. The reason for this may be different in each case, but the accumulation of a bad delta position is the end result. If you are ever in any doubt at all (about any aspect of your position), first hedge your delta risk. Hedging the delta buys time. Other things can hurt, but delta causes the most pain in the least amount of time.

For an option trader, an unacceptable delta position will generally arise from an error in a position or a trade, or the delta generated by gamma as the underlying changes. This is not the same situation as a directional trader who has made a trade that turned out to be incorrect. Do not ever try to breakeven or make money on an error. You did not enter the trade for any valid reason. The first thing to do is to get out of it. It may be that the position is so large or illiquid that it will take time to trade out. This will obviously give time for reflection and it may well be that the trader can determine that the trade is more likely than not to go his way. However, this does not provide a counterexample to what I said first: the overwhelming priority should still be to get out of the position. This type of situation just makes the exit more likely to be profitable.

GAMMA

Gamma in itself is not a risk. However, positions with large gamma will pick up deltas (and hence acquire risk) quickly. We examine in Chapter 5 how gamma changes as a function of time and underlying price. But the easiest way to see the effect of gamma on an option position is by using the risk slide.

A risk slide shows how the position evolves as a function of the underlying price. To make one, we reprice the portfolio at a range of different underlying prices. Consider the option position in Table 13.1.

We delta hedge this by buying 700 shares. The risk slide for this position is shown in Table 13.2.

TABLE 13.1 An Option Position

Strike	Call Position	Put Position
80	0	10
85	0	8
90	0	0
95	−20	−18
100	−15	0
105	10	0
110	23	1

The underlying is trading $100, interest rates are 2 percent, and there are 90 days until expiry.

So, if the underlying price drops to $80, our position will be long 558 deltas and will have lost $5,220.

A couple of assumptions have been made to produce this.

- We need to make some assumption about how implied volatility moves as a function of the underlying. But as we explore in Chapter 8, all option traders need to make this decision anyway. This choice is important. The slide of Table 13.2 assumed that the volatility curve was fixed. The curve is shown in Figure 13.1.

So if we are keeping this skew fixed and the price drops to $80, the ATM volatility will rise from 40 percent to 54 percent. If we use a floating skew curve, the entire curve shifts down. This will cause all of the greeks to change (as we discuss in Chapter 5) and our P/L can also be substantially different. The slide when floating the volatility curve is shown in Table 13.3.

TABLE 13.2 The Risk Slide

Price	80	85	90	95	100	105	110	115	120
Delta	558	392	236	119	52	37	64	118	184
Gamma	−32	−33	−28	−19	−8	2	9	12	14
Vega	−178	−231	−238	−200	−129	−44	34	94	130
Theta	31	47	54	50	38	22	6	−7	−16
P/l	−5,220	−2,847	−1,278	−406	0	204	444	890	1,639

The underlying is trading $100, interest rates are 2 percent, and there are 90 days until expiry.

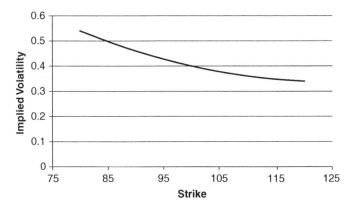

FIGURE 13.1   The Implied Volatility Curve for the Example

As we see, even though the position greeks are identical when valued against the current price of $100, they differ quite substantially at the other parts of the slide.

- We need to decide what range of underlying prices is most appropriate to use. Generally this will have some relationship to the daily standard deviation. I usually will use gradations of one daily standard deviation, but I always prefer to *see* the price expressed in dollar terms. When I'm in a hurry, or flustered, I really want to know what my risk is if the stock moves by X dollars, not Y standard deviations. Obviously these are equivalent, but the dollar change is more readily available and intuitive.

Now that we have constructed the risk slide (which is a standard feature of most option trading software), we can look along it and see if there are any places where we would lose more money than we think is acceptable. When looking at the slide in Figure 13.3, we can see that our

TABLE 13.3   The Risk Slide When Using a Floating Implied Volatility

Price	80	85	90	95	100	105	110	115	120
Delta	761	545	302	125	52	67	129	203	272
Gamma	−27	−39	−37	−23	−8	3	8	9	9
Vega	−108	−219	−259	−217	−129	−40	22	55	67
Theta	14	37	51	50	38	24	12	5	1
P/I	−5,022	−1,728	31	394	0	−467	−568	−147	772

Parameters are the same as for Figure 13.1.

TABLE 13.4 The Risk Slide after Selling 200 Shares

Price	80	85	90	95	100	105	110	115	120
Delta	358	192	36	−81	−148	−163	−136	−82	−16
Gamma	−32	−33	−28	−19	−8	2	9	12	14
Vega	−178	−231	−238	−200	−129	−44	34	94	130
Theta	31	47	54	50	38	22	6	−7	−16
P/I	−1,220	153	722	594	0	−796	−1,556	−2,110	−2,361

Parameters are the same as for Figure 13.1.

worst-case scenario is if the underlying price goes to $80 (actually it will continue to get even worse below that). There are several things we could do.

- We could sell some stock. This would somewhat equalize our risk between moves up or down. Selling 200 shares would give us the slide of Table 13.4.
- But this does not help our vega risk, or reduce the short gamma that caused us to get long the deltas as the underlying dropped. So we decide instead to buy 10 of the 80 puts. This gives us the slide of Table 13.5.

Buying those ten options did another very important thing. It made our net option position positive. We now have nine net options (the sum of all calls and puts). This is the simplest and most robust of all risk management rules. Options are good and you should always try to have a net long position. If everything goes as badly as could be imagined, being long options can only help.

This approach is also useful for looking at the effect of jumps in the underlying price. BSM theory does not think jumps exist, but they most assuredly do. And these are much more important to take into account

TABLE 13.5 The Risk Slide after Buying 10 80 Puts

Price	80	85	90	95	100	105	110	115	120
Delta	117	39	−41	−96	−110	−84	−26	51	135
Gamma	−13	−17	−14	−7	1	9	14	17	17
Vega	−21	−74	−89	−62	−6	61	123	167	190
Theta	−14	2	10	10	3	−9	−20	−29	−34
P/I	493	886	883	531	0	−502	−789	−731	−265

Parameters are the same as for Figure 13.1.

than the motion due to continuous diffusion that underlies BSM. A diffusive movement can be hedged; a jump cannot. This is just another example of an inconsistency between BSM theory and the way that it can be (very effectively) used in the real world. In the theoretical BSM world, gamma is the second derivative of the option price due to a small, continuous (and hence hedgeable) change in the underlying. In the real world a trader uses gamma to tell him his exposure to a discontinuous and unhedgeable jump.

An objection that is sometimes raised at this point is that we do not know what the distribution of returns is going to be, so we cannot ascertain the chance of reaching any particular point on the slide. While this is technically correct, it misses the point. This is not a trading decision. This is a risk decision. Can you withstand *any* possible move? The correct reasoning is not to get involved in detailed, assumption-laden, risk/return scenarios here. The correct course of action is to do whatever is necessary to stay in business. If we see a part of the slide where our loss is too great, we will need to either adjust our delta position with options or the underlying, or to buy some options so that their gamma can protect us.

VEGA

Implied volatility changes, but it usually does so far more slowly than the underlying price. Also there is evidence that it is a mean reverting parameter, so there is a good chance that a move will reverse. So vega is dangerous, but not as dangerous as gamma. There is an old saying that "vega wounds, but gamma kills."

Option traders will also have more tolerance for vega because, even if they are not actively looking to take a position in implied volatility, they feel that they are more able to actively manage this risk by trading options at favorable prices, buying them on the bid, or selling them on the offer. This view probably has some merit. It would be reasonable that a professional option trader would have a better-than-average ability to forecast and manage volatility risk.

There is an aspect of vega risk that is sometimes referred to as "skew risk." As we note in Chapter 8, the implied volatility curve's slope does not change enormously. Generally at least 75 percent of the change of implied volatility can be attributed to a change in the level of the whole curve. Sometimes a trader will enter a trade that is ostensibly designed to profit from a change in the slope of the implied curve. For example, he may buy a 30-delta put and sell a 30-delta call on the basis that he expects the curve to steepen. After delta hedging, this leaves him flat delta, gamma, and vega. His risk slide is shown below in Table 13.6.

TABLE 13.6 The Initial Risk Slide

Price	90	92.5	95	97.5	100	102.5	105	107.5	110
Delta	−872	−505	−228	−58	0	−52	−201	−430	−717
Gamma	162	130	90	46	1	−41	−77	−105	−124
Vega	534	455	333	177	2	−178	−349	−498	−617
Theta	−420	−355	−252	−120	29	183	330	458	561
P/I	2,991	1282	384	49	0	−42	−337	−1,109	−2,531

The risk slide for a position consisting of long 100 of the 30 delta put and short 100 of the 30 delta call for an underlying of $100, rate of 2 percent, time to expiration of 30 days, and an implied volatility of 50 percent. With these parameters, the put strike is 94 and the call strike is 109.

But he is only *initially* flat vega, As the underlying moves, he will accumulate a significant vega position. In this situation, his change in vega due to a move in the underlying will totally dwarf any change in implied skew. Let's look at the relative size of these effects. According to equation 8.10, an average daily move for this stock would be about $2.5. So, according to Table 13.6, this expected random move makes him $49 if it is a break and loses him $42 if it is a rally (assuming it takes place fast enough that we can ignore theta). But we also expect implied volatility to move, and applying the approximation of equation 8.7 (as we discuss in Chapter 8), we expect that a 30-day implied volatility of 50 percent would have a daily standard deviation of about 6 vols. Now about 75 percent of this (or 4.5 vols) will be in the overall level of implied volatility. This means that if the price moves about as much as we expect ($2.5), and volatility moves about as much as we expect (4.5 vols), we could expect to make or lose about

$$P/L = 0.5(\$49 + \$42) + 0.5(\$177 + \$178) \times 4.5 = \$846.5$$

In contrast, the amount of vega in the 30 delta put is $10 and in the call is $10. So if the underlying stayed at $100, we would need a skew shift of 40 vols to have a P/L that was in any way comparable to the random slop we would expect due to normal underlying and volatility moves.

This analysis ignores an important point. Implied volatility will quite probably decline if the stock market rallies (this relationship between volatility and underlying is far more complex in the case of commodities) and the position will make money. But this is not the same as making money from the skew. As always, make sure you understand where your edge really is. The relationship between the overall volatility level and the movement of the underlying is very important. The movement in the slope of the implied curve generally is not.

Another aspect of vega risk is calendar risk. This occurs when we have an option position in one month, which is offset by a position in another month. For example, we might be long one-month options and short two-month options. These can be far riskier than the total vega seems to indicate.

We see (in Chapter 5) that it is necessary to weight vega, because the volatility of implied volatility increases as expiry approaches. This is well known, but using a poor weighting of vega is not normally the problem with calendar spreads. The bigger issue should be obvious, but often seems to be forgotten: different things happen in different months. Different commodity option expirations might actually have different crops as an underlying, or the oil underlying a later expiration might still be in an oil tanker or even in the ground. In equities, earnings announcements, special dividends, FDA announcements, or legal disputes will all affect some expirations far more than others.

Part of the art of successful option trading is knowing when one can safely aggregate positions with different expirations and when one cannot. And in any event, always look at the individual expiration vegas as well.

Finally, do not forget that eventually the front position will expire, leaving you with only one half of the spread. Failure to plan for this inevitability is surprisingly common.

CORRELATION

Correlation is sometimes a direct input into an option pricing formula (examples include quanto options, outperformance options, or basket options), or the basis of a trading strategy, such as dispersion trading. In these cases we can define a measure of sensitivity toward correlation. This is normally called correlation vega.

Another situation where traders are exposed to correlation is when they decide to normalize their greeks, expressing them in terms of a base product. For example, the delta of a Microsoft (MSFT) position might be expressed in terms of QQQQ shares. The mathematics of this is simple enough.

Consider the example where we have a stock A with price $S_A = 100$, and an index I with price $S_I = 1,000$. A has a beta relative to the index, $\beta = 1.2$. This means that if the index moves up one percent, A moves by 1.2 percent. If we are long 1,000 deltas (whether shares or through option deltas) of A, and the index moves one percent, our profit is given by

$$p/l = \$0.01 \times \beta \times S_A \times 1,000 = \$12 \times S_A = \$1,200$$

And for each unit of the index ETF we hold short our loss will be

$$p/l = -\$0.01 \times 1{,}000 = \$10$$

So, to be hedged, we need to hold a short position of 120 ETFs. Equivalently our delta in terms of the ETF is given by

$$\Delta_I = \beta \frac{S_A}{S_I} \Delta_A \tag{13.1}$$

To normalize gamma into ETF terms, write down the change in the option value as a Taylor expansion.

$$dC_A = \Delta_A dS_A + \frac{\Gamma_A}{2} dS_A^2 + \ldots \tag{13.2}$$

But

$$dS_A = \beta \frac{S_A}{S_I} dS_I$$

So

$$dC_A = \Delta_A \beta \frac{S_A}{S_I} dS_I + \frac{\Gamma_A}{2} \beta^2 \left(\frac{S_A}{S_I} \right)^2 dS_I^2 + \ldots \tag{13.3}$$

The gamma term has to be

$$\Gamma_I = \left(\beta^2 \frac{S_A^2}{S_I^2} \right) \Gamma_A \tag{13.4}$$

We could normalize vega in a similar way, but we would in this case need to know the "volatility beta," telling us how much volatility in one product moves in response to a move in the other.

The simplicity of this theory hides some fairly terrible risks. Correlation is troublesome to measure and is neither particularly stable nor a particularly good way of measuring codependence (refer to Appendix B). I would generally say this type of normalization should be avoided unless you are trading products that are exceptionally highly correlated, such as some equity indices or ETFs, or different interest-rate futures. Further, if correlation is high enough to do the normalization in the first place, I would be sorely tempted to set the correlation to one to avoid measurement errors.

RHO

Individual option traders very seldom hedge rho. A trading firm normally has many traders and many more positions, and the interest rate risk is better hedged at the firm level. This is because rate risk has some characteristics that other risks do not.

- Option traders are generally not looking to make bets on the direction of interest rate changes through their rho position. If they wanted to make an interest-rate bet, this would be more effectively done with bond or eurodollar options or futures. Rho really is a risk with little associated reward.
- Rho is fungible and can be aggregated across all products denominated in a given currency. A firm needs only to hedge the net position, not each individual position.

Sadly, rho cannot be hedged very well. In theory, the rho of a five-year option will be hedged by trading a five-year, zero-coupon, riskless bond. However in practice there probably is not a bond of exactly matching duration, let alone a zero coupon bond. We have already mentioned that no interest-bearing security is risk free. Furthermore, option positions tend to be funded at the overnight rate no matter what their duration. There really is not an effective way to hedge exposure to the overnight risk, so a rho hedge will always have this basis risk.

STOCK RISK: DIVIDENDS AND BUY-IN RISK

Let's look at the situation where a company announces a special dividend. Assume the stock is trading $100 and we are long 1,000 of the one-year 80 strike calls. Assume interest rates are zero and implied volatility is 30 percent. The value of the option is 23.53. If the company announces a dividend of a dollar the value of the call drops to 22.73. We immediately lose $80,000. Note that being hedged in the underlying will not help here. The dividend is a benefit to those owning the stock, not to those owning the options.

This does not occur often. but it can be a big problem when it does. In 2004, Microsoft paid a special dividend of $3.08 when the stock was trading $29.97. Beware of companies that are sitting on a lot of cash.

It is of course perfectly possible to be hurt if we are long stock and an expected dividend is cut. However, the option market seems to be better at predicting this. Generally rumors of dividend cuts begin to circulate well in advance of the actual reduction and the option conversions begin to price in the lower rate. Finally, normal dividend yields tend to be much lower than special dividends, so the cutting of a normal dividend will not be as costly as the announcement of a special.

An even nastier situation occurs when a stock becomes hard to borrow and we are short stock. Initially this means that the short stock rebate is reduced. Next we will actually be charged for shorting the stock. This is unpleasant and costly, but we can deal with this by adjusting our synthetic dividend rate. The final stage is when our short stock is bought in. This means our clearing firm forces us to cover our short stock position. This leaves us unhedged, so we will also need to unwind some of our option position. Being forced out of a position is never good.

THE EARLY EXERCISE OF OPTIONS

We have seen that American options are always worth at least as much as European options. Generally they will be worth more. This is due to the early exercise option that they contain. If we do not know when to exercise this option we will not gain any benefit from owning it and paying for it. In fact, if we do not exercise it optimally, we will have paid too much.

There is evidence that a substantial proportion of American options are not exercised at the optimal time. Part of this can be explained by transaction costs. We will see how this can affect our decision later in this section. But traders also seem to become confused about exercise, and some of the "irrationality" of exercise decisions is simply due to faulty thinking and mistakes.

Deciding whether or not to exercise involves a simple process. You compare the alternatives and choose the better one. Either you hold the option or you do not. Whether you have hedged the option or own a portfolio of many options is of secondary importance to this basic question (we will look at these complicating factors later, but they are only complications and should not distract us from the central issue).

Simply put, you exercise early if what you will receive has a higher payout than what you pay, and the difference is more than the time value of the option. If interest rates are zero, then money has no payout. If the underlying also has no payout (for example, a stock with no dividends), then neither calls nor puts should be exercised early. If the underlying has a positive payout (for example, if it is a stock with dividends or a bond with coupons), we may be in a situation where calls may be exercised early. If the underlying has a negative payout (for example, physical commodities with storage costs), puts may be exercised early. When interest rates are nonzero, money also has a payout, so puts may be exercised even on underlyings that have no payout or a positive payout. Now we look at some examples to clarify this situation.

Exercising a Put on a Stock

A put is exercised to avoid the interest costs of holding the shares until expiration.

Example Let's say the underlying is $100 and we own the 120 put. There are 30 days until expiry and the interest rate is 5 percent. If we do not want to change our short delta position in the market, we can choose to do one of the following.

- Hold the option
- Sell the option and sell the underlying
- Exercise the option

Selling the option and the stock will incur transaction costs and we will end up with the same position as if we exercised, so we really need to compare holding the option to exercising it.

If we exercise the option, we become short the stock from $120. So we can invest the cash from this sale for 30 more days than we could if we held onto the option. So our interest received is

$$\text{Interest} = \$120 \times 0.05 \times 30/365 = \$0.49$$

This is the amount we are foregoing if we do not exercise. So we should exercise the option if it is trading less than 49 cents above intrinsic value.

From this example, we see that we would tend to exercise options that are further in the money and when interest rates are higher. Further, the relevant rate is that at which we can invest the proceeds from our short sale.

For a given underlying price, volatility, and interest rate we can find the critical strike, X^*, above which it is advantageous to exercise a put by numerically solving the equation,

$$rX^*T = P(X^*) - (X^* - S) \tag{13.5}$$

This directly equates the amount we gain from interest income (the left-hand side) with the amount that we lose from foregoing the put's volatility value (the right-hand side). One such curve as a function of time is shown in Figure 13.2.

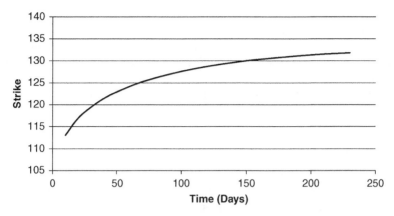

FIGURE 13.2 The Critical Strike for Put Exercise as a Function of Time
The underlying was 100, interest rate was 5 percent, and volatility was 50 percent.

A complication is that we will seldom have a position that consists of a single put. We will often be in a situation where we need to buy a call of the same strike as the put so that our risk profile is not too badly altered. In this case the cost we need to consider is the call price, so equation 13.5 becomes

$$rX^*T = C(X^*) \tag{13.6}$$

Because of the American put call parity relationship (equation 3.55) this gives a higher strike. This is shown in Figure 13.3.

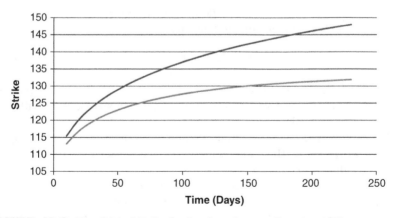

FIGURE 13.3 The Critical Strike for Put Exercise as a Function of Time
Parameters are the same as in Figure 13.2. The upper curve gives the strike when we need to cover with calls. The lower curve gives the strike when we do not need to cover.

This is an example of a situation where we need to take the entire position into account when we decide what to do with a certain option. But we need to realize that if we cannot exercise a deep-in-the-money option because we require its protection in our portfolio, we will be paying for this.

The exercise decision is dependent on the risk of the entire position, not just what is "best" for the single option.

Exercising a Call on a Future

We do this for the same reason as exercising a put on a stock. The long future position requires no cash outlay so it is cheaper to hold than the option. The analysis is exactly the same.

Exercising a Call on a Stock

Given that we saw that puts are exercised to short a stock, why would we want to exercise a call and be forced to buy a stock and pay carry? Here the stock could have a benefit associated with it that the option does not: a dividend. As we want only the dividend we will exercise the call as soon as possible to the record date, the date where the holder of the stock receives the dividend. Exercising any earlier means that we have to hold the stock longer than necessary. Here the exercise decision comes down to whether the option is worth more to us alive or exercised. If we exercise the option, we receive the intrinsic value and the dividend, but lose the remaining volatility value of the option. Or we can hold the option but we have to value it against the exdividend value of the stock with one day less to expiry. So the critical value for the strike is given by

$$C(S - D, T - 1) = S - X^* \tag{13.7}$$

Example Let's assume we have a stock trading at $100. It is paying a dividend of one dollar and we own the 30-day call struck at 90 with rates at 5 percent and volatility of 30 percent. Currently this call has an intrinsic value of $10. With 29 days remaining and an underlying of $99 the option will be worth $9. As the value when exercised is greater, we should exercise the call and receive a dollar.

Another situation where we might want to exercise a call is where the stock is hard to borrow and we have to pay a fee to short the stock. As we have already seen, this is the same as if the stock paid a continuous dividend, so holding the stock gives us a benefit that does not accrue to the owner of the call. Because this benefit is paid continuously, the analysis is similar to that of deciding to exercise a put.

Testing whether or not to exercise a call on an easy-to-borrow stock is simple. It only needs to be done immediately before dividends are paid, and typically only before the last dividend in an option's lifetime is paid. Exercising calls on futures or puts on equities for interest-rate income, or calls on hard-to-borrow stocks, is more likely to be overlooked because it needs to be checked every day.

The Dividend Spread

The fact that many options are not exercised optimally leads to trading opportunities. One way to take advantage of these opportunities is to do a dividend spread. Here two traders trade a call spread where both options are deep in the money. At the appropriate time each trader exercises his long call. It might seem that there is no money to be made here but this is not true. The way that option sellers are assigned when an option is exercised means that there can be profit here.

Options are assigned according to the amount of open interest that they represent. Let's say the open interest in a strike is 10,000. A trader who is short 1,000 will be assigned 10 percent of the options that are exercised. Let's consider the example above and assume the traders swapped 1,000 of the 85 and 90 calls with the underlying at 100. Each strike has an open interest of 10,000.

Both traders exercise 1,000 calls. Let's assume that only 75 percent of the open interest is exercised, because some option holders do not exercise optimally. This means that each of the traders in the dividend spread will only be assigned on 750 of his short strike, giving him a net profit of 250 times the dividend as he collects the dividend 1,000 times and only needs to pay it out 750 times.

Because this relies on other people failing to exercise, it is necessary to pick strikes with large open interest. We know that each of the traders participating in the call spread will exercise, so for the trade to be reasonably profitable they need to be only a small proportion of the open interest. If the strikes chosen have small open interest the trade may have to be so small that the profit is negligible.

The correct timing of exercise decisions is a great example of the necessary attention to detail that being a competent option trader requires. You have to exercise when you are supposed to; you have to be aware of when others may not, and you have to avoid egregious mistakes.

Example On September 29, 2009, Chesapeake Energy (CHK) paid a 7.5 cent dividend. The October 2009 12.5 calls were a clear exercise candidate as the stock was trading $28.17. The open interest in these calls was 39,000. None were exercised. The total value of the dividends that the call holders failed to collect was $39,000 \times 100 \times \$0.075$, or $292,500. September 28 was Yom Kippur and many traders were either not at work or were covering unfamiliar positions for someone else. We cannot know that the Jewish holiday caused this oversight, but it seems likely that someone has something extra to atone for in 2010.

SUMMARY

- Option trading is largely a matter of risk management. Making money is easy. Keeping it is the mark of a competent professional.
- Attend to risks in order of the amount of potential damage they contain.
- Try to evaluate risks in a robust, nonparametric way.
- Being long net options is the most robust form of risk control.
- If in doubt, remember the Rodriguez* rule, "Do not have more than three positions of the same sign together." So do not be short four consecutive strikes. Do not be short four consecutive expirations. Do not be short rho in four consecutive months, and so forth.
- Bad risk management will lead to one catastrophic failure. Good risk management leads to many small, inconsequential failures.

---

*Named after a trader who repeatedly drummed this saying into me.

Conclusion

Trading is difficult. But it is not a mystical ability and it can be learned. Here we have broken the trading process into the parts that a professional trader needs: an understanding of market structure, an understanding of the instruments he trades, a way to capture edge, and a methodology for managing risk. This is necessary for all traders, not only those who specialize in options. It is also the approach that the large option trading firms have been built upon.

Knowledge of market structure is probably the aspect of this approach that most distinguishes professional traders from amateurs. This is sometimes dismissed as being merely administrative. It certainly is administrative but to be dismissive to this aspect of trading is to invite failure. A solid understanding of infrastructure can directly lead to profits. For example, negotiating a better funding rate than one's competitors allows a trader to become a lender to other option traders by actively making markets in boxes. Good infrastructure also makes risk control easier. It may seem trivial to have the phone number of one's clearing firm on hand, but knowing this can easily save money in the event of technical problems. If in doubt, it is better to be overcautious when it comes to such mere administration.

The fact that we need knowledge of options in order to trade them should be obvious. Exactly what knowledge is worth acquiring does not seem to be as apparent. A trader does *not* need to know how to derive an option-pricing model, but he does need to have a very solid understanding of the assumptions the model is based on. In addition to knowing of the assumptions behind a model, a trader must know what happens to option values (and the associated greeks) when the assumptions begin to hold more loosely or to break down completely. Fischer Black, one of the inventors of the Black-Scholes-Merton formalism, once wrote a paper on "the holes in Black Scholes." It is no exaggeration to say that knowing these holes is how an option trader makes money.

Similarly, being able to perform the calculus to obtain, for example, the derivative of gamma with respect to time will not make a trader any money. This type of exercise might be useful in exams or in interviews but no trader needs to do this type of thing in the course of his business. However, a trader needs to be intimately familiar with the behavior of the greeks. In our example, he absolutely needs to know what happens to the gamma of an option as time passes. He needs to understand the shape of the curves we saw in Chapter 5, even if he cannot derive the equations. Remember, how a greek is calculated depends on the model, but options actually have greeks no matter what model we use. It is these model independent greeks that traders need to know. We trade options, not models.

Any successful trading methodology must have an edge. This is something that gives our trades their positive expected value. Most professional option traders have two separate edges: They try to capture the bid ask spread and they try to trade implied volatility against realized volatility. Market makers focus more heavily on the first of these. They aggressively scalp options to capture the spread while remaining generally aware of whether implied volatility is rich or cheap relative to realized volatility. Position traders have the opposite focus. They primarily focus on their implied volatility position, but use market making techniques to somewhat mitigate their transaction costs.

Hedging captures mispriced volatility. This transforms the options from directional bets into volatility trades. Hedging is a trade in the underlying, but we are not trying to make profitable directional trades. We are trying to manage our volatility trade in the cheapest possible way. Working on improving the cost effectiveness of hedging is probably the single most effective way a trader can add to his overall profitability.

Dynamic hedging makes volatility trading very path-dependent; it is quite possible to predict volatility correctly and lose money. This dissonance between being correct and making money makes volatility trading an inherently statistical business. This is also why we should try to hedge as much risk as possible with other options: static hedging.

But to know how much risk to hedge we need always to remember our goal. A pure market maker would be happiest with no inventory at all. The next best thing would be to have all of the greeks hedged with other options and only have a small residual risk to dynamically hedge. Conversely, a position trader wants to have vega risk. If he wants to profit from the deviation of realized and implied volatilities he cannot hedge all of his risk. He needs instead to dynamically hedge, possibly using only options to protect against extreme jumps.

The entire field of risk management needs to be viewed in the same way. What constitutes a risk is very dependent on the overall business plan. If a market maker can make money by trading actively each day, then he has no need to be exposed to any catastrophic risk at all. Buying back options as he approaches expiry may be a statistically poor trade, but it makes sense given his source of edge (scalping rather than positional trading) and his utility function. For a positional trader things are a little different. He is actually paid to evaluate bets such as these. This is his source of edge. He therefore needs to accept commensurately more risk and protect against bankruptcy by better sizing and diversification (positional traders do not need to be as active as market makers in each product so it is more feasible for them to trade options on more underlyings).

These things are necessary but not sufficient. Reading a book on trading will not make you a competent trader any more than reading a medical text will make you a surgeon. Probably the most important differentiators between successful traders and unsuccessful ones are hard work and perseverance. If someone keeps reading, keeps practicing, and keeps asking questions, they have a good chance of eventually becoming competent and consistently profitable.

There is no end to this process. You can keep learning but you will never have learned all there is to know. The markets keep changing. But all knowledge is not equal, and knowing what to learn is a very important skill. Do not waste energy looking for a great new technical indicator or trying to develop an encompassing macro-economic view of the economy. Look into the microstructure wrinkles of the markets. Force yourself to look into the boring details. In the markets, if something is easy, it will at best be useless, and probably just wrong.

Finally, you need to do the stuff that your parents probably told you about. Get a good night's sleep. Get to work on time. Concentrate. Work hard. Be lucky.

Distributions

The distribution of a variable gives the relative number of times each outcome occurs in a given number of trials. The function that describes the probability that a given value will occur is the probability density function. A completely equivalent characterization is the cumulative probability that a given value or any smaller value will occur. This is called the cumulative distribution function (sometimes just referred to as the distribution function).

EXAMPLE

One of the most useful distributions is the normal distribution (also known as the Gaussian distribution or the bell curve). This is a continuous distribution that describes many situations. It is also mathematically tractable. Its probability density is given by

$$n(x) = \frac{1}{\sigma \sqrt{2\pi}} \exp\left(-\frac{(x-\mu)^2}{2\sigma^2}\right) \tag{A.1}$$

This has two parameters: a location parameter, μ and a scale parameter, σ.

An example of this distribution is shown in Figure A.1.

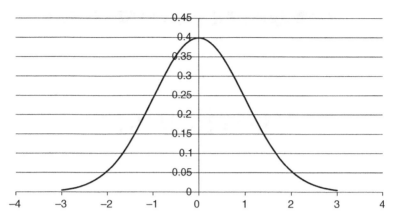

FIGURE A.1 A Normal Distribution with $\mu = 0$, $\sigma = 1$

For a normal distribution, approximately 68 percent of outcomes are within one standard deviation of the mean, 95 percent are within two standard deviations, and 99 percent are within three standard deviations.

Most other distributions need more parameters to fully describe them.

MOMENTS AND THE "SHAPE" OF DISTRIBUTIONS

The mean and the variance provide information on the location and width of a set of numbers, and hence give information on the appearance of the distribution. The mean and variance are the first two *statistical moments* and, as option traders, we will also be interested in the third and fourth moments, skewness, and kurtosis.

Quantifying the Center

The mean is meant to give us information about the center of the distribution. Inaccurately, it answers questions such as "What is a typical value?" or "What can we expect?" For discrete distributions it is defined as

$$\overline{x} = \frac{1}{N} \sum_{i=1}^{N} x_i \tag{A.2}$$

where N is the number of elements and x_i is each element.

There are other measures of central tendency, most notably the median and the mode. The median is the value such that 50 percent of outcomes are above it and 50 percent are below it. The mode is the most common

TABLE A.1	The Measured Heights of 11 Professional Athletes
5'3"	
5'6"	
5'3"	
5'3"	
5'5"	
5'2"	
5'5"	
5'5"	
5'3"	
5'4"	
7'6"	

value in the data set. Each of these statistics have uses, but people tend to run into trouble when they assume they are all approximately equivalent. A common example of this is the statement that 50 percent of people are above average. This is simply untrue. A correct statement would be that 50 percent of people are above the median. This is not just academic quibbling. Consider this example: We measure the heights (in feet and inches) of eleven professional athletes. The results are given in Table A.1 and these are displayed in Figure A.2.

The three central tendency statistics are:

Mean = 5'6.3"
Median = 5'4"
Mode = 5'3"

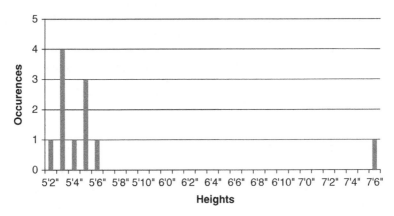

FIGURE A.2   The Corresponding Distribution of Height

As we see, only one person is above average, and the mean does not really give a very sensible summary of the data in any sense. Only one person is close to the mean. The problem here is that ten of the athletes were jockeys (the entries in the 2009 Belmont Stakes) and the eleventh person was the basketball player Yao Ming. This is of course a contrived example, but it clearly shows why we need to both have some fundamental understanding of our data and to then use the most appropriate statistical measure.

If we are making a trading decision, the "most appropriate statistical measure" will be highly dependent on the exact trade we are considering. For example, assume that we are structuring a bet on the height of a random person from the group. It pays a dollar if we are right and costs a dollar if we are wrong. Because it pays even money, the fair value for this bet would be the median: we will be equally likely to be right or wrong. But if we had a wager with a linear payoff that paid a dollar for each inch the person deviates from our guess, we would be interested in the entire distribution. We could only be 2 inches below the median (losing $2), but we could be 26 inches above it (winning $26).

In this case, there is one extreme outlier that *skews* the results. In fact skewness is the name of the normalized third moment (it may seem illogical to skip the second moment, but the odd moments measure asymmetric features, which is what we are discussing here). For a sample, skewness is defined by

$$\gamma_1 = \frac{N}{(N-1)(N-2)} \sum_{i=1}^{N} \frac{(x_i - \overline{x})^3}{\sigma^3} \tag{A.3}$$

It has been normalized by dividing the third moment by the cube of the standard deviation. This is done so that it will be independent of variance. This procedure allows us to isolate higher order differences in distributions.

Skewness measures asymmetry around the mean. Positively skewed distributions have more extreme large values. For example, the distribution of athletes' heights in Table A.1 has a skewness of 3.2.

Quantifying the Width

We also need measures of the width of the distribution. Just as the mean is blind to certain aspects of the location of a distribution, similar problems occur when we try to measure the "width," "scale," or "variability" of a distribution. Here again there are many ways of doing this.

There are two slightly different questions to answer here:

- How spread out are the values near the center of the distribution?
- How spread out are the tails of the distribution?

Different statistics will give different weights to these two elements and the choice of what to use often comes down to the relative importance of these to the question the analyst is trying to study.

There are several common measures.

The variance (of a sample) is defined as

$$s^2 = \frac{1}{N-1} \sum_{i=1}^{N} (x_i - \overline{x})^2 \tag{A.4}$$

It is the average of the squared distance from the mean. Squaring the distance from the mean gives more weight to extreme measurements. For example, a measurement that is one unit from the mean will add one to the sum, whereas a point 5 units from the mean will add 25 to the sum. This means that variance can be very sensitive to the presence of tail elements. By definition, there are few of these events, so variance suffers from fairly severe sampling issues.

The standard deviation is defined as the square root of the variance. This is easier to conceptualize than variance as it has the same units as the original data.

The mean absolute deviation (MAD) is defined as

$$MD = \frac{1}{N} \sum_{i=1}^{N} |x_i - \overline{x}| \tag{A.5}$$

Because the deviations are not squared here, this estimator places less weight on extreme values than the variance and standard deviation. However, the use of the absolute value function makes this a more difficult estimator to perform analytical calculations with.

The median absolute deviation is defined as the median of the deviations from the median.

$$MAD = \text{median} \left(|x_i - x_{\text{median}}| \right) \tag{A.6}$$

This is even less affected by extremes in the tail, because values in the tails have less influence on the calculation of the median than they do on the mean.

Each of these statistics attempts to capture the variability of the entire sample and they each do so by weighting different parts of the

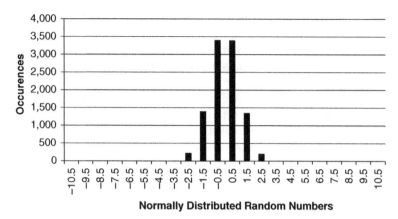

FIGURE A.3 A Histogram of Random Numbers Drawn from a Normal Distribution

sample differently. We could also attempt to use completely different measures for each part of the distribution.

The range is defined as the largest value minus the smallest value in sample. This is based only on two values, the extremes. The variability of the center of the data is not measured at all.

The interquartile range is defined as the value of the 75th percentile minus the value of the 25th percentile. This attempts to measure the variability of the center of the data and provides no information about the tails.

We next look at some examples, to see why we need different measures. We generated histograms of 10,000 random numbers from different distributions. We chose a normal distribution, a Cauchy distribution, and a uniform distribution. The definitions of these distributions are not as important as what they look like.

The first histogram (Figure A.3) is a sample generated from a normal distribution. The standard deviation is 1.003, the median absolute deviation is 0.6746, and the range is 7.80.

The normal distribution is symmetric. It has well-behaved tails and a single peak at the center of the distribution. The median absolute deviation is a bit less than the standard deviation due to the lesser weight given to the tails. The range of a little less than 8 indicates that the extreme values fall within about 4 standard deviations of the mean. If your data are approximated well by a normal distribution, then it is reasonable to use the standard deviation as the spread estimator.

The next histogram (Figure A.4) is a sample from a Cauchy distribution. The standard deviation is 393.79, the median absolute deviation is 0.986, and the range is 54,206.

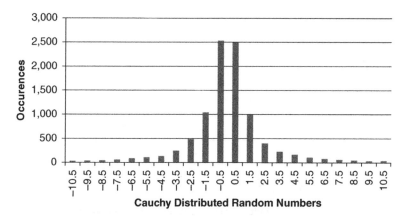

FIGURE A.4 A Histogram of Random Numbers Drawn from a Cauchy Distribution

The Cauchy distribution is also symmetric. But it has heavy tails and a pronounced peak at the center of the distribution. The Cauchy distribution has the unfortunate property that collecting more data does not provide a more accurate estimate for the mean or standard deviation. That means that, for this distribution, the standard deviation is useless as a measure of the spread. But just from looking at the histogram, it is clear that just about all the data are between about −5 and 5. However, a few very extreme values cause both the standard deviation and range to be enormous. Note though that the median absolute deviation is only slightly larger than it is for the normal distribution. In this case, the median absolute deviation is clearly the better measure of spread: It is more representative of what is going on in this case.

The final histogram (Figure A.5) is a sample from a uniform distribution. The standard deviation is 1.148, the median absolute deviation is 0.994, and the range is 3.999.

This distribution has a limited range. It has truncated tails. In this case the standard deviation and median absolute deviation have closer values than for either the normal or the Cauchy distribution.

So what measure should we choose in practice? As always, the answer is, "it depends" and, most important, it depends on what we think the underlying distribution really is. And of course we do not actually know that. We are trying to figure that out from the data.

Statisticians consider two types of robustness. In a general sense robustness is a lack of susceptibility to the effects of nonnormality. *Robustness of validity* means that the confidence intervals for a measure of variability (e.g., the standard deviation) have a 95 percent chance of covering the true value of that measure of spread no matter what the true

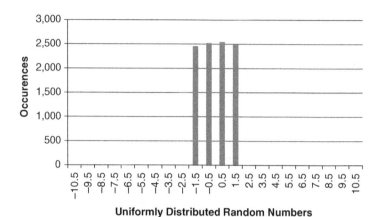

FIGURE A.5 A Histogram of Random Numbers Drawn from a Uniform Distribution

distribution is. *Robustness of efficiency* refers to high effectiveness when dealing with fat tails. So confidence intervals for the measure of spread are nearly as narrow as the best that could be done if we knew the true shape of the distribution.

The standard deviation is an example of an estimator that is the best we can do if the underlying distribution is normal. However, it lacks robustness of validity, so that confidence intervals based on the standard deviation tend to lack precision if the underlying distribution is in fact not normal.

The median absolute deviation and the interquartile range are estimates of scale that have robustness of validity. However, they are not particularly strong for robustness of efficiency.

If you think that your data are reasonably approximated by a normal distribution, then using the standard deviation as the estimate of scale is a sensible thing to do. However, if your data are not normal then using one of the alternative measures would be better.

Quantifying the Tails

We have seen that distributions can vary widely in the amount of mass they have in the tails. It is often stated that this is measured by the standardized fourth moment, kurtosis. The kurtosis of a sample is

$$\gamma_2 = \frac{(N+1)\,N}{(N-1)(N-2)(N-3)} \sum_{i=1}^{N} \frac{(x_i - \bar{x})\,4}{\sigma^4} \qquad (A.7)$$

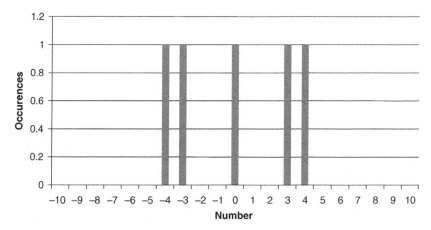

FIGURE A.6   Distribution A

The normal distribution has a kurtosis of three, so we sometimes subtract three from kurtosis to obtain excess kurtosis. This is the amount of fat tails a distribution has relative to the normal distribution (annoyingly, some people refer to excess kurtosis as kurtosis, so we often have to check).

I have referred to kurtosis as measuring "fat tails" or "peakishness." It does do this, but it is also more subtle and interesting.

To see this, let's consider two very simple distributions, shown in Figures A.6 and A. A.7.

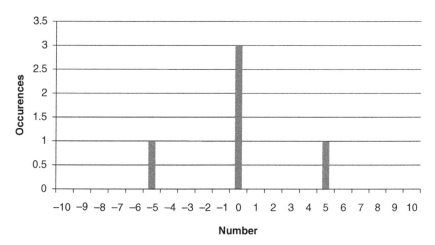

FIGURE A.7   Distribution B

Distribution A is

$$-4, -3, 0, 3, 4$$

Distribution B is

$$-5, 0, 0, 0, 5$$

These both have zero mean, zero skewness, and a standard deviation of 3.54. They also look very different. A has a kurtosis of 0.392 and B has a kurtosis of 5. It can be shown that kurtosis is at a minimum when the distribution is perfectly bimodal, so increasing kurtosis is a measure of how much the distribution departs from bimodality. To make a distribution less bimodal, mass must both be shifted toward the middle and toward the wings. So distribution B is both more peaked and more tail heavy (fat tails imply thin shoulders, as well).

All of this is important for a trader. Distributions arise in many aspects of trading, but they are most important for an option trader when thinking about pricing models and tracking results. Now that we have established a basic amount of knowledge, we will return to specifics in those sections.

Correlation

C orrelation measures the degree of linear dependence between two normally distributed variables. For a population it is defined by

$$\rho_{xy} = \frac{E((x - \mu_x)(y - \mu_y))}{\sigma_x \sigma_y}, \tag{B.1}$$

where μ_x is the population mean and $E(.)$ is the expectation.

And if we have a finite sample, our best estimate is given by

$$r_{xy} = \frac{\sum_{i=1}^{N}(x_i - \overline{x})(y_i - \overline{y})}{(N-1)s_x s_y} \tag{B.2}$$

where $\overline{x}$ is the sample mean, N is the sample size, and s_x is the sample standard deviation. Both ρ and r are between negative one and one.

Correlation has an appealing relationship to regression. Consider the scatter diagram of Figure B.1.

The regression line that best fits this data is shown in Figure B.2.

The line has three properties:

1. Its intercept
2. Its slope
3. Its "goodness" of fit

Correlation is related to the second two properties. A positive slope tells us that if one variable increases, the other does as well. In this case

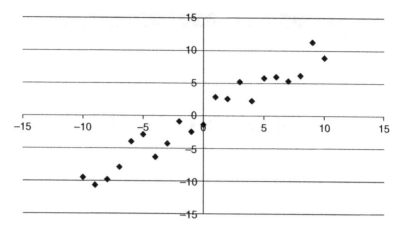

FIGURE B.1 A Scatter Graph of Two Variables

correlation is positive. A negative slope tells us that if one variable increases the other decreases. In this case correlation is negative.

Correlation is bounded by negative one and one. If the data is well described by a line, the magnitude of correlation is high. If the data is not very linear, the magnitude of correlation is low. In the case of Figure B.1, the correlation coefficient is 0.9686, indicating that a straight line describes the data very well. As always, this is very context-dependent. In finance, where we are often using correlated instruments to hedge, "highly correlated" might mean anything with a magnitude greater than 0.9, "moderately correlated" might mean a magnitude between 0.7 and 0.9, and anything less than 0.7 would be "low correlation."

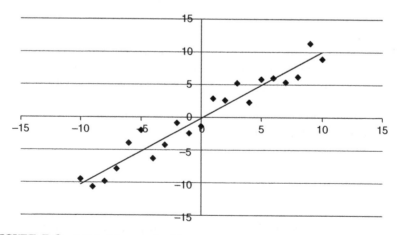

FIGURE B.2 A Fitted Regression Line

A variable that has a more intuitive interpretation is the square of the correlation coefficient, sometimes referred to as the coefficient of determination. This tells us the proportion of the variance in y_i that is accounted for by a linear fit of x_i to y_i. This is defined by

$$r^2_{xy} = 1 - \frac{s^2_{x|y}}{s^2_y} \tag{B.3}$$

Here $s^2_{x|y}$ is the squared error of the linear regression of x on y.

$$s^2_{x|y} = \frac{1}{N-1} \sum_{i=1}^{N} (y_i - a - bx_i)^2 \tag{B.4}$$

For example, the statement, "a stock's return is a function of the market return with an r-square of 0.6" can be interpreted as saying that 60 percent of the variation of the stock's return can be explained by the variation of the market, and the remaining 40 percent needs to be a function of something else.

Correlation tends to be very poorly understood and open to frequent misinterpretation.

- **Correlation is not causation.** This is very frequently stated and equally often misunderstood. It does not mean that correlation between two variables cannot be interpreted as evidence that there is a causal link between the two. It just means that the presence of correlation does not, on its own, prove such a link. We would then need to do further research and identify a plausible mechanism linking the variables.

  A financial example of spurious correlation is the "Super Bowl Indicator." This theory holds that if a team from the AFC wins the Super Bowl, the stock market will have a bad year, and if a team from the NFC wins the Super Bowl, the stock market will have a good year (the original theory was based on the old AFL and NFL). This theory has worked rather well. From 1967 until 2008, it correctly predicted the direction of the market (proxied by the Dow Jones Industrial Average) 34 out of 42 times.

  The reason we should not believe that this strong historical correlation is predictive of future performance is that there is absolutely no reason to believe that the outcome of a football game should have any effect on the yearly return of the stock market. Before trusting a correlation, you must believe in a fundamental reason for the relationship to hold.

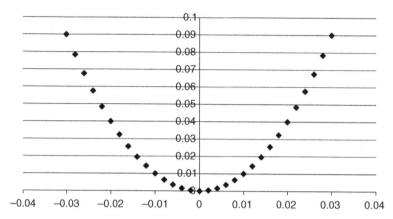

FIGURE B.3 Data That Has a Clear Relationship and a Low Correlation

- **Correlation measures the degree of linear association.** Variables can have a low correlation yet have a very clear and strong relationship. An example is shown in Figure B.3. Here the correlation coefficient is only –0.258, but the relationship is obvious.
- **Correlation does not tell us "things are moving together."** It specifically says that the fluctuations have a relationship. The variables may still drift apart. Figure B.4 shows two "price" series, whose returns have a very high correlation (0.9994), but are clearly moving in opposite directions.

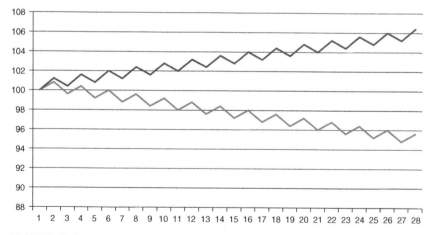

FIGURE B.4 Highly Correlated, Divergent Series

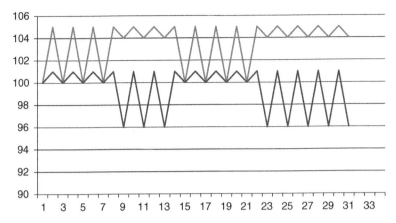

FIGURE B.5 An Example of Positively Correlated Returns and Negatively Correlated Volatilities

A similar observation applies to volatilities. Highly correlated return series need not imply that the volatilities are highly correlated. In fact, we can have close to perfectly correlated returns and still have total independence of the volatilities (this is a central assumption of most multiasset option pricing formulae). Correlation of returns implies something about the codependence of the *direction* of fluctuations. Correlation of volatilities implies something about the codependence of the *size* of fluctuations. Consider the situation in Figure B.5. Here the returns are positively correlated (a correlation of 0.4), but the

TABLE B.1 Anscombe's Quartet

X1	Y1	X2	Y2	X3	Y3	X4	Y4
10.0	8.04	10.0	9.14	10.0	7.46	8.0	6.58
8.0	6.95	8.0	8.14	8.0	6.77	8.0	5.76
13.0	7.58	13.0	8.74	13.0	12.74	8.0	7.71
9.0	8.81	9.0	8.77	9.0	7.11	8.0	8.84
11.0	8.33	11.0	9.26	11.0	7.81	8.0	8.47
14.0	9.96	14.0	8.10	14.0	8.84	8.0	7.04
6.0	7.24	6.0	6.13	6.0	6.08	8.0	5.25
4.0	4.26	4.0	3.10	4.0	5.39	19.0	12.5
12.0	10.84	12.0	9.13	12.0	8.15	8.0	5.56
7.0	4.82	7.0	7.26	7.0	6.42	8.0	7.91
5.0	5.68	5.0	4.74	5.0	5.73	8.0	6.89

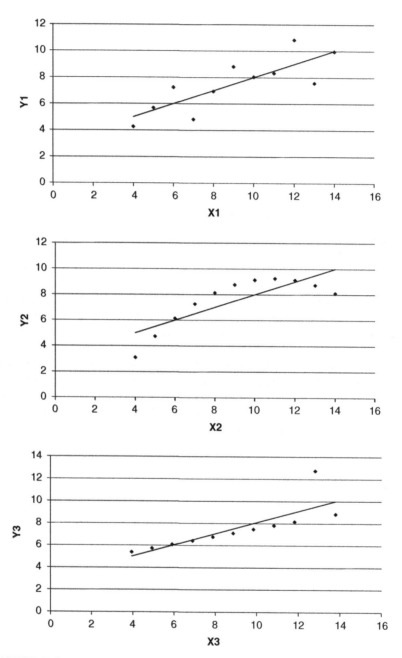

FIGURE B.6 Anscombe's Quartet

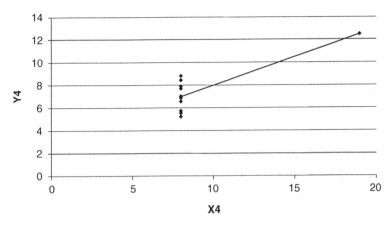

FIGURE B.6   *(Continued)*

volatilities are negatively correlated, as one series is quiet when the other is noisy.

- **When we calculate correlations, we need to use synchronous observations.** If we were to calculate the correlation between the German DAX index and the S&P 500 using the closing price of each index, we would get a result of about 0.58. However if we used synchronous data, we would obtain a correlation of about 0.9. This is far more indicative of the true interdependence of the markets.

- **Correlation on its own cannot tell us much about the relationship between variables.** A famous example of this is Anscombe's Quartet. The data is given in Table B.1.

Each x variable has a mean of 9.0 and a variance of 10.0. Each y variable has a mean of 7.5 and a variance of 3.75. The correlation between each set of x's and y's is 0.816 and the linear regression line for each set of data is also identical: $y = 3 + 0.5x$.

Each group is displayed as a scatter graph in Figures B.6.

The first set looks to be normally distributed and would be a good candidate for regression analysis. The second set looks to have a strong but highly nonlinear relationship. The third set has a very good linear relationship with a single outlier. The fourth set also has a single outlier, but the y values seem to be totally unrelated to the x values.

A model that characterizes coassociation by correlation may be a good one, but only if the data is bivariate linear. Often there is much more going on. The first thing to do with any data is to look at it!

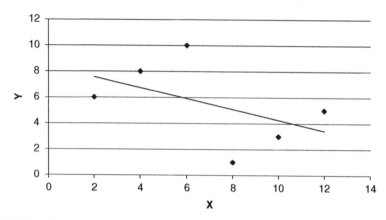

FIGURE B.7   An Example of Simpson's Paradox

- **Be careful when drawing conclusions from the amalgamation of separate groups of data.** It is quite possible for two subsets of data to have positive correlation, yet the whole set to display negative correlation. This is an example of Simpson's paradox. An example is shown in Figure B.7.

  Here both halves of the data have a correlation of one, but the overall data set has a correlation of –0.4739.

Glossary

all or nothing (AON) This is a type of limit order that is to be filled in its entirety or not at all.

American option An American option is one which gives the holder the right to exercise at any time up to and including its expiration. In practice American options can be exercised only at one specific time on each trading day.

American Depository Receipt (ADR) A negotiable certificate issued by an American bank representing a specific number of shares of a foreign stock held by the bank.

arbitrage ("arb") A trade that results in a risk-free profit.

arbitration A dispute settling process between market participants.

ask Relating to the price at which a market maker is prepared to sell a security.

Asian option An option whose underlying is an average of prices of a given security.

assignment When an option holder exercises an option, the opposite side of their position change is referred to as *assignment*. Assigned options are randomly allocated amongst the option sellers.

automatic exercise A provision in an option contract that specifies it will be automatically exercised at expiration if it is in-the-money by a certain amount.

at-the-money The strike price equal to the spot.

at-the-money forward The strike price equal to the forward.

back months Expirations other than the first month.

back office The department in a financial institution that processes trades and handles delivery, settlement, and regulatory procedures.

back spread A position where you buy more options in one strike than you sell in another.

backwardation A term used in commodity markets to refer to a futures curve where longer dated contracts trade lower than the spot price.

basis The relationship between a future and the underlying cash market.

basis point A one-hundredth of a percentage point. It is often used to describe changes in interest rates.

basis risk The risk associated with holding a position in the cash market, hedged by one in the futures.

basket option An option where the underlying is a collection (basket) of instruments.

bear a trader who thinks the market will decline.

Bermudan option An option that can be exercised on a set number of days up to its expiration date. So named because it is somewhere between an American option and a European option.

bid Relating to the price at which a market maker is prepared to buy a security.

bid/ask spread The difference between the bid price and the ask price.

binomial model An option pricing model that assumes the underlying can make only one of two possible moves in each time period.

Black-Scholes-Merton (BSM) model An option pricing model that uses the principle of no arbitrage to derive a partial differential equation for the value of an option.

block trade A large prearranged trade.

box An option position consisting of a long conversion in one strike and a short conversion in another. Used as a hedge of interest rate risk.

broker Someone who executes a trade for another person's account.

brokerage A firm where brokers work. Also known as a brokerage house or brokerage firm.

bucket shop A brokerage firm that internalizes the order of a customer without executing them on an exchange, so named because orders go "into the bucket." It is illegal to operate such a firm in most states of the United States.

bull a trader who thinks the market will rise.

butterfly An option position with positions in three equally spaced strikes. It would consist of one option at the lowest strike, short two at the middle strike, and long one at the upper strike. A call butterfly is made of calls and a put butterfly is made of puts. It can also be viewed as the difference between two spreads.

calendar spread An option strategy consisting of a long position in one month and a short position in another. Also known as a time spread.

call An option that gives the holder the right to purchase the underlying at a specific price.

call-around market A market structure where brokers arrange trades by phoning different market makers. Once the trades are agreed they can either be crossed on an exchange or agreed as OTC trades.

call spread An option strategy consisting of a long position in one call and a short position in another.

carry cost The expenses incurred while a position being held.

cash settlement A contract that is settled cash rather than the physical underlying. Most index options are settled with cash.

CBOE Chicago Board Options Exchange

CBOT Chicago Board of Trade

charm The partial derivative of delta with respect to time.

Christmas tree An option position made up of a long call and short calls at two higher strikes.

clearing All the parts of the trading process that take place between the initiation of the trade its settlement.

clearinghouse A financial institution that provides clearing and settlement and acts as a central counterparty.

close Pertaining to the closing time of the underlying.

closing price The price of the instrument at the closing time.

closing trade A trade that closes an open position.

CME Chicago Mercantile Exchange

collar A position consisting of long stock, long an out-of-the-money put and short an out-of-the-money call.

color The partial derivative of gamma with respect to time.

combination A position consisting of more than one type of option.

combo An option position consisting of a long put and a short call.

COMEX A division of the NYMEX that trades metal derivatives.

commodity A physical substance such as metals, oil products, or agricultural products.

Commodity Futures Trading Commission (CFTC) A U.S. government agency that regulates trading in futures.

commodity trading advisor (CTA) A firm or individual who is paid to give advice on futures trading and manage accounts.

condor An option strategy consisting of a long option position in one strike, short positions in two higher strikes, and a long position in a higher strike. This can be implemented with calls to create a call condor, or with puts to make a put condor.

contango A term used in commodity markets to refer to a futures curve where longer dated contracts trade above than the spot price.

contingent order An order to execute a trade only if another trade has previously been executed.

contract   A shortened version of the term "derivative contract."

contract month   The expiration month for a given contract.

contract size   The number of units of the underlying that an option contract would deliver if it was exercised.

convergence   The decrease of the futures basis as expiration becomes closer. More generally, it can refer to the narrowing of any financial spread.

conversion   An option position consisting of long stock and an offsetting short synthetic position of long put and short call of the same strike.

corner   An illegal practice where so much of a security is purchased that its price is controlled.

coupon   A periodic payment made to holders of a bond.

covered call   A position where we are long the underlying and short an equal number of calls.

credit risk   The risk that another party may default on its obligations. This is also referred to as counterparty risk.

cross   A trade executed by a broker when he holds both the buy and sell sides of the order. Generally exchanges have rules in place to allow other traders to participate in these trades if they wish.

day order   An order that stays in effect for a single day.

deck   A broker's order book.

deep (in-the-money)   An option position that is a long way in-the-money.

default   The inability of a market participant to meet their obligations.

delivery date   The date by which the seller of a futures contact must fulfill his obligations.

delivery options   The options available to the seller of a future. These can include timing options, wildcard options, and quality options.

delivery price   The price at which the futures contract is settled when delivery is made.

delta   The derivative of the option's value with respect to the underlying. By construction, this is also the hedge ratio of the option and the trader's exposure to the underlying.

delta neutral   A strategy that has a delta of zero

derivative   A financial instrument that whose price can be derived from another.

diagonal spread   An option position consisting of a long option in one month offset by a short option of the same type in another month and another strike.

dispersion   A statistic that quantifies the mispricing between the volatility of an index and the volatility of its constituents.

dispersion trading   An option trading strategy consisting of a short position in index options offset by long positions in options on the index constituents.

dividend   A cash payment that is periodically made to the holder of a stock.

dividend yield   The annualized percentage return received by a stock holder that is generated by the dividends.

designated primary market maker (DPM)   A category of trader on the CBOE who is obligated to provide a certain amount of liquidity. This position is a hybrid of a market maker and a specialist.

dynamic hedge   A trade in the underlying to neutralize the deltas accumulated from a gamma position as the underlying moves.

electronic communication network (ECN)   A computer system that facilitates trades outside an exchange.

elasticity   The percentage increase in an option's value for an underlying price change of 1 percent.

electronic exchange   A derivatives exchange where trading is conducted by computer.

equity   (1) Stock; (2) the liquidation value of a trading account.

exchange-traded fund (ETF)   Exchange-traded closed-end funds.

European option   An option that can only be exercised on the expiration day.

EUREX   The derivatives exchange formed by the merger of the German DTB and the Swiss SOFFEX.

exchange   A Place or mechanism that brings together buyers and sellers.

exdividend date   The date at which a stock dividend is paid.

exercise   The action where the buyer of an option converts the option into a position in the underlying.

exercise price   The price at which the exerciser of an option can buy or sell the underlying.

extrinsic value   The portion of an option value that is not intrinsic value. Also known as "time value."

exotic option   An option whose features are deemed to be more complex than standard. This definition changes over time. Originally puts were deemed exotic, but now Asian options and basket options are no longer considered exotic.

fast market   An exchange declared state where trading is determined to be too fast for market participants to be held to their normal obligations in terms of speed and accuracy.

first-in, first-out (FIFO)   An algorithm that allocates trades of the basis of time priority.

fill   The result of an order execution.

fill or kill (FOK)　An order type that is canceled if it is not filled immediately.

final settlement price　The price at which a cash-settled contract is settled at maturity.

forward　An agreement between two parties to trade a certain amount of a product at a fixed price and time in the future.

front month　The first contract month.

front running　The practice where a broker executes orders for his own account before filling a customer order. This is often illegal.

fungibility　Interchangeability of contracts due to their identical nature. For example, a stock option traded on the ISE is fungible with one traded on the CBOE.

future　A standardized, exchange-traded forward.

gamma　The derivative of delta with respect to the underlying price.

give up　A process where a broker executes a trade for another trader, then "gives up" the second trader's name as the counterparty even though he did not execute the trade.

Globex　The electronic trading arm of the CME.

good until canceled　An order that remains active until it is either filled or canceled.

greeks　A collective term for the partial derivatives of option values with respect to their parameters.

guts　A strangle constructed from in-the-money options.

haircut　The margin charged by a clearing firm to its customers.

hedge　A trade that offsets another risk.

hedge fund　A fund that is open to wealthy investors that undertakes a wider range of trading activities than traditional long-only investment funds.

high　The high price of a trading period.

historical volatility　The volatility calculated from historical underlying prices.

horizontal spread　An option position that consists of a long position in one option and a short position in another that differs only in the expiration date.

ICE　International Commodities Exchange.

implied volatility　The volatility parameter that allows an option pricing model to match the market price for an option.

index　A group of stocks whose prices are aggregated according to a published formula.

initial margin　The amount of money a customer must deposit in a margin account when entering a new position.

interest　Money paid when borrowing.

interest rate   The annualized percentage return received by a lender.

in-the-money   An option that would have value if it were exercised. A call is in-the-money if its strike is below the underlying price. A put is in-the-money if its strike is above the underlying price.

intrinsic value   For calls, the underlying price minus the strike price. For puts, the strike price minus the underlying price.

iron butterfly   An option position that is synthetically equivalent to a butterfly, but is constructed from out-of-the-money options. For example, a long strangle and a short straddle would make an iron butterfly.

iron condor   An option position that is synthetically equivalent to a condor, but is constructed from out-of-the-money options. For example, a short put spread and a short call spread would make an iron condor.

ISE   International Securities Exchange.

jelly roll   An option position consisting of a long synthetic in one expiration offset by a short synthetic in another.

kurtosis   The fourth moment of the return distribution. A normal return distribution has a kurtosis of three. A kurtosis greater than this is indicative of a distribution that is leptokurtic, or has "fat tails."

leaning   (1) A market making technique where a trader will make note of a large resting order to use as a possible stop; (2) having a directional bias.

long-term equity anticipation product (LEAP)   A long-dated equity option at the CBOE.

leverage   The use of borrowed money or derivatives to increase the potential return of a trade.

LIFFE   London International Financial Futures Exchange.

limit order   An order that can only be executed at the specified price or better.

linkage   The option linkage plan is a program that guarantees an equity option customer will get filled at the best available price.

liquidity   The ability of a market to absorb large orders with reasonable market impact.

local   An exchange trader who trades his own account.

locked limit   A market that has been closed because it has reached its price limits.

long   Having a position that benefits from a rising market.

lot   A portion of a trade.

low   The low price of a trading period.

maintenance margin   The amount of margin that must always be held in an account. This is generally a smaller amount than the initial margin.

manipulation   Illegally tampering with the market in order to make a profit.

margin   The difference between the market value of a position and the loan from the clearing firm.

margin call   A demand for additional funds by a broker.

marked to market   Using the current market price of a security to determine its value for accounting purposes.

market impact   The amount that the bid (ask) price moves in response to a sell (buy) order of a given size.

market order   An order that will be executed with no regard for the price.

market on open   A market order at the open.

market on close   A market order at the close.

market if touched   A market order whose execution is triggered when the specified price is touched.

market maker   A trader whose trading strategy involves quoting a bid and an offer for a security.

mark to model   Using the output of a pricing model to determine the value of a security for accounting purposes.

merger   The combining of two companies.

moneyness   The relationship of an option's strike to the underlying price. This can be expressed as an absolute difference, a ratio, the logarithm of the ratio, or the number of standard deviations.

Monte Carlo   A computational technique that involves the use of random numbers to derive a sample.

naked option   An option that is unhedged.

net present value (NPV)   The present value of the expected future cash flows minus the cost.

notional value   The total value of a derivatives positions underlying assets.

NYMEX   The New York Mercantile Exchange.

NYSE   The New York Stock Exchange.

Option Clearing Corporation (OCC)   The institution that is the issuer and guarantor of all listed option contracts.

one cancels other (OCO)   Contingent orders where the filling of the first cancels the other.

odd lot   An order for a block of an unusual size.

offer   Relating to the price at which a market maker is prepared to sell a security.

open   Pertaining to the opening time of the underlying.

opening trade   A trade that opens a new position.

open interest   The total number of derivatives contacts traded that have not yet had an offsetting transaction.

open outcry   The method of trading used on nonelectronic exchanges where traders call out the details of each buy and sell order, so that it is available to all other traders.

OPM   "Other people's money": trading with borrowed funds.

option   A derivative contract that gives the holder the right, but not the obligation, to buy or sell the underlying at a given price either on or before a certain date.

option class   The call options or all the put options for a particular underlying.

option premium   The amount that an option buyer pays to the option seller. For stock options, this is quoted on a per share basis.

option series   Options on the same underlying with the same exercise price and maturity.

order   An instruction to a broker that commits the issuer to the specified terms.

order ticket   A form (paper or electronic) giving the details of an order.

out-of-the-money   A call (put) whose strike price is above (below) the current forward price.

out trade   A trade that does not clear because of a disagreement between the counterparties.

over-the-counter (OTC)   A decentralized market where participants trade unlisted securities directly with each other and not through a centralized clearinghouse.

path-dependency   A situation where the value of an option depends on the price history of the underlying rather than only its instantaneous value.

payoff   The amount given to a winning trade.

payoff diagram   A graph of the value of an option position at expiration as a function of the underlying.

portfolio insurance   A dynamic trading strategy designed to replicate a long put position, so that the value of the portfolio does not fall below a certain amount.

position   A trader's market commitment.

price limits   Limits on the size of daily price changes that are set by futures exchanges.

proprietary trading   Trading for a firm's own account.

put   An option that gives the holder the right to sell the underlying at a specific price.

put/call parity   A relationship that connects the values of calls and puts with the same expiry, strike and underlying.

put spread   An option strategy consisting of a long position in one put and a short position in another.

quoted price   The highest bid and the lowest offer.

quoting   Providing a continuous, two-sided market.

range   The difference between the high and low prices for a given period.

ratio spread   An option position consisting of an unequal number of longs and shorts.

rho   The partial derivative of the option price with respect to the interest rate.

realized volatility   The actual volatility of the underlying.

replication   The process where the payoff from a portfolio is matched by constructing a synthetic portfolio from other instruments.

resting order   A limit order; generally one that is not close to the current market.

return   The change in the value of a portfolio over a given time period. This can be expressed in absolute, logarithmic or percentage terms.

reversal   An option position consisting of short stock and an offsetting long synthetic position of short put and long call of the same strike. Also known as a reverse conversion.

risk neutrality   A pricing concept where one assumes that the current value of all financial assets is equal to the expected value of the future payoff of the asset, discounted at the risk-free rate.

risk reversal   An option position consisting of a long put and a short call at a higher strike.

roll   (1) The action of moving a position to either a different maturity (rolling forward) or to a different strike (rolling up or down); (2) abbreviation of jelly roll.

round trip   The purchase and sale of the same security in a short time period.

scalping   A trading strategy that aims to make a lot of trades for small gains.

seasonality   A persistent cyclicality in time.

seat   Position of membership on an exchange.

Securities and Exchange Commission (SEC)   The federal agency that regulates the securities industry.

settlement   When payment is made for a trade.

settlement price   A price that is used to calculate gains and losses in margin accounts and invoice prices for deliveries.

shading   The process where a market maker will slightly bias his bid and offer prices from the true market in order to reflect his desired position.

short   Having a position that benefits from a falling market.

short covering   The purchase of securities by short sellers to cover those that were borrowed for the short sale.

short interest   Total number of shares that have been sold short. Often expressed as a percentage of the float.

short selling   Borrowing a security for the purpose of selling it and repurchasing it later to return to the owner.

short squeeze   When short sellers are forced to buy in their positions either because of margin calls or because the owners call the shares back. This drives the market prices higher, exacerbating the losses on the short positions.

skew   (1) The third moment of the underlying return distribution. Normally distributed returns have zero skew. If the skew is negative the mean is lower than the median, and we will have a greater chance of encountering large negative returns; (2) An implied volatility curve where higher strikes have significantly lower implied volatilities.

smile   The implied volatility curve as a function of strike or moneyness.

spoofing   Making a deliberately misleading quote.

standardized portfolio analysis of risk (SPAN)   The risk measurement system used by most exchanges to calculate the worst expected daily portfolio return.

specialist   A member of an exchange who is designated to maintain a "fair and orderly market" in a security. This is a combination of a market making and brokerage position.

speed   The partial derivative of gamma with respect to the underlying price.

spot   Relating to the cash price of the underlying.

spread   (1) The difference between the bid price and ask price of a security; (2) a strategy that involves the simultaneous sale and purchase of similar securities.

squeeze   A period when a security rapidly increases in price as weak hands are forced to liquidate.

static hedge   A hedge that is designed to not need rebalancing.

stop   An order to trade at the market when a certain price is touched.

stop limit   A stop order that initiates a limit order.

strike   The price at which the underlying may be bought (sold) if a call (put) option is exercised.

stupid   An option position comprising calls (or puts) of the same expiration and different strikes. Sometimes also called a strip in Europe.

straddle   An option position consisting of both a put and a call of the same strike and expiration.

strangle   An option position consisting of both a put and a call of the same expiration and different strikes.

strap   An option position consisting of a puts and two calls of the same expiry and strike.

strip   An option position consisting of two puts and a call of the same expiry and strike.

swap   Originally a derivative where counterparties exchange cash flows. Now applied to a wide range of derivative products other than simple forwards, futures or options.

synthetic   An option position that replicates the underlying by holding a long call and a short put of the same strike and expiry.

takeover   The transfer of control of a company from one group of shareholders to another.

teeny   An option that is struck far out-of-the-money.

Texas hedge   A trade that increases the risk of the original position.

theta   The partial derivative of the option price with respect to time.

tick   The smallest allowable price change.

ticking   Improving another market maker's quote by the minimum amount.

tied order   An option order where the counterparties also exchange the delta hedge.

time decay   Theta.

time spread   A calendar spread.

time stamp   The time at which a trade is executed or an order is entered.

time value   Extrinsic value.

trailing stop   A stop that is adjusted as the market moves in the direction of the trade. For example, a trailing stop on a long position will be moved higher as the market rallies.

tree   (1) The evolution of the underlying as modeled in the binomial model; (2) abbreviation of Christmas tree.

underlying   The asset that the derivative contract is priced from.

value at risk (VaR)   A procedure for estimating the probability that the portfolio loses some specified amount in a given time period.

vanilla option   An option with no unusual features.

variance   The second moment of the return distribution.

variation margin   The additional deposit required to bring a trader's equity account up to the initial margin level when its balance drops below the maintenance margin requirement.

vanna   The partial derivative of delta with respect to volatility.

vega   The partial derivative of the option value with respect to volatility.

vertical spread An option position which consists of a long position in one option and a short position in another that differs only in the strike.

VIX The CBOE volatility index.

volatility The square root of variance.

volatility trading Making trades to capture the spread between realized and implied volatility.

volga The partial derivative of vega with respect to volatility.

warrant A long dated call option issued by a company on its own stock.

"with a tick" Giving a broker some leeway in the price of a limit order.

yield The percentage rate of return of a stock paid out in dividends, or the effective rate of interest paid on a bond.

Index

Bold number refers to definition

Printed and bound by CPI Group (UK) Ltd, Croydon, CR0 4YY

16/04/2025

14658501-0003